An Autobiography of George Washington

as told to Edith Ellis, *scribe*

Foreword by Caroline Myss

CMED Publishing

An Autobiography of George Washington
as told to Edith Ellis, scribe

© 2005 by CMED Publishing Company
Oak Park, Illinois

Cover Design by Colleen A. Daley
Interior Design & Printing by
Chauncey Park Press, 735 N. Grove Ave., Oak Park, IL 60302.

Printed on #55 Natural White Glatfelter Text
by Spring Grove Mills on a Mann-Roland 28 x 40 offset press.
Text and headlines set in Adobe Caslon Pro.

Library of Congress Control Number: 2005924266.
ISBN: 0976968002 Perfectbound
International ISBN: 9780976968009 Perfectbound

1. Washington, George   2. Psychic Studies
3. Cherry Tree Legend

Dedication

*To the People of the United States of America:
May they always hold to the
Founding Vision of this great Nation—
Freedom, Justice, Virtue.*

Contents

WITH GRATITUDE AND BLESSINGS

I have no doubt that if Edith Ellis were alive today, she would be writing the Acknowledgments rather than me. So on her behalf, let me thank all of you for trusting in her ability to channel the spirit of the Founding Father of America, a risky task to say the least. She would also thank her dear assistant, Harriet von Tobel, who worked at her side for years, organizing all of the information that flowed through Edith on an almost daily basis. Edith, of course, did not live long enough to learn what became of her manuscript. She, no doubt, would be astonished to learn how Harriet cared for this rare piece of channeled history for the rest of her life, always with the intention of finding a way to keep a promise to George Washington to see that his autobiography would be published one day. So I, too, am deeply grateful to Harriet for what in the end became a part of her life's work – to care for this manuscript until she could find a publisher. Not many people would work for decades to see the fulfillment of a promise, much less to a spirit.

In addition to Edith Ellis and Harriet von Tobel, who are the real stars of this project, I consider the following to be the *George Washington Team:* Jean Etter, a life-long friend, worked on the Washington project in the early days with me, and without her, I could never have found Harriet von Tobel again, much less acquired the manuscript. Her enthusiasm, devotion, dedication, and outrageous sense of humor did not and will never go unappreciated. Amy Myss, my dear sister-in-law, put in endless hours of editing, typing and organizing this manuscript. She worked those long, long hours with me as only a sister would. And in one of those fun incidents of synchronicity, Amy, who is a DAR (Daughter of the American Revolution), discovered that her ancestor, Nathaniel West, fought in the American Revolution. My heartfelt love and gratitude goes to Charles and Sue Wells, who did editing, as well as layout and printing – in short, they put the book together with diligence and perfection. I relied upon Charles and Sue like a right and left hand, not only because they put the book together, but also because, in addition to being a wonderfully talented printer-designer team, Charles Chauncey Wells is also an American Revolutionary historian and author of *Preachers, Patriots, and Plain Folks.* As a historian, his expertise was invaluable to me. And to Colleen Daley, who did a brilliant job of cover design, my thanks and loving appreciation for always being there. I am grateful also to Sharon Mullins who spent hours proofreading the text.

And to David Smith, my business partner and dear friend, my thanks for believing in this project and supporting it with unbounded enthusiasm, as is your style. David and I are also very grateful to Hay House, a company that profiles spiritual integrity, and to Reid Tracy, president of Hay House and Donna Abate, editor of the Hay House Myss Newsletter, for their very generous support of this project – and all my projects, for that matter. So on behalf of the *George Washington Team* and myself - we are very, very honored and blessed to be able to make this book available to you after a sixty-year-long journey.

Caroline Myss

FOREWORD

The *Autobiography of George Washington* represents a most extraordinary piece of America's Sacred Contract. The spirit of George Washington made contact with Edith Ellis in 1944, requesting that she take down his autobiography. When her sojourn with George Washington began, Edith was a woman in her mid-seventies suffering from severe glaucoma. Harriet von Tobel, who today is a delightful and highly energetic 83-year-old woman, was in her mid-twenties in 1944. She provided secretarial assistance for Edith who channeled this remarkable piece of work over the course of 110 days. The *Washington Autobiography* is a masterpiece of intrigue, but equally extraordinary is the content that came through a nearly blind woman who had no formal training in history. I met Harriet in 1983 when the manuscript first arrived at Stillpoint Publishing Company, founded by two colleagues and me in that same year. She submitted the manuscript for consideration for publication and that began an adventure that has gone on for twenty-three years, leading to the opportunity to finally bring this rare piece of mystical literature to the public. For Harriet, it marks a type of closure on her sixty-year commitment to Edith Ellis and George Washington to see that his autobiography made it into America's public domain.

My own story with *The Autobiography of George Washington* is its own saga, from working with it 23 years - ago in preparation for publication, to losing track of the manuscript for twenty-years. Then, once I decided to write *The Sacred Contract of America* (more about that further on), I lamented its absence like the loss of an old friend. I had lost touch with Harriet, although she no longer had possession of the manuscript either. But as it happened, or as "providence" would have it, as Washington would say, Jeannie just happened to be traveling with me on one of my out-of-country seminars. Jeannie and I had worked together at the publishing company. She was also a part of the Washington project from the time Harriet's manuscript arrived. I mentioned to Jeannie how much I could use the Washington manuscript now that I was going to write *The Sacred Contract of America*, but that I felt it was far too late to ever see it again. And besides, I added, I didn't even know if Harriet von Tobel was still alive, much less where she was living. Jeannie grinned as she replied, "Oh, she's alive. I'm still in touch with her." That was the beginning of the mini-drama through which I re-acquired this manuscript, and once again Jeannie was a vital part of it. Without a doubt, this was the most exciting piece of work that ever came into our hands because it symbolized so very much, not the least of which was that communication with "the other side" was absolutely possible. Then, to have a document whose author from "the other side" was the first President of the United States of America and the man considered to be THE Founding Father was like being connected to cosmic electricity. Every day was an enchantment while working on this manuscript, and work we did.

ENDLESS DISCUSSIONS took place as to how to approach this material, beginning with the most essential question: Was it fraudulent? Was Edith Ellis just a clever woman who managed to create an extraordinary piece of work? After all, Edith Ellis, in addition to being a highly reputable channel who had other channeled books published through Knopf Publishers in New York, was also a successful playwright, although none of her plays were

*Edith Ellis, at right, of New York City ((1874–1960), channeled
Washington's message and works with her young assistant, Harriet Von
Tobel, who typed the manuscript from Edith's notes.*

historic in nature. These channeled books were written through
her connection with a spirit who identified himself as Wilfred
Brandon, who said he lost his life at age nineteen during the
American Revolution. If Edith Ellis was a fraud, where on earth
did she get her facts, especially those mini-facts that weren't easily
available in history books during her era? For example, how could
a woman who never loaded a musket describe it so perfectly, along
with the smell of gunpowder? And how could she possibly know
what it was like to pursue the British through the cold woods in
knee-deep snow while carrying the heartache of watching an army
of starving men walking behind you? The facts that Edith Ellis
would have had to retain in her mind would have challenged the
memory capacity of even the best historian.

Consider, for example that Edith Ellis was born shortly
after the Civil War and thus her education was typical for a woman of her generation; she was hardly a scholar of history. And we
all know the Internet did not exist in 1944, so her ability to access

a wide database of knowledge outside her field – and all within 110 days – was severely limited. And then there was this compelling fact: at the time she accomplished this amazing feat, Edith Ellis was nearly blind, which is why she required the secretarial assistance of our dear Harriet von Tobel, who was, of course, quite a young woman in 1944. As Harriet recalls, Edith Ellis "channeled" material from George Washington during the day. She "heard him" in that subtle fourth dimensional voice that those who cannot hear it will never understand because it is absolutely indescribable. Then Harriet took her handwritten notes and neatly organized and typed them each evening. As an author, I must say that if Edith was writing a piece of fiction, she did an incredible job of knocking out pages and pages per day of intriguing information without a break. (My editor would adore me if I could pull that off.) My only explanation, after reading this manuscript so many times, was that she must have been in touch with some source other than her own imagination – it's just too remarkable an accomplishment.

At any rate, now let's return to 2002 where I was lamenting the loss of this precious manuscript because I was in the beginning creative throes of *The Sacred Contract of America*. I just adore Divine intervention and the hand of destiny—or as Washington calls it, "Providence." Jeannie had joined me on one of my workshop tours out of the country and one day while chatting, I told her about my new book idea and remarked about how I wish I had held onto a copy of our Washington manuscript, even though I would not be able to use it anyway because I did not own the rights to it. But at least I would have it as a type of reference, or for psychic company, so to speak. And then I said, "And I don't even know how Harriet is, or where she is anymore." Jeannie looked at me with that casual grin of hers and said, "I do. I've kept in touch with her all these years."

I about flew out of my chair when I heard that. Chills ran down my body. I was on fire with enthusiasm. I wanted Jeannie to phone Harriet right then and there, from Greece, and ask her if she had a spare copy of the original manuscript. Well, that didn't happen. But what did happen was that through one wondrous bit of synchronicity after another, within a few months, the manuscript was back in my hands – Whew – at last.

᠅

LET ME RECALL A BIT OF WHAT took place with this manuscript during the years we worked on it at the publishing house. As publishers, we were most concerned about authenticity. We did not want to publish a piece of "channeled fiction," and channeled material, to say the least, is high risk. I'll elaborate on the nature of channeled material a little later, but let me say at this point that we went through an extensive, and I mean extensive, process of research with the Washington material. We enlisted the aid of an attorney who had superb research skills, and together we entered the world of American Revolutionary history and the scholarly work of most of the leading Washington historians. For months and months – over a year – we took each fact that Washington stated and sought to verify it. Did Timothy's Tavern really exist? Did Washington have a brother named Charles? He said that he intensely disliked that famous Gilbert Stuart portrait of him—did he ever comment on that while alive? Did he develop smallpox in Cuba? Did he have a childhood friend name Corliss? Some facts were very easy to double check: yes, Washington did have a brother named Charles. But here's one that we may never find out, and it was statements exactly like the following one that caused us to discuss again and again the risk factors involved in publishing this manuscript. According to the material that Edith Ellis channeled, George Washington stated:

"I was 75 when I died – not 67, as I am recorded. I was born in 1724 - not 1732. All records that I know of have been based on British accounts, which were never really authentic."

Washington went on to state that his actual birth date is recorded in the family bible. We weren't, of course, able to verify that, but these types of statements were more than a bit arresting and they gave us reason to reconsider time and again whether we wanted to go through with publishing this material. Yet, such discrepancies also suggest that if Edith Ellis were attempting to create a fraudulent document, that goal would have been far better served had she kept to the known facts of conventional history. She was putting her entire effort at risk by making such outrageous claims—unless, of course, she wasn't the one making them.

❀

IN THE END, WE AT THE publishing company produced a book entitled *The Missing Pages*. It was a mixture of the material of Washington's combined with inserts by Washington historians. We ended up deleting a substantial amount of the original manuscript. In short, we gutted it for the sake of authenticity, convention and editorial safety. After all the years of hard work, research, and patriotic excitement that we had invested in *The Autobiography of George Washington*, the project never saw the light of day, which is something I do not at all regret. We had taken the spirit out of it, and if I may say so on behalf of Washington, we took out his personality and kept in only the earthly details that would support believability.

Now, once again, I have the opportunity to bring *The Autobiography of George Washington* to the public. In order to fully appreciate this material, however, the nature of channeling needs to be elaborated upon as it is such a misunderstood domain. And secondly, but by no means less important, it is vital to discuss why this manuscript is important to us at all. What type of information can it possibly contain that would be of any interest to anyone? What reasons did Washington have for contacting Edith Ellis in the first place with his request that she take down the recollections of his lifetime that he felt were so important to share with his fellow Americans?

❀

UNDERSTANDING CHANNELING
AND
CHANNELED LITERATURE

BECAUSE *The Autobiography of George Washington* is channeled, it opens a door into a realm of literature and cosmic activity that requires some measure of explanation. Not everyone is familiar with channeled literature and others who know about channeled material often maintain a highly skeptical viewpoint of it, which is completely understandable. In fact, I encourage healthy skepticism at all times because it is so easy to be seduced by the world of psychic activity. And all that I can say to you, should you decide to read the entire book, is that ultimately it remains a mystery as to whether the spirit behind this manuscript is truly that of George Washington. I certainly cannot make that statement with absolute confidence, and for that reason alone, I could have once again decided not to release this manuscript to the public. But then I considered the history of this manuscript and its contents and decided to let you, the reader, decide its worth and value and authenticity. I offer it to you because it exists as a piece of the mystical history of this nation, and that is the most authentic statement that I can make about *The Autobiography of George Washington.*

❀

BUT LET'S CONSIDER for a moment that channeling, the ability to make contact with a spirit and become a vessel of communication, is real. People who seek spiritual guidance, after all, are in fact opening themselves to a form of channeling even if that is not the word they use to describe it. Channeled material has always been available. In fact, there has never been a time that I can think of when cultures were devoid of channeled material. (I'm tempted to ask, 'What isn't channeled?' when it comes to great pieces of music, literature, science, art, architecture, medicine, acts of heroism, and devotions of love.) Back in the 1970s and 80s, a number of authors became quite popular on the scene for their channeled work, such as Jane Roberts and the Seth material and Helen Schucman for *A Course in Miracles*, which is a deeply respected piece of channeled information. Scriptures and sacred literature are channeled material. If you want to get into a highly refined description of what qualifies as channeled literature, Church spokespeople prefer the word "inspired" when describing the source of sacred literature, which is fine—call it what you will, a rose by any other name is still a rose.

People have always—and I mean always—tried to find ways to pierce the veil between worlds, to connect to angels and guides on the "other side." So the question is not so much, "Is channeling possible?" because it is. The concern is whether the channel one is working with is authentic or a fraud. Secondly, even if a channel is authentic, does that mean that all the information coming through that channel is accurate? My experience in this field has been that people are all too quick to assume that if someone is a channel, the source they are in touch with is good, holy, pure, wise, perhaps an angel, and most certainly infallible. It's easy to understand how such an assumption has evolved, of course. We associate the invisible realm with God and angels and guides. But the fact is the invisible realm is murky psychic territory and very, very few channels are actually clear vessels, just as very, very few healers can actually channel a quality of light that can heal an illness fully and completely.

That tendency to assume that the entity that someone is channeling is incapable of communicating an error is our misconception and a projection of our illusions about the spiritual domain. Death by no means makes a soul enlightened any more than it elevates an individual to the rank of angel or guide. I'm hardly an expert on the social network of the nonphysical world, but I know enough to understand that human beings do not automatically become enlightened masters once they leave their physical bodies. If that were the case, all doctrines promoting reincarnation would have to be cancelled out as there would be no need to return for continued life cycles of learning for we would have accomplished all that in one lifetime. People also assume that the spirit of someone who has passed over should somehow retain the same personality characteristics that they held while alive on earth, including being able to maintain the same speech patterns.

Washington states early on in his autobiography that we, the readers, should not expect him to speak in language patterns and mannerisms of the 18th century because he doesn't exist there any longer – he has shed the trappings of that era, so to speak. His tone, his language, and his approach to his life is far more reminiscent of an older man sitting by a fireplace recalling a long and dramatic life rich with accomplishments, than a spirit who has returned to impart divine wisdom. That, let me emphasize, is not his stated purpose. Washington lived during an era when the British were America's adversaries and slavery was still a part of the culture. Washington was a soldier who fought battles in the French-Indian War as well as the Revolution, and he recalls those battles with the same fervor as a soldier returning from battle today. At first, I have to admit, I found the casualness with which he presented his memories of killing men in battle, for instance, to be almost shocking, until I reminded myself that Washington was clear from the onset of his autobiography that his purpose was to recall the details of his physical life, and these are the details of his physical life. At the same time, Washington's recall of his love for Martha and for America is more than enchanting.

※

IN OUR EAGERNESS TO validate our connection to these nonphysical beings, we long for indicators of proof of authenticity, such as language patterns, and that is completely understandable. But I recall in reading *A Course in Miracles* that the language and phrasing of its content hardly reflected what I imagined the voice of Jesus to sound like; yet Jesus claims to be the "real" author behind the text. One needs to adjust constantly to the world of the beyond. Also, and this is somewhat of a technical note about the process of channeling, when a link is made between a spirit and a human being capable of receiving impressions or information from the fourth dimension, that information still has to "incarnate." As such, the impressions have to make their way into the earth plane through the psyche and intellect of the mind of the human scribe. The quality of the impressions must rely upon the sophistication of the scribe's vocabulary as well as historic associations. In other words, rarely can a "pure" channel be found. Even the most sacred of scriptures have discrepancies due to the differences among the individual scribes. At the end of the day, we must acknowledge that there is a cosmic filter that exists between our world of time and space and literal history, and that other dimension in which all history blends into the grand scheme of eternity.

Even understanding that, however, I still knew that the discrepancies in all channeled material, including the Washington material, could be most alarming. *Then I realized something that has served me well ever since, which is that we have more than one history.* All of us have a physical history, but we also have an emotional, psychological, intellectual, psychic, spiritual, and collective unconscious history. We are a product of several historic paths moving along simultaneously. If you were to write your personal history according to each of those categories, you would indeed end up with seven separate historic paths that overlapped, but each would tell different versions or interpretations of the same event. Your physical history would record an event, but your emotional history would articulate how you felt about that event. Your spiritual history would record how that event impacted the content of your soul. You might well end up with seven versions so different that one would hardly believe they were all rooted in the same event. But that is the nature of life and consciousness. It is a complex matrix of perceptions and interpretations of the events of our lives.

WHY NOW?

GEORGE WASHINGTON HAD a genuine spiritual purpose in contacting Edith Ellis. He felt that the time had come to share with Americans the content of his heart and soul as he felt that he had denied Americans this part of his life while alive. Washington clearly stated that his intention in wanting to communicate his autobiography was that he felt that he had denied Americans any insight into his emotional being while alive, and into the way he felt about this nation and all that he experienced, such as the fear and horror of his time at Valley Forge. Our image of him historically is that he was a frozen figure. That, he felt, hardly did him justice. This goal eclipsed the need to recount the details of physical events, as he felt that others had accomplished that task. He was doing only what he could do. Further, from the spiritual plane the facts of those events were no longer important. What one takes to the "other side" is represented by what a person comes to realize about the truth in life as opposed to one's ability to remember the small day-to-day details of one's physical life. Fair enough, say I. (Besides, most people cannot recall what they had for lunch yesterday much less what they did two hundred years ago...).

America was entering a dangerously vulnerable period of time; Washington felt when he worked with Edith Ellis, that it was a time when the country was coming close to losing contact with its founding vision. Washington believed that if Americans reconnected with his spirit, and with what he had experienced during the struggle for this nation, the enduring bond he had established between himself and his beloved nation would help to reawaken the founding spirit of America. But curiously Washington wasn't referring to the psychic climate of 1944, when America was at the height of its pride and glory, filled with the honor that comes from having won two wars against two enemies. He was looking ahead, down the road in the decades following World War II. He was looking at us.

Washington said he came back to share the content of his heart and spirit because he felt he might inspire Americans to feel a passion for this nation again lest we lose our way, lest we lose the vision that inspired the birth of this great nation. It's obvious we are living in a time of great change; we are living in an atmosphere as volatile perhaps as what our forefathers and mothers must have felt when they anticipated what they would have to go through to bring forth a new beginning, a new nation, a new spiritual paradigm, for that is what America represented in 1776.

We are very much at the crossroads of a new spiritual paradigm and most certainly America is once again at the forefront of a revolution. This time it's global. The stakes are higher, the consequences far more lethal, but the power of America's vision remains intact if we as a nation reconnect with that vision.

※

AN AMERICAN *DaVinci Code*

I BELIEVE THAT THE exploration of *The Sacred Contract of America* must begin with a sojourn into the mystical history of this nation because it is the only nation which has a political theology rooted in a cosmic belief in its own Divine destiny. America was born of mystical vision mixed with a fervor for freedom. We love the symbolism of the pyramid on The Great Seal and the fact that so many of our Founding Fathers were members of a secret esoteric society, the Freemasons. We love the fact that there was an element of cosmic consciousness involved in the minds of these men and women who laid the foundation of America. And we love that part of America's birth that first connected this nation to power of destiny. *The Autobiography of George Washington* is a part of America's mystical history for many reasons, not the least of which is that Washington speaks so passionately of his contact with the spirit of destiny in these early hours of America's birth.

Where did such a belief originate? George Washington was one such man as were Thomas Jefferson, Benjamin Franklin, John Adams, Alexander Hamilton, Thomas Paine, John Hancock, Paul Revere, and Sam Adams, among so many others whose forceful characters and spirits grounded a vision that a nation could exist where freedom of spirit reigned supreme. These people believed themselves to have a destiny, and the lives of many would indeed indicate that a destiny did direct their footsteps on this earth. That they all lived at the same time – such outrageously powerful personalities with such individual geniuses – is curious in itself, quite frankly, but that each had a specific genius required to build a new nation bears all the markings of Divine design. To my way of thinking, they were political mystics cleverly disguised as extraordinary mortals, burdened with all the hardships of ordinary life, including all the essential character flaws that go along with being human.

But that element of mysticism – that deep passion they shared for carving a way of life that gave way to the rights of their spirits - is a most revealing window into the souls of these men. They were in touch with a power much greater than themselves that flooded into their psyches and souls and, during times of great desperation, even angelic visions were experienced, as Washington describes during his trials at Valley Forge. In fact, it was said that during the horrible winter of 1777, Washington experienced a profound vision that gave him the strength to endure that winter and the coming years of the war, and that he told some of his soldiers of that vision. One of them, Anthony Sherman, repeated the story to a newspaper reporter who published it in 1864. It is worth sharing, not only because it so beautifully speaks of the mystical consciousness that was prevalent during the American Revolution, but also because Washington refers to this in his autobiography. The following is the journalist's account of Sherman's story, which validates in vivid detail the vision that Washington recalled again through Edith Ellis:

"The last time that I ever saw Anthony Sherman was on July 4th, 1859, in Independence Square. He was then ninety-nine, and becoming very feeble; but though so old, his dimming eyes rekindled as he looked at Independence Hall, which he said he had come to gaze upon once more before he was gathered home … (he said),

"Let us go into the hall. I want to tell you an incident of Washington's life – one that no one alive knows of except myself; and if you live, you will before long see it verified … "From the opening of the Revolution, we experienced all phases of fortune – now good and now ill, one time victorious and another conquered. The darkest period we had, however, I think, was when Washington, after several reverses, retreated to Valley Forge, where he resolved to pass the winter of 1777. Ah! I have often seen the tears coursing down our dear old commander's care-worn cheeks, as he would be conversing with a confidential officer about the condition of his poor soldiers. You have doubtless heard the story of Washington going to the thicket to pray. Well, it was not only true, but he used often to pray in secret, for aid and comfort from that God, the interposition of whose divine providence brought us safely through those dark days of tribulation.

"One day – I remember it well – the chilly winds whistled through the leafless trees, and though the sky was cloudless and the sun shining brightly, he remained in his quarters nearly the whole afternoon alone. When he came out I noticed that his face was a shade paler than usual, and there seemed to be something upon his mind of more than ordinary importance. Returning just after dusk, he dispatched an orderly to the quarters of the officer I mentioned who was presently in attendance. After a preliminary conversation, which lasted some half an hour, Washington, gazing upon his companion with that strange look of dignity he alone could command, said to the latter, "I do not know whether it was owing to the anxiety of the mind, or what, but this afternoon, as I was sitting at this very table engaged in preparing a dispatch, something in the apartment seemed to disturb me. Looking up, I beheld standing opposite to me a singularly beautiful female. So astonished was I – for I had given strict orders not to be disturbed

– that it was some moments before I found language to inquire the cause of her presence. A second, third, and even a fourth time did I repeat the question but received no other answer from my mysterious visitor than a slight raising of her eyes. By this time I felt a strange sensation spreading throughout me. I would have risen, but the riveted gaze of the being before me rendered volition impossible. I essayed once more to address her, but my tongue had become useless. A new influence, mysterious, potent, irresistible, took possession of me. All I could do was to gaze, gaze steadily, vacantly at my unknown visitant. Gradually the surrounding atmosphere seemed as though becoming filled with sensations, and grew luminous. Everything about me appeared to rarefy – the mysterious visitor herself becoming more airy and yet even more distinct to my sight than before. I now began to feel as one dying, or rather to experience the sensations which I have sometimes imagined accompany dissolution. I did not think, I did not reason, I did not move; all were alike impossible. I was only conscious of gazing fixedly, vacantly at my companion.

"Presently I heard a voice saying, "Son of the Republic, look and learn," while at the same time my visitor extended her arm and fore-finger eastwardly. I now beheld a heavy white vapor at some distance, rising, fold upon fold. This gradually disappeared, and I looked upon a strange scene. Before me lay spread out in one vast plain all the countries of the world – Europe, Asia, Africa and America. I saw rolling and tossing between Europe and America the billows of the Atlantic, and between Asia and America lay the Pacific. "Son of the Republic," said the same mysterious voice as before, "look and learn." At that moment I beheld a dark, shadowy being, like an angel, standing, or rather floating mid-air, between Europe and America. Dipping water out of the ocean in the hollow of each hand, he sprinkled some upon America with his right hand, while he cast upon Europe some with his left. Immediately a dark cloud arose from each of these countries and joined in mid-ocean. For a while it remained stationary and then moved slowly westward, until it enveloped America in its murky folds. Sharp flashes of lightning now gleamed throughout it at intervals, and I heard the smothered groans and cries of the American people. A second time the angel dipped water from the ocean and sprinkled it out as before. The dark cloud was then drawn back to the ocean, into whose heaving waves it sank from view. A third time I heard the mysterious voice saying, "Son of the Republic, look and learn." I cast my eyes upon America and beheld villages and towns and cities springing up, one after another, until the whole land from the Atlantic to the Pacific was dotted with them. Again, I heard the mysterious voice say, "Son of the Republic, the end of the century cometh; look and learn."

"At this the shadowy angel turned his face southward, and from Africa I saw an ill-omened specter approach our land. It flitted slowly and heavily over every village, town and city of the latter, the inhabitants of which presently set themselves in battle array, against each other. As I continued looking, I saw a bright angel, on whose brow rested a crown of light, on which was traced the word UNION, bearing the American flag, which he placed between the divided nations, and said, "Remember ye are brethren." Instantly, the inhabitants, casting from them their weapons, became friends once more and united around the National Standard.

"And again I heard the mysterious voice saying: "Son of the Republic, the second peril is passed; look and learn." And I beheld the villages, towns, and cities of America increase in size and number, until at last they covered all the land from the Atlantic to the Pacific, and their inhabitants became as countless as the stars in heaven, or the sand on the seashore. And again I heard the mysterious voice saying, "Son of the Republic, the end of the century cometh; look and learn." At this the dark, the shadowy angel placed a trumpet to his mouth and blew three distinct blasts; and taking water from the ocean, he sprinkled it out upon Europe, Asia and Africa. Then my eyes looked upon a fearful scene: from each of these countries arose thick, black clouds that were soon joined into one. And throughout this mass gleamed a dark-red light, but which I saw hordes of armed men, who, moving with the cloud, marched by land and sailed by sea to America, which country was presently enveloped in the volume of cloud. And I dimly saw these vast armies devastate the whole country and pillage and burn the villages, towns and cities that I beheld springing up. As my ears listened to the thundering of the cannon, clashing of swords, and shouts and cries of the millions in mortal combat, I again heard the mysterious voice saying, "Son of the Republic, look and learn." When the voice had ceased, the dark shadowy angel placed his trumpet once more to his mouth and blew a long and fearful blast.

"Instantly a light as of a thousand suns shone down from above me and pierced and broke into fragments the dark cloud which enveloped America. At the same moment I saw the angel upon whose forehead still shone the word UNION, and who bore our national flag in one hand and a sword in the other, descend from the heavens attended by legions of bright spirits. These immediately joined the inhabitants of America, who I perceived were well nigh overcome, but who immediately taking courage again, closed up their broken ranks and renewed the battle. Again, amid the fearful noise of the conflict, I heard the mysterious voice saying: "Son of the Republic, look and learn." As the voice ceased, the shadowy angel for the last time dipped water from the ocean and sprinkled it upon America. Instantly the dark cloud rolled back, together with the armies it had brought, leaving the inhabitants of the land victorious.

"Then once more I beheld villages, towns, and cities springing up where I had seen them before, while the bright angel, planting the azure standard he had brought in the midst of them, cried with a loud voice to the inhabitants: "While the stars remain and the heavens send down dew upon the earth, so long shall the Republic last." And taking from his brow the crown on which still blazed the word UNION, he placed it upon the standard while the people, kneeling down, said, "Amen."

"The scene instantly began to fade and dissolve, and I at last saw nothing but the rising, curling white vapor I had first beheld. This also disappearing, I found myself once more gazing upon my mysterious visitor, who, in the same voice I had heard be-

fore, said, "Son of the Republic, what you have seen is thus inter-
preted. Three perils will come upon the Republic. The most fearful
is the second, passing which, the whole world united shall never
be able to prevail against her. Let every child of the Republic learn
to live for his God, his land and Union. With these words the vision vanished, and I started from my seat and felt that I had seen
a vision wherein had been shown to me the birth, progress and
destiny of the Republic of the United States. In UNION she will
have strength, in DISUNION her destruction."

"Such, my friends," concluded the venerable narrator,
"were the words I heard from Washington's own lips, and America
will do well to profit by them ..." [Charles W. Alexander (Wesley
Bradshaw), Washington's Vision (Philadelphia: C.W. Alexander
and Co., 1864), pp. 98-99.]

IN A SENSE I CONSIDER *The Autobiography of George Washington* to be somewhat like an American *Da Vinci Code*. However,
this manuscript is real, and it suggests that many of the mystical
legends that make up the founding years of this nation have their
roots in actual events. Visions like the one Washington was said
to have had at Valley Forge cannot be proven, but then again, how
much of history can be indisputably proven? Furthermore, consider how many of our life beliefs are based upon stories that will
never be proven, like whether there were three kings who paid
homage to an infant in a manger or did Siddhartha ever really sit
under a Bodhi tree? Myth or real? and do you care? What is worth
noticing is how much power these legends and myths have had
in forming your reality. People die on the battlefields every day
because of their allegiance to myths that cannot be proven. When
you come down to it, few things in life can actually be proven true
and even then, what is true tends to have a short lifeline – just ask
any scientist. Today this is true and tomorrow it's not. Myths have
a way, however, of outlasting physical facts that are continually
edited as more are discovered. There is something about the power

contained within the myth that grabs hold of our spirits and feeds us in a way that is impossible for the dense container of earthly facts and information. We adore myth because it suggests a power hidden behind the scenes, a force greater than ourselves operating within the Universe as a whole and governing our own lives. We would be empty creatures were it not for our myths and legends.

Washington spoke about his vision at Valley Forge to Edith Ellis, as you'll read in his autobiography. He was desperate as he watched his men starving to death. He wondered if the vision of freedom alone was enough to keep these men going and then, in his hour of greatest need, as he said to Ellis, an angel came to him.

Washington was hardly the only American to have experiences of Divine intervention. According to Manly P. Hall in *The Secret Destiny of America*, the Declaration of Independence was not only a mystical document, but the signers of the Declaration were urged on by an apparition from the balcony of Independence Hall. Faced with the death penalty for high treason, the men in the State House at Philadelphia in 1776 debated for several hours, with the doors locked and a guard posted. Abruptly, according to Manly's account, a confident voice from the balcony, which many believe to be the voice of Master Spirit St. Germaine who watches over this nation, advised them:

"Sign that parchment! Sign, if the next moment the gibbet's rope is about your neck! Sign, if the next minute this hall rings with the clash of falling axes! Sign, by all your hopes in life, or death, as men, as husbands, as fathers, brothers, sign your names to the parchment or be accursed forever! Sign, and not only for yourselves, but for all ages, for that Parchment will be the textbook of freedom, the Bible of the rights of man forever…"

Suggesting that the hesitant founding fathers might be "the awful clouds which veil the brightness of Jehovah's throne," the speaker cited recent battles by the colonists at Bunker Hill and Lexington as evidence of God's will that America be free. When he finished, the delegates rushed forward to grasp the historic quill. Once the signing was accomplished, they sought to find the unknown orator and thank him for his efforts. But he had vanished, despite the locked and guarded door. (Manley P. Hall, The Secret Destiny of America (Los Angeles: Philosophical Research Society, 1978), pp. 164-172.)

Numerous other stories, myths, and legends exist that most certainly suggest that America was a nation conceived by Divine design with a Contract deeply tied to Sacred intent and guided, as Washington often said, by the hand of Providence. Sacred intent by no means makes a nation superior any more than it does a person. But it does infer that there is a cosmic obligation in place that calls upon the people of a free nation to act with an intense degree of responsibility for conscious action, thought, and deed because we can, and because that is what freedom of spirit gives us the right and power to do. America was created to inspire and protect the human spirit. This nation was conceived as a place of enlightenment for all humanity – so believed Benjamin Franklin, Thomas Jefferson, so many others – and of course, George Washington.

❀

THE SACRED CONTRACT OF AMERICA
&
The Autobiography of George Washington

I WAS INTRODUCED TO The Autobiography of George Washington in 1983. The story is one of the best adventures of my life, one that is obviously ongoing. But I was separated from the Washington manuscript for almost twenty-one-years and would have remained separated from the manuscript except for 911, the grim event that re-directed the future of humanity. As a way of sharing how extraordinary I believe this manuscript to be, I felt that recalling my own history with The Autobiography of George Washington was a story worth telling. No doubt 911 effected most people in some way. For me, my already passionate sense of patriotism became even more passionate. Shortly after 911, I was on a book tour for *Sacred Contracts,* traveling cross-country for what seemed like forever. One evening, as I was watching the news, I began wondering about the Sacred Contract of America and about the extraordinary events and individuals that inspired and shaped the founding of this nation. My editor suggested I write an op-ed piece for the New York Times on the subject but as I began outlining what I had intended to be a provocative op-ed piece, an outline for a book emerged: *The Sacred Contract of America.* Because the subject matter of this book ignited my quest to acquire the Washington manuscript once again, and because you are a part of the Sacred Contract of this nation – and therefore everything George Washington lived for (and lives on for) – I decided to write an extensive piece explaining the significance of America's Sacred Contract and why *The Autobiography of George Washington* is perhaps one of the most divinely guided pieces of American literature since the American Revolution.

My inspiration for exploring the *Sacred Contract of America* took shape as the result of two life-changing events, one personal and one global. The first was writing the book, *Sacred Contracts,* which introduced the idea that assignments or agreements were made prior to each of our births that organized the events of our physical lives. That each of our lives was nothing more than a random act of fate in which we lived in hope of occasional acts of Divine intervention was just too preposterous a notion for me, as preposterous perhaps as the idea might seem to some that we are given Sacred Contracts whose energy directs the unfolding of the opportunities and challenges of our lives. A belief in God is built into the theory of Sacred Contracts because a person is obviously making an agreement with someone or something cosmic, whereas a person is free to muse about the existence of God – any type of God – if life is seen as nothing more than a potpourri of random events. I deeply and profoundly believe that every single life is here by Divine design and that each of us has Sacred Contracts that must be – and will be – attended to during the course of a lifetime.

Many, many times I have witnessed a person's life become transformed when, during a moment of profound cosmic understanding, they recognize the difference between that which they *want* to do and that which they *must* do. Most often the *must do* choices of our lives require the most courage and the most faith because that's the nature of a Sacred Contract – they are the agreements you've made with the Divine that require a union with the Divine in order to succeed. As a person becomes aligned to the life force of his or her Sacred Contract, they can intuitively sense the energy field around one of their Sacred Contracts. That ability to recognize an intimate thread of cosmic animation redirects their life forevermore. Meaning and purpose become internalized into their fiber. The study of Sacred Contracts at the individual level consumed me because the cosmic domain of life pulsates with so much tactile divinity. Individual purpose and meaning are no longer theory; they become facts that direct the course of one's life.

※

THE EVENTS OF 9/11 inspired my wanting to take the study of Sacred Contracts from the individual level to exploring the organization of cosmic events within the scope of nations and global dynamics. Do nations have Sacred Contracts? Are events on the global level as choreographed as they are on the individual level? How could they not be? Our inability to understand a mechanism sophisticated enough to organize the cosmos and all that occurs within the territory of the cosmos does not preclude that such coordination exists behind the scenes. Nor does our need for events to make sense preclude cosmic design. We ponder the moral, ethical, and spiritual purpose behind events that unfold with horror on our earth and cannot imagine that such events are planned – or allowed – to occur. Wars, for example, are such events, as are tsunamis and earthquakes that take the lives of hundreds of thousands of *innocent* people. What exactly qualifies for the label *innocent*? That we do not see a legitimate *evil* reason why they should suffer? We adhere to a theology that believes heaven operates – or should operate – according to our laws of justice, which essentially can be summed up with "an eye for an eye." Application of our limited code of justice as a measure of the standard of fairness of the Divine is preposterous, but that doesn't stop us from doing our cosmic calculations and trying to find the way to pierce the veil between dimensions in order to grasp even a hint of why things happen as they do on this planet. Whether we will ever accomplish a foothold into a cosmic understanding that satisfies all of us is doubtful, yet we cannot stop ourselves from pursuing the mystery of why things happen as they do, because that is what life is about – the pursuit of mystery.

For me, exploring the Sacred Contract of America meant entering into the pursuit of the mystery of the founding of this extraordinary nation. Long before I began to pursue the research necessary to write a book examining the Sacred Contract of America, I believed America to be a sacred nation. It could be said, of course, that all nations are sacred because that is certainly the truth from a cosmic perspective. America, however, stands out in the arena of the sacred in that it was so consciously inspired by philosophies and spiritual principles (not religious, but spiritual), as is articulated in depth further on. I knew it was a nation steeped in mystical roots, but not until I saturated myself in the sacred literature and writings of America did I even come close to touching, sensing, and embracing a fragment of the "founding spirit" that possessed these first Americans. For one thing, I recognized that our founding Fathers and Mothers were political mystics disguised in the necessary costumes of the times. I have listened to people present arguments over their faults as men, as leaders, as racists – and they had their faults, most certainly. But to my way of thinking, their flaws make their accomplishments all the more extraordinary. If they had been fully formed Beings of Light, what would there be for the ordinary among us to admire? And why do we demand that those who inspire us be perfect while they are here on earth – or suffer the consequences of our wrath? So, flawed they were, but they were also Illuminates – individuals who were impassioned with a vision that a nation could exist in which the rights of the human spirit were honored above all else. As I read through the mystical literature of America, it occurred to me repeatedly that it was precisely because of this extraordinary spiritual vision that so much Divine intervention took place; Heaven wanted America to be born. Now, four years into this project, I have acquired a library of literature on the mystical history of this nation, including files and papers that I had no idea even existed. For all the arguments that can be placed on the table about what America has done during its brief lifetime, the fact is that its beginning will always remain mystically extraordinary.

I HAD INTENDED THAT The Sacred Contract of America would be presented solely as a book, but during these past four years, the vast amount of research required to write that book and the substantial time required to do justice to the organization of that material made me realize that more than a book was required. I also realized that The Sacred Contract of America is both historic in nature and a living entity. Sacred Contracts are real. They are not physical, but they are real. That something is not physical is hardly a measure of whether or not it exists. Your Sacred Contract is as real as your breath. America's Sacred Contract is equally real, equally an energetic source of life. It is the pulsating spirit behind the vision that inspired the American Revolution and that spirit has never ceased to radiate its subtle influence and grace. The Sacred Contract of America manifests in a complex mixture of this nation's mystical history along with the historic and political events that we all know took place and continue to take place in every second of every day.

And then there are the people whose lives and personalities have risen to the forefront because there was something about them that represented elements of the American spirit – at its best and in its shadow. Just consider this mixture: Daniel Boone, Wild Bill Hickok, General George Custer, Abraham Lincoln, Teddy Roosevelt, John F. Kennedy, J. Edgar Hoover, Martin Luther King, Jr. Helen Keller, Rosa Parks, Robert E. Lee, General Dwight David Eisenhower, Charles Lindbergh, Edgar Allen Poe,

Emily Dickinson, Henry David Thoreau, Ralph Waldo Emerson, Walt Whitman, Jonas Salk, Thomas Edison, Alexander Graham Bell, Chief Seattle, Sitting Bull, and Walt Disney - an endless list of individuals who represent just a very, very few of the countless archetypal characters that embody America's electric and free spirit. I could have continued the historic list forever (and I have yet to add one living example).

But now consider that *you* are a part of America's Sacred Contract. The spirit that first awakened in our Founding Mystics, as I like to think of them, runs through your spiritual DNA. It is a part of your Sacred Contract because you are an American. And even if you are not an American by birth, but are drawn to be here in some way, a part of the energy of this nation's Sacred Contract is merging with your own with every breath you take. Consider the archetypal patterns that comprise the stellar chart that is this nation: Entrepreneur, Judge, Slave-Master, Victim, Prostitute, Saboteur, Orphan Child/Adopting Motherland, Visionary/Inventor, Rescuer/Liberator, Rebel, Warrior, Pioneer. Both in their power of Light and in their shadow, these archetypal patterns are active within the soul of America as strong and dominant (operative word – dominant, as other archetypes are certainly influential) energetic currents.

✿

No MATTER WHERE I went during these past four years, members of audiences asked me about the status of the book, *The Sacred Contract of America*. The public eagerness to have me complete this book went beyond ordinary curiosity; there was a low-grade desperation or sense of panic and loss in their voices. I did not want to wait until I finished the massive task of combining all of this information to release to the public what I had already discovered, most particularly about America's mystical history, because it is that part of this nation's heritage that needs to be animated the most at this time. *More than anything else, we need to connect once again to the psychic and spiritual currents of power that so inspired our Founding Fathers and Mothers.* I do not believe I am alone in my thinking, for a couple of reasons. First of all, during the past four or five years, a plethora of books on our Founding Fathers have poured out of publishing houses, including biographies on John Adams, Abigail Adams, Benjamin Franklin, Thomas Jefferson, Alexander Hamilton (one of my favorite people), Aaron Burr, a book on the Founding Brothers, and of course several on George Washington. Why is that? Are we as a nation experiencing some yearning within the core of our collective spirit to reconnect to the sacred thread that they wove so carefully into the earth of America's new soil? Some force is at work behind the scenes other than clever marketing in a few publishing houses.

Perhaps there is a mystical explanation – an outrageous mystical explanation that stretches the limits of anyone's imagination – even mine. A physician named Walter Semkiw, M.D., released a book entitled, *The Return of the Revolutionaries* in which he states quite emphatically that the Founding Fathers and Mothers have "returned." They have reincarnated because America, their beloved nation, needs their guidance once again. They are now living among us. Is that true? Who knows? Who can prove such a claim? And that really isn't the point. The point is that such a book – such an outrageous idea – would be introduced into the public domain simultaneously with the flood of biographies of the Founding Fathers and Mothers. It is the simultaneity of the publications of these many books that one needs to ponder as much as, if not more than, the content, because even if the content is bogus, the author was responding to some need in the American collective, as were the authors of all those biographies, to bring the Founding Mystics back into view.

Without a doubt, something from the time, the era of the American Revolution – a spirited patriotism, perhaps, or the recognition that it requires conscious effort to maintain freedom or a mixture of many such motivations – something of that time has returned. I believe Washington's autobiography is a part of the mystical literature meant to be unveiled to America at this time - a piece of a grand cosmic plan. The time is now right.

It is my hope that *The Autobiography of George Washington* will enchant your imagination and your curiosity about both Washington and about the mystical side of history and The Sacred Contract of America.

This line drawing is taken from an 1802 edition of *The Washingtoniana*, published by Wm. Hamilton, Lancaster, Pa., printer, who produced all 411 pages in hand-set type. The book is a biography produced after Washington's passing in 1799 and includes eulogies, orations, poems, his most valuable public papers and his last will and testament. Such George Washington commemorative books were common.

CHAPTER ONE

BOYHOOD

❧

Early Years

DICTATED AUGUST 30, 1944

So MANY MISSTATEMENTS, wittingly or unwittingly, have been made regarding me and my father, that I wish here to set down the facts of my life – and some of his – as they truly were.

I was 75 when I died – not 67, as I am recorded. I was born in 1724 – not 1732. All records that I know of have been based on the British accounts, which were never really authentic.

I shall set down all that seems to me of value in my early years. Much was written about me, long after the writers had forgotten how and when and where the events happened. No justice was ever done my father or my younger brother, both of whom were closely associated with me in all my efforts and shared in my views. Indeed, I owe the foundation of all that formed my character, my beliefs, and my political action to my father.

The dreadful blight that the story of the 'Cherry Tree' has laid upon my personal character I can only attribute to Parson Weems' imagination. So far as I know, cherries were *not* grown on our plantation. All children decently brought up were thoughtful in that day as in this and priggishness was not considered an embellishment to character. Religion, however, exacted perfection of conduct from all who professed it. Taradiddles were probably frequent among young and old. Thrashings were not invited by small boys—not by me, at any rate.

※

My EDUCATION began at the age of four, when my elder brother began to teach me my letters. I must have been a dull pupil, for I well remember the cuffings he administered every time a lesson was undertaken. He never quite abandoned the idea that I was a born dullard, nor did my subsequent career redeem me in his eyes. Often, my mother would rescue me from his scholarly rages, mingling her tears with mine.

Lawrence Washington
SAR Collection, Lexington, KY

By the time I was five, my mother took over the task of my education and started me on the road to spelling and reading with a primer, with helpful illustration. Her patience and gentleness accomplished results where my brother had failed.

By the time I was nine, I was reading such books as I found in our home. These were somewhat limited, consisting mostly of the Scriptures, two volumes of Shakespeare's plays, a copy of *Pilgrim's Progress,* and a publication called *The Gentlemen at Home and Abroad,* the author of which seems never to have been guilty of a spontaneous action in his life. Another volume was a book of sermons by a Divine who had so little faith in human nature that he exacted a rule of conduct that was a virtual spiritual straitjacket, any departure from which invited a future spent in everlasting hell fire. There was a book called *The Huntsman's Friend.* This was my favorite reading. Another well-thumbed volume was called *Careless Days,* which set forth the story of a lad who so neglected his lessons for fishing, nutting, swimming, and 'bird nesting' that he came to be a worthless habitué of taverns, and his end was deplorable beyond description.

There were periodicals called, if I remember, *The Agriculturist*, and a weekly newspaper, *The Signal*. Now and then, a guest would leave some sort of periodical so that there came to be a miscellaneous collection of various kinds, such as animal care or family medicines. One that fascinated me was called, if my memory serves me, *Friends of Liberty*. It was in this pamphlet, when I was about twelve, that I got my first gleam of consciousness of what political liberty really meant. Until then, I had never heard a political discussion. My father and our neighbors talked of Britain at home, airing their views on whatever measures were taken that affected taxes and prices of their produce. The shipping rates were also a subject such debated. The authors of these pamphlets I paid no attention to. Books, to my mind, seemed to write themselves and, except for Shakespeare and the authors of the Holy Scriptures, I never, to my knowledge, heard the authorship of any of these writings mentioned. This gave to what one read a fixed authority.

When I was ten, a tutor came to live with us, and from him I learned a smattering of Latin grammar, mathematics, and English history, with such occasional subjects as botany, geography, and chemistry. My brief interest in these subjects was the study of mathematics. History bored me, for it dealt only with the ancients, those civilizations in the past that seemed too remote from life in Virginia to matter.

At thirteen, I was sent to a school in the neighborhood where I learned many things outside the school room - cock-fighting, boxing, wrestling, and little else. Our lives in the open had made us a restless lot for the instructors to deal with. However, I spent a year and some months at this institution, then decided against any more of it. My father agreed that I was never intended for a scholar, and permitted me to leave. I was a tall lad and seldom at ease behind a desk, towering above most of my school fellows. On a horse or with gun on my shoulder, I held my own with the men. There in the classroom, small lads could best me in every subject but mathematics. I longed to be in the open, free of their gibes at my lanky fingers and my stumbling attempts at Latin.

❀

CHERRY TREE LEGEND

DICTATED AUGUST 31, 1944

IN A FEW MONTHS I had wearied of work on the plantation which consisted of the stable duties, making and mending harnesses, and other such tasks as are common to such a large and busy estate as ours. My father had under cultivation almost 600 acres, aside from timberland of 40 acres.

I saw myself becoming a mere farm hand, and that I had no idea of being. My dreams were all of a career as a civil engineer —in that work my mathematical talent (my only one discovered so far) could be put to use.

Then, too, I loved the open and wished to always be on the move. My father had a friend, a Mr. Collins, who was a civil engineer and I was apprenticed to him.

At first, a natural shyness made me a rather unpromising pupil, I am sure. However, Mr. Collins was a most patient man and when I would stumble over my problem, he would come to my rescue with a perfect good nature. He, in a great measure, set the pattern of manhood for me, and I never regretted that choice.

Soon, I was through with the pedagogic part of my studies and happy to carry the chain, as he was a very competent and popular surveyor.

What happy days they were! Those many delightful mornings when by seven we were in the fields and on the roads, with all Nature sending forth her perfumes and her loveliness making over a show of beauty for our delight! My special task to carry the chain was so simple that I often lay for an hour on the roadside among the growth of sweet-scented things and, gazing at the great sky panorama, I meditated on the marvels of this world and the glory of our planet. I saw in it all a divine and perfect artistry that made me long to express in some way my love for it all. I wanted to make people open their eyes to the glory and grandeur of our Country, to make them adore its bounty and its beauty. Oh, how my heart used to swell as I would think upon this and often I turned on my face and kissed and tried to embrace this sweet Earth that was mine.

Yes, I claimed it for my own and vowed to love it, to cherish it, and to try to serve it all my life long! I had no idea how I could do this, but I felt within a surge of power that seemed to my young mind the answer to my longing.

When Mr. Collins would whistle and I would rise to my feet, he would laugh and say,

"Well, George, have you been asleep?"

My answer was a shy,

"No, sir, I was just looking at the sky."

He would answer that with another laugh, saying,

"My boy, you should be an artist and paint those skies you love to contemplate."

The days were very long. We halted for a lunch about 4 o'clock, an interval of more than nine hours since our breakfast which, of course, was a hearty one consisting of sausages, eggs, and birds and often rabbit pies with plenty of good hot bread and coffee. I saw in my own home sometimes as many as a dozen dishes piled with hot food.

Bounteous Nature was here again being shown me and, when grace was spoken, my thoughts would fasten again on the great bounty we enjoyed in this Country.

I was not religious and not a poet, only a simple youth whose mind and heart were running to meet his destiny.

Often now, as I look upon the boys who can never know life as I lived, and who are bound in a tight and impervious civilization that makes light of the things which formed my early years, I pity them for all they have been denied in a land that could still offer so much of her beauty and wonder to her sons, if they but sought it.

Well, I was on my way to manhood and well remember how I felt when my father came to my room one night and, sitting beside my bed, revealed to me the mystery of all human existence. I feared for what he was about to say. I knew those mysteries. I had cared for too many of our animals not to know that they shared with the human species the laws of generation. My poor father was at a loss as to how to broach the subject. My brothers had been of a different disposition and were more communicative and less reserved and far more in his confidence.

My mother was the one to whom I went to say my prayers, while my brothers knelt with my father as we gathered each morning. It may seem strange to our moderns that we had no food until we had gathered in a room and read a chapter from the Scriptures and knelt in prayer, asking for help to make of the coming day a profitable one in mind, body, and soul.

This over, we were allowed to talk our heads off if we wished, and breakfast was a battle of voices. Our own family had, aside from mother and father and brothers, some distant relatives —a great aunt of my father's, three cousins (a girl and two lads), and four slaves who worked in the house. Today, of course, we would not have slaves—and that is as it should be; but in my time, we did. We had not yet awakened to the evil of slavery. We had in the kitchen a table for the field hands and they were as noisy as we; and so as the slaves attended our wants and passed through the open door to the kitchen, we all made such an uproar that to be heard one had to shout.

My poor mother often would pick up her table bell and ring it for silence, saying,

"My conscience! What a noise! Can't you all speak without shouting?"

Then, for perhaps three minutes, we would keep our voices down, but soon all were roaring again at the top of their voices. The sound was a happy one. My father was the noisiest of all, for his chest was powerful and he had a voice that rang out clarion clear. My mother seldom spoke unless first ringing our bell, and then in quiet tones saying what she wished.

My own place at the table was beside her, on her left. The old great aunt, Lucinda Washington, sat opposite me. The old lady fortunately was stone deaf and seemed never to know of the racket about her. She was a famous cook and gave her opinion at every meal as the merits or demerits of the food on her plate. This was also a morning custom. The small fry, as my three distant cousins were called, took no part in the noise. Children were trained to be silent at the table when their elders were present, but they were speedy eaters and, soon asking to be excused, could be heard in the yard yelling like Indians.

We seemed to recall that they were happier at night when at the evening meal each was asked how he or she had spent the day. My mother was the questioner. My own pleasure at this little ceremony never lagged. Their young voices were so sweet as they told of their adventures, after their lessons with my mother, watching birds, running races, giving the chickens their share of food, or perhaps building a little house out of the fallen limbs in the woods where they played they were frontiersmen. One lad, Charles, said one evening,

"Aunt Mary, I played I was a big Chief, and I made Mark give me his hatchet." Mark – being a slave who was not much older. We asked what he had done with the hatchet, and he said,

"I can't tell a lie. I chopped down one of the small trees with it."

This was, of course, forbidden; and Master Charles was forthwith sent to bed in the midst of the evening meal. So much for that ridiculous old tale that has been a curse to me.

CHERRY TREE STORY HAS A LIFE OF ITS OWN

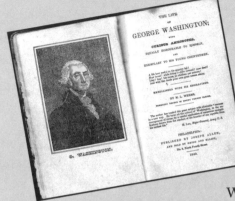

The Rev. Mason Locke Weems did not include the Cherry Tree Legend about George Washington until the 4th edition of *The Life of George Washington*, published in 1840. He says he received the story as "related to me 20 years ago by an aged lady, who was a distant relative (to Washington), and when a girl, spent much of her time in the family."

While both Washington, in this book, and later historians in their research, discredit the story, it had a life of its own when it was read in *McGuffey's Eclectic Second Reader*, used by 80% of America's schoolchildren. "I cannot tell a lie," many a grade school child repeated for generations.

A similar legend concerns Abraham Lincoln. It seems Lincoln had borrowed a book from a friend and put it into a chink in the log cabin wall when he went to bed. Later that night, a snowstorm soaked through and ruined it. Lincoln was so honest that he is said to have split logs for rail fences for a full day to pay for it. The book: *The Life of George Washington*.

We are unsure if Weems himself personally knew Washington. He did serve at Pohick Church at which George Washington was a vestryman or church elder. However, when he arrived in 1800, Washington had been dead a year. But, because Weems served at Washington's church, he had credibility as being associated with Washington and many believed he knew about his life in great detail.

Painting of Parson Weems on display at the Weems-Botts Museum, Dumfries, Va.

CHRISTMASTIME

DICTATED SEPTEMBER 1, 1944

THE WINTER MONTHS were spent hunting and in such ways as were social. My father was a famous sportsman who loved to tramp through the fields and forests in search of small and large game. Deer was plentiful and so was bear. The skins of the latter gave up much comfort under our feet in winter, as well as for rugs beside our beds. Deerskins were used for saddles and to make moccasins and rude coats, or we wore them whole over our shoulders, as protection in rainy weather.

We shot various raccoon and squirrel. The latter was eaten while its skin made warm caps. Much was done with the fat of the bears, we polished our boots and oven; and with a dash of scent, used this as a pomatum on our hair. Bear's grease also kept the harness pliable, and we spent much time and labor polishing our saddles and bridles, as well as the driving harness.

I disliked this work but, while at home, it was my task - assigned by my father to me alone.

We found a variety of uses for our feathered game. My mother made many lovely articles from the breasts of the wild geese and duck. Our great feather fans used to keep the flies from the table as they were waved over our heads by black boys.

We also had a collection of stuffed birds that we had shot. My older brother made an artificial aviary for them in one of our vacant rooms.

This same room was also a storage place for our guns and powder horns, our extra skins and such articles as we used in hunting and fishing.

All this seemed to me a delightful part of our life, a sense of the goodness and bounty of Virginia and the mysterious lands that lay beyond us, but which I could only imagine.

The time that seemed best of all in the winter was the Christmas festival. My mother would begin to prepare for this at the coming of frost in October. We boys she would command to bring in the nuts, hickory, walnut, and butternut, along with the groundpeas or goubers, which now you call peanuts. Later we would have a cracking-bee sitting on the floor and pounding the nuts open on flatirons. Then came the hard job of picking out the nutmeats.

We were apt to try to get out of this, but our mother would only have to say,

"You need expect no cakes or candies for Christmas if you do not pick out the nutmeat."

This was enough to send us disgustedly at our task. We picked the popcorn in August and hung it on the rafters because Christmas was a time for shaking the long-handled popper over the open fires, sometimes three of us at it and then pouring the corn into the milk pans where the salt shaker was used to complete the labor.

We had no time for kitchen quoits or playing chess or checkers in the evenings of December. Too much was to be done to provide for Christmas. We had the apples to gather and the windfalls to sort—some to go to the cider mill and the rest to be stored in the dry vat where they would be cool.

Mincemeat had to be chopped and all the boys, with kitchen aprons tied about them, patiently chopped the meat, apples, and fat for two puddings, which were boiled in the great copper washboiler.

We were also kept at our task by the old slave, Mammy Banty. She got this nickname because she was under five feet and never weighed a hundred pounds. She only shared her authority over us with our mother. In the kitchen she was supreme, and my mother second in command. Mammy Banty was always in a mood to believe we had some mischief in mind and never relaxed her vigilance when we were carrying out our tasks for Christmas. She seemed to think we were natural born demons, whose sole purpose was to defeat her in her culinary creations. All we could say or do never removed her suspicion that we were "jost natchual bown debbels."

We loved to tease her and carried our reputation as far as we could, and enjoyed her beratings.

Once the food was prepared, the turkeys grown, and the heavy meats hung in the smoke-house, we turned to the happier task of cutting the holly, the mistletoe, and the laurel—and the great Christmas tree. Our home was open house for visiting friends and relatives from the week before Christmas until Boxing Day. Quilts and blankets were hauled down from the attic and skins carried to the loft in the barns, for boys could sleep anywhere.

Beds were given to the grownups and the girls and small fry slept on the floors and sofas. As many as could be accommodated took refuge in the hall that ran through the center of the house. Young ladies occupied our parlor and children were tucked into corners of the bedrooms.

The house was not a large one, I suppose no more than twenty rooms, and the family numbered usually a dozen, without a guest.

The slaves, of course, had their own quarters. Only Mammy Banty slept in the house in a small room off the kitchen, where she became a sort of watchman against any depredations. We always trimmed the hall and erected the Christmas tree there. The young ladies watching us were the arbiters of all the decorations and ordered us about peremptorily. Now and then, one would be made to pay for her hardness with a kiss.

Christmas Eve – I find myself deeply moved by the memories of those Christmas eves, when my father would read to us all the story of the Christ's birth. We would assemble on the stairway and he would stand before the tree, bright with candles, colored paper parcels, and cotton bells hung from the branches.

We knew the story well, but my father would read it in such fashion as to make it seem new, wondrous, and poignant.

We thought of the Man to grow from that Babe in the manger and His teaching of the love of men, one for another - as the one thing to end man's cruelty and bring that peace on Earth, which down the ages has been the dream and hope of humanity.

Each year, as I sat on one of the upper steps of the stairway in the shadows, I pondered on the great dream. Here in Virginia men enjoyed plenty. There was no need for lies, greed, robbery, or murder. Yet such things happened.

Why?

A man need only work with the blessed Earth and the bounty supplied. The land was cheap and could be had on such terms as barred no man from owning the acres needed to support his family with all necessities.

Often before the carols were sung, I would pray that this message of Christmas peace on Earth and good to all men might come to be here in our own blessed land.

※

IN PIONEERING TIMES, it was well known that boys and girls were supposed to be out on their own as soon as possible. In my youth, boys usually married before they were twenty and girls as young as fourteen or fifteen. At twenty, an unmarried girl was "an old maid."

As for myself, I was physically precocious as my beard indicated – a man at fourteen. We were a hardy lot, and were treated as grown-ups as soon as we could plow a field and hunt with success. We had little spare time for school attendance. Education in good families went along at home, some members of the family starting the boys at four or five, and the girls at about the same age. When we could read, write, and calculate, there was usually a tutor brought to the home for further instruction of the boys and a governess for the girls - this when it was a planter's family. Townspeople sent their boys to school from the age of five. If a boy was to take up a profession, he might go on to college or, in case of the legal profession, enter the office of a local lawyer for training, later to take his examination before a Board of Examiners. My brother, Lawrence, was never suited to the planter's life, and at the age of forty became a lawyer and practiced in Richmond.

※

POOR PROSPECTS

DICTATED SEPTEMBER 2, 1944

ALL THIS TIME, I was conscious that something was lacking in my life. I needed a strong emotion to urge me to action. I was a lazy fellow, loving to lie in bed until 8 o'clock, then sheepishly appearing to Mammy Banty and begging for some breakfast, which she readily prepared while lecturing me on my evil ways.

My father often said,

"George, you are becoming the laziest fellow. Why don't you make up your mind what you wish to do and get at it? I shall not try to tell you what you should do. You must decide that important matter for yourself."

I suffered deep humiliation when these well-meant reproofs were administered, and wished sincerely that I really knew what I was best fitted for. My career as a civil engineer had not yet advanced beyond that of a chain bearer. I read what was at hand, but the result shed no light to guide me, and so I drifted. When I was not helping on the plantation, I was roaming the fields and forests with my gun, trying to make up in some way for my listlessness. When I had reached the age of fifteen and a little more, I met a man in the village who appeared in my eyes as a very great character. His name was Lightfoot. He was about forty, and a very fine type of manhood.

This man had been abroad, and was a most accomplished teller of his adventures. These embraced life at the various courts of Europe, as well as valorous exploits in many battles. It seems he was one of those Irishmen who would fight for any cause or country, merely for the joy of fighting. I questioned the truth in many of these stories, but it was safe to say the man had been a wanderer in many lands. One of the exciting tales was that of a lad of seventeen who became a great general – no less a person than

Wellington. I was fired by this romantic figure and decided that I, too, could make a career as a soldier.

When I spoke of this to my father, he was so shocked that he refused to even discuss the subject. I was only the more intent upon this as I met opposition. It all came to nothing at the time, and only after another year was the way opened for me to join the militia in a campaign against the depredations of the Indian tribes that came over the mountains. In that year, I was merely a farm hand and no more. I saw no future for me beyond taking up wild land to be had on long terms and slaving away as I saw so many men doing, who had no capital to start with. We at home were busy and working for my father without pay. The little we had to spend we earned by selling pelts to the local market. Perhaps two pounds a year was all we ever spent, this at the sweet shop or the tavern or a bet on a cock-fight.

My older brothers were in the same place as myself. One had married, and his father-in-law presented the bride and groom with 50 acres of good, cleared land. The other two boys were still laboring for their keep at home.

My mother often wept at their poor prospects, and she sometimes said,

"This Colony has no future for any boy. You should choose your work and go to Massachusetts. In Boston or Philadelphia you would find suitable occupation."

One brother acted on her advice to that end and he became a very successful man as a merchant, and junior partner after years of apprenticeship.

My older brother remained at home and as years passed, took my father's place on the plantation which he was entitled to inherit.

I mention this to show you the difficulties of the young men of that time, reared in plenty, but with small chance of personal achievement. All was there for the taking, but no boy, reared as we were, saw himself starting from scratch.

The Virginia Colonel
Engraving after a 1772 painting by Charles Wilson Peale.
Courtesy National Archives

Chapter Two

YOUTH

⚜

A Virginia Volunteer

Dictated September 3, 1944

What a commotion on the farm when I came from the village one August evening and told my family that I had joined the Virginia Volunteers, an infantry company that was being formed by an ex-Colonial in the British Army who had emigrated to this Country some years previous.

My mother fainted. My father seemed to lose his power of speech for the moment. My three brothers broke into a roar of laughter. Old Mammy ran in to tell me I was never to darken her kitchen again. The other servants were silent, but looked terrified. My small cousins clapped their hands and were the only ones to applaud my decision. It seemed strange that a military career should be so unpopular because our peaceful county was never a scene of battle. Soldiers to our neighbors meant a lot of rowdies making a hell of a noise at taverns and making illegitimate children for tavern maids, who only shoved them off on the county to support in the poorhouse.

Such a thing as honor, not to say glory, never entered their minds in their picturing of a soldier's career. The militia was made up of youths like myself and a few middle-aged men who liked to get away from home and be paid for doing so.

Our officers were elderly men who made a business of raising the patriotic spirit of each county in the Colony, and were far from possessing the technical knowledge that should be there as leaders of men who must risk their lives for the general good.

We met to drill on the village common. Since our work was fighting Indians, we did not make a great feature of precision footwork. We all were good shots. Healthy bodies and keen eyesight were the chief requirements. My own case was not typical. My comrades were mostly from very poor families who were glad to find a haven and a living in taking service with the State. All were reckless young daredevils who were able to defend themselves in hand-to-hand conflict with the enemy.

Wrestling was a sport that prepared a youth to meet his enemy and, perhaps, to grapple with him so closely as to disarm him. I, myself, was considered an expert wrestler and had a powerful back and grip.

Our weapons were three: a musket, a knife, and a dagger. The knife was used as a handy weapon when the fighting was close. The dagger, to be thrown at the enemy. We practiced dagger-throwing until we could hit a bull's eye in the target at 40 paces. This required not only correct aim, but unusual arm strength and muscular control.

In these days when we watch, as many of us do, a baseball game and note the power and precision with which the ball is thrown to cover the plate, I think what great dagger-throwers the pitchers would make.

We also had to learn how to defend ourselves against a skilled tomahawk-thrower. A small shield of steel about a foot in diameter was worn on the left arm.

In closing with an Indian, the main thing was to disarm him of his greatest weapon, the tomahawk. We first tried to invite his attention as if by accident in hope that he would throw his weapon at our heads, which was always his aim. When he did, we would leap to one side as the tomahawk left his hand, and throw our dagger at his heart. Both missing, we each drew our knives. These were hunting knives with a horn handle and a blade a foot long. The Indians had wooden handles wrapped with skin thongs and the blade somewhat shorter than ours.

Closing in, each grappled with his left hand and arm, with his right raised to strike. We often wrestled for several minutes before either gained an advantage. The legwork of the wrestler made the difference between life or death. The excitement was even greater if we had an enemy who endeavored to shake our nerves with his war cries.

❊

I HAD LITTLE TIME for adventure after I enlisted, but was taken at once to the nearest Fort, which was near Baltimore. We marched there, and were at work in three weeks from the day I enlisted.

Our uniform outfit consisted of two pairs of woolen stockings, two pairs of flannel underdrawers, three flannel undershirts and four pairs of moccasins. It was mostly forest that we marched through and, when we met the enemy, we wore a hunting shirt made of deerskin, fringed down the arm and at the bottom. The shirt was long enough to keep our thighs warm. A pair of linsey-woolsey trousers were supported by thongs over our shoulders, the latter of bearskin an inch wide. A pair of leggings wrapped about the leg and fastened with narrow strips of skin, tied in a row of bow knots down the outside of the leg which we fitted by ourselves. A knapsack and musket were furnished by the State. We made our bullets at the Fort during training. In our knapsack we carried a pencil and paper for writing home and usually, as in my case, a small Bible, two or three needles and skeins of thread, two or three little trinkets or souvenirs, and such odds and ends as we fancied.

We had no military tailor or quartermaster to supply ready-made garments. Each man provided and supplied his own outfit. This was the stumbling block to many who could not raise the two pounds the outfit cost, even when we shot and killed the deer ourselves. Socks, shirts, drawers, trousers, and moccasins all had to be made to fit, and women did that work. We also had to furnish a pair of woolen blankets.

Our home had an attic filled with piles of skins of deer, bear, and small animals. The skins made into hunting shirts, moccasins and leggings. We raised sheep, and my mother and the slave women dyed the wool, spun it into yarn, and wove it into cloth. The same was true of the cotton. Socks were knitted.

We were also to provide ourselves with a powder horn and three pounds of gunpowder. All this was easy for me. We made our own gunpowder by the hundred weight, and I had my own hunting knife, powder cask, and horn. We wore on our heads the coonskin or squirrel hat with the skin, the tail going over the back of the neck as a protection.

All in the matter of home supplies was no difficulty, so my only worry was in the attitude of my family – which became almost too hard to bear before I got away.

My mother, it seems, had a religious prejudice – as well as a social one – against soldiering, and her weeping and prayers were constantly to be heard. My father kept a grim silence that spoke as loudly as my poor mother's moans. My brothers jeered and sneered and predicted a future for me as a besotted and crippled member of the community, supported by public charity. My little cousins, fortunately, admired my temerity and often gave me whispered words of encouragement.

Mammy Banty was less antagonistic than I feared she would be and I became the recipient of her choicest viands. She wept at the thought of the spare diet and lack of feminine care that my future promised, and begged that I would come home at frequent intervals so that she might "fatten me up."

All this wore on me, and I was eager to be off.

THE DAY I LEFT for Baltimore was a day of mourning in my home, and I was all but crushed by the sorrow I had occasioned. However, my determination did not weaken and, as were the goodbyes, I went off feeling that I had done the best I could and would yet justify myself. I was offered so much to eat on the way by Mammy Banty that it would have filled two saddle-bags. I was to ride my own favorite horse to the village, and there leave her in charge of the tavern-keeper until one of the family came after her later in the day. I was off at daybreak.

As I rode in the dawn, I felt the pang of separation from my horse. A rider always from my fifth year, a saddle seemed my home. Now I was to be a foot soldier, and the joy that only a horseman knows would be gone from my life. I even stopped and laid my head forward on Dilly's neck. The whinny she gave seemed to tell me she understood and was sharing my grief at parting. I wept tears in these last hours of leaving home with all its happiness.

Dilly stopped, and turning her head she seemed to say, "I wish I could go with you."

I dismounted and going to her head, I put my arms about her neck and, laying my face against her head, I wept bitterly. She tried to comfort me by little soft whinnies and tender caresses as she nuzzled her soft mouth against my cheek.

All my life, I have remembered Dilly's sweet and loving goodbye. No human seemed to understand as she had. I never saw her again. She died the next year of a sad malady, but her memory has lived down the years and I cherish our last moment together still, after centuries.

Arriving at the village, I found I was late and my old Colonel gave me a dressing-down in such language as few men are able to command in a rage. Vituperation, with him, had become an art with the added virtue of scientific results. From that day, on I was promptness itself and I also exacted promptness in others.

We were fifteen in all when we started off an hour later for Baltimore.

INDIANS

DICTATED SEPTEMBER 5, 1944

MY FIRST IMPRESSION of the Fort was disappointing. I had always imagined a large building, such as pictures I had seen of the old European forts.

This was only about twenty yards in all, with stockades and a building of two stories with openings for cannonading and a platform that was outside, for musket shooting. We slept in the lower part and were fed in the open. Our beds were made of a sack of straw and our blankets were the only bedding. My father had told me of the hardships of soldiering, but I did not fully realize how primitive the conditions would be.

We fed upon whatever we could kill. No very great hardship for that, for we did the same at home, but it was a different matter when we had to cook our own food at a campfire without Mammy Banty's culinary wizardry in our kitchen. However, we were young and strong and the food soon became a habit. Nature, as ever, adapted herself to conditions.

Often I spent long nights awake, meditating on the great joys of a good bed and a variety of food. Soon, however, I ceased even thinking of the past and lived only in the passing moment. Letters I wrote gave as favorable a picture of our life as I could while keeping within a reasonable distance of the actuality. We were so high spirited that, unless on combat duty, we managed to enjoy ourselves as youth will always do when living together. We were not all congenial, and paired off in comradeship with each other. My "buddy" (as you call it here today) was a chap named Corliss, a big fellow almost as tall as myself but with a heavier frame. Dark and with a charming voice, he was a fine, boon companion. Corliss sang the songs of the day, both hymns and the songs heard in the taverns. The latter songs were ribald, and for that reason all the more popular with his audience.

Corliss came from a poor family in the south of Virginia

where he had grown up the eldest of sixteen children. He always declared he joined up to rid himself of baby tending. His father, a poor planter, had never even been to school. Corliss taught him what lessons he himself learned as he went along. These lessons got no further than the second primer where words of two syllables were pictured and spelled. He could only calculate as far as the multiplication table. Still his mind was eager and strong, and it pleased me when he shyly asked me to aid him in mathematics. This I was delighted to do, for I feared growing rusty and felt I might need this branch of study sometime in the future. The desire to make fun of all serious things was strong among the boys, and so we always stayed away from the others for these lessons. It was from the poor families that the defenders of the State were recruited. I seemed to these simple chaps to be an aristocrat, but they respected me for my wrestling and my marksmanship.

We invented games such as we could play with our equipment. We whittled out checkers and chessmen. I could play chess, as my father declared it was an excellent exercise of the mind and had taught us all the game, but it was the least popular of all with my comrades. Checkers, dominoes, and cards were the usual games played. The best times were when we had leave to go into the town to see there the sights, purchase tobacco, sweets or whiskey, and flirt with the maids in the shops.

Two of our number were noted for the great amount of liquor they could carry. This doubtful accomplishment made them feel superior to those of us who had to stop at two or three fingers of the corn-whiskey that was dealt out to us at three-pence a glass. All the dancing we got was on the Common on Saturday night when a fiddler would call off the figures. Not many of the town boys participated. They disliked us and gave us the right of way so that we romped with the girls while they stood and looked critically on.

WHEN WE WERE ORDERED away after a few months' training period, we thought we were heroes. We marched out of Baltimore where the townfolk lined the way and cheered us on. The British flag was carried by one of us, while a fife and drum on either side led us. We broke ranks after a march of seven or eight miles and bivouacked on the bay. Then for the first time, I slept beneath the stars to the sound of waters. I recall how excited I was at all the strange sounds: the lapping waves, the sound of the sentry pacing nearby, the faint call of the watch - all this to be my life's daily round for years to come.

As I lay awake on my blanket, I began to weep. Why, I could not tell. A sense of my helplessness under the vast starry sky swept over me. I felt impotent, insignificant, and even lost in a world that seemed too vast for me to ever comprehend. Corliss lay next to me and he, too, was awake. I remember he said in a whisper,

"By God, George, we are not much of anything in this world, are we?"

I could only assent to this. We talked in our ignorance of what life was. Both of us were full of wonder at the mystery that lay ahead. We were trained to fight savages who were warriors from the cradle. Of course, today I would never dare to think of our brother and sister Americans in such terms. But I am recalling who I was then and how I saw the world so long ago. Could we face and outfight them, or were we going to meet a foe that would make an end of us before we had reached manhood? We both were confident we could hold our own, man to man with an Indian, but we were so few. Our company, but two-hundred strong, might have to face three times their number. Anyway, we at last fell asleep, but all too soon the reveille sounded.

We marched each day at daybreak and bivouacked at noon for breakfast, which we now had furnished us. This consisted of hard baked bread, a slice of bacon, and such vegetables as the commissary could purchase from the planters. We cooked it all together, vegetables and the bacon for flavoring, in our camp kettles. Each man cooked his own. We drank tea furnished us, a quarter of a pound a week. An hour's rest and we were off again, our faces to the South and West.

We stopped at nightfall and were given a ration of one quarter pound of meat, tame or wild, and a quart of dried beans. These had to be soaked for two hours before they could be sufficiently softened to cook. That two hours was hard to bear. Hungry as wolves, we had to wait upon the beans. We sometimes furtively gnawed at our bread to still the pangs of hunger. Once we had eaten the rations, we were ready for sleep.

We first untied our leggings and removed our moccasins, washing our stockings in the nearest brook or stream and put them to dry. If damp in the morning, we had our reserve pair. Soap was given us, two ounces a week. We washed our shirts and underdrawers on Sundays, usually a holiday. This meant rest, playing games, singing, or rambling about in search of game, for we were in a wild and very sparsely settled part of the State.

We lived in hope of meeting adventure, but beyond a bear hunt now and then, we found none. We were six weeks scouting around the foot of the mountains before we met the enemy. Doubtless, their own scouts had been watching us from the time we left the settlement. One incident betrayed us. That was when Corliss drove a spike into the ground and forgot to remove it when we left. He liked to hang his cap and hunting shirt on this short pole. This, in the semi-darkness, gave an impression of a man on his knees.

Our Colonel, when he observed it, gave Corliss a fine admonition and threatened to make an object lesson of him if he repeated the offense. We thought at the time the Colonel was making a mountain out of a molehill, but later we understood his wisdom. When we had reached the foothills of the mountains that lie to the West, we found traces of Indian camps - bits of their food, the bones of wild fowl, fish bones, and ashes of campfires. The Colonel gave us an address to the effect that now we were facing danger every moment of the day or night. He doubled the sentries and shortened the period of sentry duty in order that there should be always vigilance. We were on the alert and a bit jumpy.

Nerves steady enough in training and on the march became taut. We said little but I think each boy like myself and Corliss, who confided in me, was trying to keep down his fears and attempt a bravado he was far from feeling.

❦

It was on the night of January fifteenth that we got our first dose from the enemy. All of us were wrapped in our blankets, with weary limbs stretched out, sleeping as only dog-tired men sleep. A sudden shrill cry like that of a loon rang through the stillness and darkness, and we were awakened immediately by the sentries prodding us. Into our leggings, which were not well tied, and our moccasins, we got on our hunting shirts and caps and were ready with our arms, but poorly fortified with empty stomachs to meet the foe.

We saw nothing but, as we took refuge behind the nearby trees, we saw a flash of a musket in the near distance. We held our fire as our Captain ordered until we could sight the enemy. We had nearly succumbed to exhaustion from the strain of standing behind the trees, when a single tomahawk was flung nearby one of the boys and grazed his shoulder. A yell like a thousand screech-owls followed and half a dozen Indians came into sight. They zigzagged through the forest and all we could do was wait until we could close with them.

Our Captain ordered us to take to our hunting knives and be ready to close with the advancing Indians. They did not know from which tree the next man would expose himself, so they tried to look in every direction. I managed to get my knife out by turning sideways and was ready for business. Corliss was next to me behind a nearby tree, when an Indian appeared just behind him. I called to him to jump and he did so. That exposed the Indian, who tried to get away, but I grabbed my musket and caught him fair. He fell with a yell. This was the start of a fight that lasted for three hours or more. When it was over, two of our boys were dead and five wounded. We counted seven Indians who were killed, and how many wounded, we could not know. Apparently we won, for they were not able to continue the attack and withdrew with their wounded.

Our Colonel gave us his best encouragement and said,

"My boys, you have now tasted blood. You have acquitted yourselves well. We must now expect constant battle, so be ever on the alert and rest when you can. Eat when and where you can. I can only say that you will soon learn how to smell the enemy far off. When this is so, we shall have the victory nearly won."

❀

WELL, WE WERE A pretty scared lot that day and few could sleep. We held this wood position and waited for another attack. We wept over the bodies of our dead comrades and dug their graves. We buried them, wrapped only in their blankets and such tree bark as we could scale off and tie together around them. The Colonel read the burial service over them at sun-down. So ended our first lesson in active warfare against an enemy so subtle, so trained, that we seemed like children. Most of us had never seen an Indian. Unlike the other Colonies, Virginia had cleared most of the territory in the East, at least of the Indians.

The friendly tribes lived in Delaware, Maryland, and what is now the State of Tennessee. All we knew of them came by way of stories of the old settlers and we were unaware of all our Founders had learned of the ways of Indians in warfare. We believed them to be afraid of gunfire. That, of course, is nonsense. They feared nothing.

Whatever may be said of the American Indian of that time, his courage, endurance, and fearlessness were second to none. He was wise beyond the white man in the ways of Nature and such methods of fighting as he was accustomed to. His body was a perfect one in beauty, grace, agility and strength. His unerring eye and trained ear were instruments far superior to ours. His love of his homeland gave him a strength of mind and body that at times seemed superhuman. What could we present that matched them? Merely our youth, our skill in wrestling, and our white man's courage, based upon reason even more than instinct.

While we awaited the second attack, we were mostly quiet and thoughtful. I was the one put to the task of sentry that night. Never since have I known such terror. All the more that I must not show the least trace of it. I was given orders to leave our camp and make a wide detour encircling it. With my height, that meant crawling on hands and knees and keeping watch as I tried to make progress, with as little noise as need be, among the trees. When I had been perhaps two hours creeping along, I came near a sleeping Indian. He seemed to be a youth like myself, tall and slim. I saw him move an arm as if to reach his gun and, at that, I sprang upon him and drew my knife. He was taken unaware but so agile that he got to his feet and threw his arms around mine. I then kicked his leg out from under him and he fell, with me on top. His next move was to get his right arm free. I took my knife and plunged it into his shoulder. He screamed, and then lay quiet. This took me off guard and I rose, upon which he seized his tomahawk and flung it at my head. I ducked just in time and at the same moment charged towards him, throwing him to the ground where he lay, when I found myself in the midst of several of my comrades who had heard the Indian scream and came at once on the run.

My Captain was not with them and when we brought our prisoner in, he reprimanded my comrades for going to my aid without orders. He said we might have all been killed if the Indian's screams had brought his tribesmen to help him. This, we saw, was good sense, but it saddened us to think we could not come to aid our comrades in mortal danger.

We dressed the wound of the prisoner, and he was tied to a tree where he was fed and given water. He seemed quite philosophical and even smiled when I said in English, which perhaps he might have understood,

"I am sorry that I had to do it." He grunted and nodded.

All night a sentry watched him as he let him sit and sleep, leaning against the tree he was tied to. Twice he tried to wriggle free, but each time the sentry presented his musket and so the prisoner gave up these attempts. All were now on the alert and ready for anything. We lay there four days and three nights before we again were attacked.

Our Colonel said,

"They will come if we wait long enough. We know our ground, and better here than on strange territory."

❀

WHEN AT LAST WE heard their battle cries, we were ready, each man set to avenge his fallen comrades. We fought all night in the moonlight. We saw sunrise with seven men killed and two taken prisoner, eighteen wounded. How many Indians were killed we do not know. Fifteen were found. We took two prisoners and, of course, never knew how many we had wounded. Corliss got an arrow through his leg at the calf. This lamed him for the rest of his life, but he continued on duty. We were now veterans, so we thought, ready to meet the enemy day or night. We saw no Indians again for three weeks.

Then, they came in force. We met a stinging defeat with ten killed and fourteen taken prisoner with twenty-two wounded. We found forty Indians and took six prisoners. This ended the campaign as the Indians withdrew. An exchange of prisoners was made and, after a few weeks in camp, a treaty was signed and we returned to Baltimore.

MARYLAND

DICTATED SEPTEMBER, 6, 1944

WE WERE VERY PLEASED to be back at the post and once more have leisure to go into the town to dance, drink, and carry on like the young hellions we were. Corliss had to sit by and make love to his girl instead of being the prize dancer of the regiment, which place he filled before he was wounded. Corliss, however, was a game fellow and never complained, but made the best of his life as he saw it. Fortunately, it was but a limp. His handsome face and fine physique were enough to make him a favorite with the girls. The rest of us rather envied him his success until one maid carried her fondness for Corliss to the extent of presenting him with a pair of twin girls.

We all felt the disgrace of the poor chap and adopted the babies as regimental luck pieces. The girl - whose first name was Lizzie - was quite pleased at the whole affair. Corliss feared what we used to designate as a "shotgun wedding," with an irate father, brother, or grandfather holding the gun. But none appeared to champion Lizzie's right to a wedding ring and so all went on merrily as before, except that Lizzie had to take her place in the ranks of paupers at the poor farm until the twins were old enough to crawl about the tavern floor where she tended the bar, a role she was filling when Corliss won her heart and her virtue.

A few other incidents had colored the history of that campaign and several of the boys were made husbands against their will. However, they bore the affliction as best they could, and longed to be again away and fighting Indians. Such had been the amorous and more than reckless conduct of our regiment that the Colonel made it the subject of a tirade during which he was bold enough to prophesy that we were headed straight for the devil and would find ourselves at a rope's end, unless we mended our ways. This sermon, delivered in strong language punctuated by numberless oaths, not to say curses, gave us a terrible and nerve-shaking fear that for at least a week kept us from our familiar habits. We drank more and loved less. My own bill for whiskey that week ate up my month's pay.

✻

WHEN WE FINALLY were ordered out, it was to fight in Maryland where the Indians were newly freed from their promise of peace contained in a treaty now ending. Several homes had been burned and women carried off, children massacred, and meat stolen. We were filled with rage that made us eager to avenge our people. Perhaps no element is so needed to arm and give courage to a fighting man as the sense that he is an avenger. Our boys at that time had full knowledge of the cost every Colony had paid in human suffering for the privilege of life there. Some were still disfigured from the old days when no man went to sleep without his gun and knife beside him. The women, also, had to defend their homes when the men were on a hunt or selling their pelts. We were well fortified by this rage and we did not weaken it by telling ourselves that the Indians owned all the land. We knew there was plenty for all, but unfortunately no one was wise enough to approach Indians with the respect due to the original people of this land. We have no words to fully express the meanness and contemptible manner in which later the Indians were robbed, cheated, and made to live like the poorest of all men in the Country. These tribes were filled with magnificent people. These were our friends, and often fought with us in later times. We now love and revere many of their great Chiefs and leaders. Their high sense of personal honor, their sacred regard for their word and a wholesome sense of decency made them far superior to the miserable and crafty whites who, under a political guise, reduced these great people to a condition far worse than even slavery. No amount of cruelty practiced for sheer gain ever broke their pride. Even today some of them retain the manly virtues and fine rules of conduct of their ancestors. They have still the ideal of manhood that has, of late years, become so seldom seen among our people as a whole.

But now, let me continue into my memories as a young soldier.

※

WELL, OFF WE WENT with high hopes of catching the enemy unawares this time. Unhappily, Indians never leave off their vigilance. These were warriors of years' experience who knew every move made against them. My squad was as good as any, and I was sure of them in a skirmish. Still, we were but raw boys at fighting with only three battles or skirmishes to our credit. We were as tough as the next, but not as experienced as the foe. We got a taste of his quality the third day out of Baltimore. We had marched all night and were sleeping in a clump of woods near a small stream. Our sentries were exhausted and had failed to note the passing of a canoe filled with Indians who discovered our camp and went quickly down the river to the nearest Indian village and there gave out the news. It was not yet sunrise when a yell gave us the first warning that the enemy was upon us. Of course, we had slept with all our clothes and footwear on, and with our weapons next to our hands. Still, it is not easy to gather one's wits when so suddenly awakened after a sleep of exhaustion. I was calling the men when an arrow went past my ear and grazed my hair. Another flew over my left shoulder and hit a man in the chest. I saw it and wrenched it out before he even knew what had hit him.

This was our first casualty. He staunched the blood, and grabbing his gun, fought with the rest of us. We had no stretchers or hospital bases. Wounded men died as they fell or lived on fighting as long as they had the strength. No Red Cross existed and no doctors went with troops. All was confusion and, as I looked about, I saw Corliss throw a dagger and hit an Indian on his forehead just as he was aiming his tomahawk at Corliss. This seemed to terrify the six or seven warriors to be seen, and they took cover.

We went after them with the result that we lost two men as prisoners and found one killed by an arrow in his head. We did not kill a single Indian nor take a prisoner in this case. We feel sure we did wound a few in arms, shoulders, or legs as we would sight them behind a tree.

We fought all day, and by nightfall were starving and all but crazed by our weariness and nervous tension. We gathered in an open space with sentries changed every hour, as few could remain awake even that long after such a day. This fight lasted sixteen hours with no let-up and no chance for even a drink of water. We never wish to live through another such day. It took all our mental and moral courage to face what was to come.

In the middle of the night, we were awakened by our

Colonel who gave us a bite of tobacco and said,

"Chew that, and then spit it out. It will quiet your nerves."

I had never used tobacco, even to smoke, and was unaware of the solace it could be. Again he came, this time doling out rations to go in our knapsacks: a loaf of bread and a piece of fried pork. He also filled our flasks with whiskey and gave us orders to eat when we could, and never drink more than a mouthful of whiskey or it would disable us. He was an old Indian campaigner and knew what was coming. One of the boys became hysterical and began to cry and laugh, disturbing the sleepers. The Colonel went to him and gave him a punch on the jaw that sent him into oblivion for a few hours.

All night we lay quietly wondering if we would ever see the stars again. At reveille, we quietly made ready to march. We ate our breakfast as we went on, and tried to believe we were ready at any moment to meet the foe. We had probably gone four miles when an arrow sped from a rise in the land to our right, a natural rampart for the enemy. His arrow passed between us and we turned and fired at the hill. No command had been given. This was simply the men's instinct to answer the Indian's arrow. The Colonel shouted,

"Load and hold your fire until you are told to shoot."

At once we saw how foolish we had been wasting bullets, caps, powder and time on a bare hillock. Before we could load again, they came yelling on the rise at us, shooting their arrows as they came. We met them with our hunting knives, and we were so enraged that seven Indians lay dead and twenty wounded when the thing was over.

We lost five men dead, twenty taken prisoners, and five wounded. At this rate we would soon be too decimated to make a front. The Colonel then withdrew to a nearby village, and gave orders that every man was to find a billet and report to him at the tavern.

All night, I was seeking quarters for the men and only a few homes were open to us. We were obliged to sleep on the village green and to eat our cold rations there, while the children and old men stood about gaping at us.

Our Colonel was furious. He declared that if that was the attitude of the citizens, he should march his regiment back home and leave these people to fight the Indians themselves. This brought a change in their attitude and soon we were all housed in comfort, cleaning up, shaving, and in every way trying to make the best of the difficult situation of war.

❦

HOME AGAIN

DICTATED SEPTEMBER 7, 1944

ALL WE WERE SENT out to do was overthrown by the Indians themselves. They offered peace and we were glad to accept it. Perhaps we showed enough fighting spirit to make them pause before coming to grips with us again. Anyway, they appeared in three days, bearing a white cloth upon a pole. Our Colonel was near the end of his wits. He had no power to make a truce and we were in the Colony of Maryland with a Governor who had been so ungrateful, after making help of Virginia, that when it was given he only remarked,

"What a travesty on the word 'soldier.' These louts will only make matters worse."

All we had suffered had been ignored and the "louts" who had died for Maryland were not even thanked in any way by the old demon in his speech or reports. Virginia now resolved to take no further steps on behalf of Maryland and its people, and so the Indians had to ask our Colonel who they could surrender to. The Colonel, full of righteous anger at the treatment of his regiment, told them they must go to the Governor, then at a town called Salisbury. Baltimore was then a part of Virginia. So, these poor fellows with their flag of truce returned to their own camp for instructions.

In the meantime, all of us were jeered at by the native townspeople. We came to hate the very name of Maryland because they had not supported us during this terrible campaign. Later this was to bear fruit that was bitter. Only the interference of our friends who had sheltered a few of us prevented a riot. My own little part in this episode was to take the Indians to the Governor with an escort of men.

On the way, we became acquainted with these Native American men and found them rather pleasant fellows. Arriving at the Governor's mansion, a large frame dwelling, we said goodbye to our new friends and went back to camp, only to find the camp gone. They had deserted the town and gone to the river where they set up another camp and were washing, cooking and cleaning their guns, making a joke of the whole thing. The few who could not forget our missing comrades were quiet and gave little attention to the rude jokes of the others. All this came to an end in another week and we went back the way we came to the Fort in Baltimore.

In two months more, we were paid a bonus of five pounds added to our pay of one pound a month and told to go to our homes. This meant we went home to plant the new crop and aid our people. Such was the custom in those days, as the Indians usually made war after they had their own crops gathered.

Indians and the Frontier
Drawing by Darley from a painting by A. Bobbett, Sr.
Courtesy National Archives

CHAPTER THREE

YOUNG MANHOOD

A Time for Choices

As the years went by, I had come to maturity and that time of life when we feel the need of giving our emotions the outlet of passion. Many of the boys yielded to this urge and I, myself, had been frequently a victim. Now, I realized that I had so far nothing but hope, strength, and desire to offer any girl who might return my feelings. This was often the cause of hours of meditation on what my future would hold that might tempt a young woman to marry me. My mother often wrote me letters of great solicitude, lest I become a lawless marauder among women. She painted in bright colors the future if I could but find a way to support a wife and family. She said,

"My son, do not believe those who would make you a cynic about marriage. It is the bond that strengthens and enlarges the nature and gives new and untried power to any man, providing he chooses a wife who has his good and that of his children most to heart."

You will see that she was a wise and ever loving mother.

Her counsel was above all others in my estimation. No young man I knew had failed to become more of a man and a worthy member of society because of taking on the responsibility of family life. I felt ashamed to admit that I was incapable of doing likewise. I wanted to make a home and become a citizen of some responsibility. How could I do this? The soldier's life was too precarious and too poorly paid to make a decent future for a woman who might share it.

One day, while plowing the field for my father, I came to see clearly that now was the time to make preparation for the future. I saw no way, but a feeling of peace came over me - a deep sense of my own ability to make my way as a man. Our simple faith in a personal God, who was ever ready to listen prompted me to leave the plow and, while the horses rested, to kneel there in the furrowed earth and ask Almighty God to open the way for me to marry.

I was in love with a charming girl, the daughter of a neighbor. Elizabeth was a dark and glowing beauty, who was so attractive to me that she constantly occupied my thoughts. It was Elizabeth who had inspired my prayer. I rose with a quiet and peaceful heart. I felt my cause was won.

What could I do to make the approach to Elizabeth? She was a very voluble and lively girl and was inclined to be something of a tease. This was often the method maids used to attract one they wished to catch as a husband. I was well aware that Elizabeth would yield to me if I put the question, but so far I had not done so.

One night, I called on my sweetheart and, to my astonishment, found her in the depths of depression. This new aspect of her disposition was not attractive. She sulked and vowed she was sick and tired of life and never wished to live another day. Finding my presence gave her no comfort, I took my departure very soon. "This was not meant to be," I said to myself. "She is too moody a woman to make a wife for me."

ALL WAS AS BEFORE, and I drifted through that spring and summer satisfied to help my father. In the autumn, the news came that a real battle had to be found with the Indian tribes over the mountain. They had ruined the peace of the settlers all along the Valley, and in two cases burned the houses and barns. I was called to duty and in October we went into camp, this time near the mountains to the west of us. I shan't recount that brief campaign. We lost sixty men, three hundred taken prisoner, and five hundred wounded. Our defeat was complete, and we could show a record of four prisoners and sixty-two dead to offset it. The treaty that followed gave peace for only six months. In that time I was recruiting, drilling, and studying what I could of the ways and means to cope with the Indians.

Our old Colonel was dead and the man in command was a product of the European war school. This was of small use in Indian warfare. I felt no confidence in his ability or judgment. What could I do? I resigned. Now I was free and my first thought was Mr. Collins. He was still the only civil engineer in Virginia, and I asked him how I could get further instruction in that profession. He seemed a bit reluctant to give any advice or encouragement, and said,

"George, you are too fond of adventure for this profession. It needs a man of settled ways."

I told him it was the one thing I had any desire for now, and had resigned my commission in the militia. Indeed, that if he would give me another opportunity, I was sure I would not disappoint him. The outcome was that I again bound myself to him for a year, and at its close I was a surveyor of some ability.

The land was in continual litigation by contestants who were disputing boundaries. I managed to do so much work that Mr. Collins' business was quadrupled. Now I had at last found a way to make a good living and that was no longer an idle dream. However, the element lacking was the lady. I was no longer in love. All my romantic emotions for Elizabeth had vanished and no other girl had managed to awaken them. My mother felt my state was deplorable. She invited many of the neighbors' daughters to visit us, and my brother profited by marrying the only heiress among them. I liked them and amused myself playing at love, but not one lady did I desire to share my life with. All were favorable to me, and most of all, felt my family was a good one to marry into. Girls were practical then, and most of them had an eye to the main chance. This was the result of their parents' teaching. A girl who threw herself away on a poor prospect was looked down upon and often ostracized. All were fine young women, well schooled in housewifery and the arts of weaving, dyeing, spinning, knitting, and garment making, as well as kitchen work. No well brought up girl was a sloth. In those stern days, a woman's work made the home. Her simple method of healing kept the family in health. Her industry clothed and fed them. Her moral nature set the pattern for her family. Such was the Virginia woman who could hope to win for herself a desirable place in that little world.

I saw so many girls who could have made a fine wife that it was difficult to choose one. My mother said one day,

"George, you seem to be looking for a saint. They do not exist in Virginia."

I swore to her that I really desired to be married, but I felt no urge for any of these delightful girls and must wait upon Fate to choose a wife for me. I confided my experience concerning Elizabeth to her, and she vowed I was wrong to make a single instance of a passing mood the measure of a girl. My mother then set about arranging a visit from Elizabeth to our home. This culminated in a mutual dislike for each other, and the girl frankly flouted me. I was not sorry. I felt I had been in divine protection. My mother in her solicitude even spoke to Elizabeth, who up and said,

"I wouldn't have George if he were the last man on earth. He is too domineering. I want a husband who will be a companion and not my superior officer."

Well, poor Mother then gave up on me as a matrimonial failure. What I had not confided to her was that my facial disfigurement from the pock marks confirmed me in the belief that this disfigurement would always prevent any girl, who might be my ideal of a lover, from being attracted to me. I had no desire to marry one who would accept me simply to avoid spinsterhood.

In the meantime, I loved my work and was absorbed in it. I read much from Mr. Collins' library, and roamed the forest in search of game for the family. All this was pleasant enough, yet I knew life was incomplete.

※

Politics

Dictated September 8, 1944

One of the most happy events of my young manhood was when my father gave me permission to take over his share of the County business. He had taken care of the small cases of land disputes and was always considered fair in his judgments. His office was not to decide between litigants, that was the business of the Courts. He was simply an adjuster of the arguments over boundaries and tried to present the obvious facts, so that a settlement would follow. My work as a surveyor gave me a real interest in the subject. One day, a man whom we had always known came to me to ask if I would take a bribe and, when I refused, he said,

"George, you are a real patriot. You can go to the stake for a principle. Be sure you go into politics. Men of integrity are needed there. Only rascals seek political posts. Honest men have to be invited to occupy them. We think you would belong to the latter."

This set me thinking. Perhaps there was a future for me in politics. I was keen and studied what books on the subject I could get my hands on. We had an old copy of the *Pennsylvania Gazette* and I studied the editorials and the many articles contained in it. Among these, I read an article headed: "Long Lost Liberties." I was fired by it, for it told of the way we had gradually been forced by the Mother Country to give up the many original rights given the Colonies in past time. No excuse was given for this encroachment. It was simply the will of Parliament, and we had no redress. I pondered this many times and asked myself by what right had Parliament arbitrarily withdrawn our privileges and vested interests? Our own Governors were English, and they supported the Home edicts. Now we should, I thought, claim those rights and refuse to send our taxes unless they were returned to us.

Many a time I made sport of the way Governors tried to imitate the Home rulers. So warm were my arguments that they began to attract the attention of several of our neighbors. This made both friends and enemies for me. My father counseled me to keep my opinions to myself but I was not young enough to heed his admonition. I considered myself a man able to take a stand as a tax-paying citizen while I had the run of the farm home. I had acquired, by either gift or purchase, about thirty acres of good farm land offered by Virginia at the price of a pound, or five dollars, an acre. This was taxed by Virginia, then by the Home Government, and yet it was public land and still unoccupied. I got no revenue from it. I was unable to make out any excuse for the second tax, which was sent overseas, and no service of any kind was received in return.

What could a man expect who was made to contribute a tax with nothing given him in return? I concluded he could only expect further inroads on his investments if he improved upon his property. This, I found on inquiry, was to be expected and was often the case. More than all, I resented the way in which it was collected. A tax gatherer appeared twice a year and gathered all the money due England under the law. Then, when Virginia tried to collect, the owner was usually unable to pay. So the State was always the loser unless it seized the land and sold it for the taxes due. This, of course, ruined the owner and disgraced him as a defaulter. No mercy was shown by Britain, and so I made up my mind that no very great prosperity could rise in the Colonies. This opinion only deepened with the years. It was, in fact, behind all my other activities. If I was wrong, I had not yet learned how. No man has a right to any money that he has not given an equivalent for, either in money, goods, or services. Why should a government not be as responsible? Americans should never stop demanding their government be responsible to them.

Back then, we at home paid a larger tax to Britain than to Virginia. In return, we got a receipt, and nothing more. All my life, I heard my father say,

"Wait until I get Britain's tax money together."

This was what I heard when the house needed repairs, or a new piece of machinery for the fields, or a horse or cow that would have been of great benefit. Nothing mattered but the taxes for Home. My mother often wept at the way we were obliged to wear patched coats and trousers because we could not afford new, presentable garments. This was a sore point with me, and I voiced at home my resentment in strong language.

At last I was called to address a county meeting and, when I delivered it, my subject proved to be "Long Lost Liberties." I had been too long thinking out the subject to lack for words - or the feeling needed - to give them force. My audience listened attentively and at the close of the meeting, I had to beg them to let me go. Such was the swirl of questions that it was impossible to answer half of them with any thoroughness. Well, from that night on I became the leader of a faction that was pledged to work for the cancellation of the Home tax on our land. We were all land owners. I was the least of them so far as my holdings went, but they seemed to believe I had an idea that was important and could be made effective.

So it transpired that in a short time I was in demand all over the county, and even the adjoining ones to address meetings on the subject. My father feared that I would get in trouble with the Home government and tried to dissuade me from making myself a conspicuous target for the officials who were ever on the lookout for someone to prosecute and collect a fine of a few pounds. Here again was the greed of the Motherland, I thought. We had a great rally one night on the village common and there, on a chair, I spoke to the crowd. I knew all the people assembled and could call them by name, and I also knew their holdings and what they paid to Home. So I cut loose and let them have it straight. We were only half a hundred or so, both men and women, but the mayor, who owned even less than I, cried,

"This is treason! I shall report it to the Home Secretary unless you cease these seditious statements."

From that moment, I was a rebel. I never again took the oath of allegiance to Britain. My only fealty was to the Colony. I was now an outlaw.

❀

CROWN TAXES

DICTATED SEPTEMBER 9, 1944

ALL WENT AS EXPECTED in the way the Home powers acted toward the American Colonies. No mercy was shown for those whose crops had failed or whose money was too little to pay both taxes and buy life's necessities.

In Virginia, the poor were begging the government to at least lower the impost. This was a useless effort. The Governor, an official sent out to squeeze every shilling from the planters and merchants, did not even report to the Home Secretary the cases where families were made to work on the public highways to pay for their State tax while every penny realized from their meager crops went to England. The rich and the well-to-do were not happy to have the cream skimmed and only the curds left after a year's abundance.

Finally, the pressure of public opinion became so strong that we began holding meetings of protest and mailing the minutes to the Home office. This was a very tedious matter, since a month or more was required to reach the Home office by sailing vessel, and months were required for a reply.

My own case, a small and insignificant one involving but a pound, simply served as a measuring rod for those poor men whose livelihood was all in what the land produced. Most of these men would feel very happy if they had tobacco and cotton surplus after their own private needs of these crops were filled, and they could get as much as three pounds for the rest. This was to purchase the year's supply of whatever they must have in clothing or household and farm needs. Cut off his three pounds, two of them must go to the tax gatherers. Such was the state of things in Virginia, the most prosperous of the Southern Colonies.

We had no way of avoiding the taxes for the Home Office. We lacked any public works where a man's labor could pay the tax, as was the case of the State impost. A few men gathered together to petition the Governor to state the case to the Home Secretary. While they waited upon this well-paid, well-fed, well-housed, and altogether pampered public servant who was supported by the State's tax, they were received with discourtesy and even insulted. The old parasite was too pompous to even receive them personally but, after cooling their heels in an anteroom, the men were received by a secretary. This was a scandal that became a force throughout Virginia and occasioned another series of meetings in different counties, towns, and villages. It came to our locality like a match set to timber. Even the women spoke in their rage when the news came that the Governor had not deigned to receive their husbands and sons. One woman, a very old settler, set the pace by saying,

"God Almighty! Was ever a people so scorned by the man they sustained?"

All the red blood of the men present surged hotly at that and in a few seconds every man was on his feet and declaring his determination to avenge this insult. I was present. Some inner urge led me to step to the platform where a chairman presided. Even without asking the floor I burst into a tirade against the Governor that led to a movement which would bring to the Governor the realization that he was our servant and not Britain's, so long as we paid his salary. The plan was to give a memorial to him in which our grievances were set down and a declaration that unless he conducted himself toward the Colony as their paid servant, they would give him his congé and send him packing back home.

This we carefully worded and sent to him by a committee of seven of the most important landowners of Virginia. My father was one. His report of the affair was that the more prosperous citizens were received with a cool but courteous disposition and, when the old gentleman had read it, he was in somewhat of a panic. He stammered out excuses for his treatment of the first call of the poorer men who had presented their memorial. Then he said he was unwell and obliged to keep to his bed and had delegated his secretary.

One man spoke up and said,

"That is not true. I met you that very day and you were in good health."

And he described the meeting place just to prove he had really seen the Governor. The Governor was at a loss and said,

"I see you have me there. Well, present my apologies to your neighbors and say that I will report their complaints to the Home Secretary." Then, he added, "As to your own case, I can only say that you are subject to the will of the Parliament and only there can it be judged."

So we had no advocate then. The whole thing must be presented to Parliament and who could say when, if ever, it would be acted upon. My father and his friends wrote a memorial to the Commons and to the Lords and this was probably sent off on the first vessel sailing. No reply was ever received. Thus ended all hope of relief.

※

We did not realize that we were simply servants to earn money to pay for Britain's extravagance and a useless Royal Family, which is how I saw the world more than 230 years ago. We simply thought we were being exploited by the politicians and, if the King knew of our plight, he would at once see that an end was put to our wrongs.

We always opened each meeting with a prayer, which

began with supplication for the King and his Family, and calling down blessings upon them with full, loyal hearts. What followed was directed at the Home Office, the Secretary, and our local Governors. Most of the Colonies still believed in the Divine right of kings. I, myself, saw no reason to acquiesce in this accepted law as a Divine one. However, I made no point of it in my speeches or in my private conversation. I assumed that it was good policy for a sovereign to give his faraway subjects fair treatment, if their loyalty was to be counted on.

My father and his friends really shared this opinion but gave no public expression to it. They felt as I did, that only a stupid king would abuse his people who were living abroad and out of reach of the many avenues he could use to keep them on his side.

All was in chaos in the Colonies and getting worse by the week. Men declared they might as well be dead as to face a future where only slavery to the land and the government faced them. Firebrands considered rebellion and separation from the Home Country. I was among them and felt a hot heart against the cruelty of the oppressors, whoever they might be. One thing was sure: we must have relief or no progress could be made by anyone in the Colonies.

The poor - above all - must be given an opportunity to make a decent, honest livelihood from the land or all growth would stop, and soon we would be at the mercy of the Indians who counted on our extermination with no aid from Britain. We saw British officials winning the friendship of the Indians, permitting them to destroy the crops of those who were behind in the Home taxes. Seven men had their dwellings burnt to the ground by savages who scalped them and took their wives as hostages. An appeal to the Governor for troops from the British garrison to avenge this outrage brought only this,

"We cannot give protection to those Colonists who do not keep up their payment to the Home Government."

No relief was in sight. No way was found by which poor planters could meet the Home demands. At last, after years of hard toil and bitter privation, wasting means, labor, and heath, as well as courage, the poor planters began to leave the Colony. Free land was offered by both Spain and France to the West and South in the Floridas where the Indians were friendly, and to the North, in Quebec, where the French Government tax was second to the provincial tax, and very small at that. The sovereigns of Spain and France were far more interested in helping their colonies than was the British King, George II. We saw our population dwindling. Those who owned slaves and had purchased the land at a time when it was almost a grant could survive, but their children faced a bleak and barren future.

No wonder I felt there was no hope for the generation of which my brothers and I were a part! We must be free of Britain or emigrate. I loved, even worshipped, the dear land I knew so well. Virginia - to me - was a precious and priceless land, meant to nourish a breed of men of which it could only be said that we were a great and ever evolving element in the human race. I was proud of every citizen who tilled the fertile soil and wished that the King could only come and see for himself the glorious land called Virginia.

We who loved this lovely Colony were loyal Britishers, for the newcomers were still mainly from England, Scotland, and Wales. A few Irish drifted in but they were mostly attracted to the towns, where they worked as boat builders or seamen going out in the boats that did a coastwise trade among the Colonies and the West Indies. A sprinkling of Germans were found on the coast where they kept taverns or sold wares in the villages. We had also a few Scandinavians who were seafaring, and made their living as seamen or fishermen. The lasses were usually from England and Scotland, and a few Welsh. We had no racial animosity, all lived in harmony and mutual respect, with all cooperating in public affairs. What an opportunity there was for a Government to bind these people to it and to make their efforts a crowning success for the Home Country! We could have been the greatest possession ever seen on earth.

ALL WAS IN A FERMENT when a small circumstance caused Virginia to ring with cries of protest. A small planter, a man who owned several acres of land, was hauled up in the court for non-payment of taxes to the Home Government. The sum due was a pound and two shillings. The man had been ill with rheumatism and unable to put in his crops. His family - a wife and two small children, were all but starving. Only the bounty of neighbors had kept them and their livestock alive. The man was sentenced to a fine of ten pounds, in addition to his tax, or go to jail. Ill and desperate, the man committed suicide by drowning himself in a small piece of water near his home, after filling his pockets with stones.

He had left a letter stating his situation, asking aid for his family since he could no longer be of any service to them. When the tragedy became known, a meeting was held. The poorhouse became the refuge for his wife and children; and his land, home and all his simple belongings were sold, as well as his horse and two cows. The proceeds were applied to the fifteen pounds due the Government, but no accounting was given to the widow as to the amount netted for land, house, barn, and outbuildings, furniture, implements, or livestock. The widow received only a few garments and some bedding to be used to save the county the expense of furnishing these articles. This was not the first time a man had been robbed by the government in this manner. Two other instances were on public record and many more had been hushed up by the officials.

All were now sure that this sort of treatment was to be expected and no poor man had any future in the Colony. We saw a bleak and far from hopeful prospect for our youth. Spain, already making inroads on our population by her liberality and great promises to settlers, would be ever growing stronger and we could expect eventually to become subjected to her. What could we do? No one seemed to know and, I must say, I least of all. We again sent protests to Commons, Lords, and even to the King, but with no result. It was in the autumn of the year 1745 that I began a course of study on government, taxation, and similar subjects.

I found in a friend's home a fine collection of such works. They were mostly pamphlets written by thoughtful men, many of them Virginians of our own times. They gave me an insight into the use of government for benefit of the citizens and, also, the part officials played in administering the laws from the King down to the humblest man. Also, I read of the ancient republics and how they came into being as well as the forces that destroyed them.

These works were to me a great inspiration. I saw that men only made statutes, created governments, and administered— while the kings and emperors were but figureheads with which to dazzle and hypnotize the common people into submission. I saw, also, that the forces of religion and military organization were the two instruments used to hold the masses in check. My friends often discussed these matters with me and that left a profound impression upon my character. I saw that our isolation from the Home Country was giving opportunity to the officials to abuse their local authority and to prejudice the Parliament against our interests.

No more loyal subject could be found than myself until then. I had never wished to be ruled by any other sovereign than the King of England. My heart was torn with anguish when I saw we were never to be safe from the politicians who betrayed both his interest and ours.

My studies were no aid in making me less unhappy. I could think of little else than the future of Virginia and the other Colonies. All the careless days in the field and my work of surveying were over. My thoughts were constantly reverting to the instability and uncertainty of the future. When I spoke of these things to my father, he seemed amazed that I should give them such deep thought and strived to dispel my fears for the future. When I came upon a poor man who was struggling to meet his taxes, I talked with him and won his confidence. In no case was he free of anxiety and fear. What a situation it was for those who had come in full confidence in the promises made them of a future in our Colony! Most of these had believed the Home Officials, who painted life in Virginia as one that promised peace and plenty to all who cultivated even a modest plantation, with but their own labor. Many men said they had risked all in the venture and could not return to the Homeland — yet I saw no future ahead. I tried to be calm and give what encouragement I could to the poor fellows, but the facts did not admit of many fair prospects.

❀

ALL THIS TIME I worked with Mr. Collins, who shared my views, but was too timid to express them publicly.

All was seemingly quiet on the surface of life, but the forces of discontent, fear, and disillusionment were underneath; and no man of small means spoke of the future as a bright or even a safe one. When word came that a new impost was to be collected for the Home Government, we all thought the last straw had been added to the weight we already carried. This was on the importation of cloth. It was not be collected yearly but each merchant must pay it at the dock-side. This tax was again collected by him as he sold the yardage.

Many decided to wear only the homespun linsey woolsey cloth woven by the women of the family. Sheep required pasturing too extensive for small planters. However, they bought at low prices the wool of the sheep owners and the women learned to dye, spin, and weave. This, too, required capital and many were in debt to wheelwrights and the men who built the weaving frames and spinning wheels. Dye kettles were borrowed or rented for a few pence.

The merchants saw that they could sell little imported cloth outside the towns where money was freer, or at tidewater where seamen required proper cloth for their men who sailed in wintry weather. Women, also, wore plain, unbleached cotton or dyed it for their outer garments, and for winter wore mostly the linsey woolsey. For the most part we tried to use the peltry and skins and reverted to the primitive sort of costume that we had used in the earliest days, after the clothing brought from England had worn out. We made it a duty to see that no tribute was paid to the cloth importers. It became a subject of song and story, the saga of "the linsey woolsey sweetheart" in contrast with the town belle who wore the gay prints that bore the tax.

All was done to ridicule anyone who wore a cloth coat and breeches. We made it a point to appear in skins when possible with hunting shirts and linsey woolsey trousers. Well, in a month a proclamation was issued by the Governor declaring it to be illegal to hunt in certain localities or to use peltry as wearing apparel. The excuse was that wild life was being destroyed and must be preserved for future use. A tax then was levied by the Weigh-Master, who was also an appointee of the Governor. The tax was to be levied on wool and was to be collected at the sale.

❀

VIRGINIA'S PLIGHT

DICTATED SEPTEMBER 11, 1944

WE SAW THAT EVERYTHING that could be done to force us to buy cloth of English importation was being done, and soon we would have to yield. We again petitioned the King and Parliament. No reply at all was received.

Men of small holdings now began to move. "Spain and the Floridas" was their cry. Few people could find the means even for that and so sank into debt, for which their lands and belongings were seized and their families sent to the Poor House to be supported by the Colony, while the men wandered off to hire themselves as laborers, or keel boatmen on the river.

❀

AT LAST, THE SITUATION was such that the Poor House was overflowing and no one could imagine the misery of the poor inmates, destitute, who had no means of replenishing worn out garments. Their rags and tatters and the unshaven faces of the men and wild looking women, who had no decent covering, were a spectacle to make one weep. All this in a Colony that had been called "The Paradise of America." We all sent what we could of clothing to the Poor Houses, but even the planters who were well-to-do found difficulty in covering their own bodies and those of their slaves.

Many women were in such an undressed condition that they could not appear in public. Small children crept about in a state of nature. Larger ones rarely had shoes or stockings and the older men were kept out of sight as they were not needed for work and might be spared to the end that they wrapped themselves in sacks or cowhides and remained cooped up indoors. We saw such things as no other settlers were ever called upon to view in order to satisfy the greed of our political rulers. We also had the Governor at our heels constantly pouring for edicts and announcements, threatening all and sundry with arrest for poaching on wild land or for wearing skins.

One day, my father said to me,

"George, this Country must be free if it is ever to be a decent refuge for settlers."

This was the first implication I ever heard that reflected on Britain's boast of being the world's champion of free men. My whole life was spent in a community in which every citizen toasted the King before anyone touched his glass. We believed that he was divinely appointed to rule over the British possessions and that any other ruler would be a tyrant by comparison. Imagine my astonishment when my father said what implied lack of freedom in our Colony. Somehow, I had always disassociated the tax burdens from the King and the British form of government. I supposed the tax evils came from the venality of the public servants. I even exonerated the Home Secretary, believing that subordinates confiscated our letters of complaint to suit their own wicked ends. All my life, both morning and evening, prayers were said with whole hearts for the continued safety and well-being of the King and his Family, and for those who served him. We even prayed by name for the Prime Minister and those who administered the King's government. What a shock to hear my father say,

"This Country must be free if ever it is to make a decent refuge for settlers."

Free? Who is so free as a British subject?

Never had the foundation of my conviction been so shocked.

Free?

Why, no one was free, but those who were under the safe and sound protection of the British flag. I did not at the time say anything in response to my father's remark. I suppose that I was too mentally confounded by the shock of his words to form any sort of reply. When I recovered my usual composure, I did open the subject to him, saying,

"What would happen if we did not have the King as our protector?"

He looked at me as if I had suddenly gone mad, and then slowly smiled and said,

"My dear George, what protection do you get from the King?"

I was not slow in asserting that as the King's subjects, he was bound to protect us from any and all enemies. My father then asked,

"Did he ever protect us from the Indians?"

I had to admit that no British seaman or soldier had so far ever been known to give aid to the Colonies against the Indian enemies.

"What protection has he ever given us in our fight for justice against the Governor's tax levies?"

I knew he had me there, and so I had to admit we had been fleeced, abused, and no act of the King had been known to befriend or protect us in this crucial matter. My father then went on to explain where our taxes went. He said the Governor was not benefited—neither were the Home Officials. It remained to be spent by the Crown.

This staggered me. I was now awake at last to what

Colonies meant, slavery and servitude under the name of a fine new country for pioneers, whose labor was primarily to enrich the Royal Family. So, with this conclusion, I seemed to come to my full stature as a man. I was a victim of an unjust and hard political system that showed no mercy and gave no quarter. From that day, I became in my heart and mind a rebel. My father never spoke of this again, and I was not one to make it the subject of my conversation abroad. When politics and the state of the Colony was discussed, I listened and all I heard but confirmed my father's words. We had in the county an association called "The Tax Payers' Society." This was composed of the men who paid most of the taxes and levies. They knew how little was ever done by the Home Government to aid, succor, or encourage their members. The Chairman of the body was a very large landowner and the chief source of taxes in our county. He was a loyal and fine citizen who opened every meeting with a prayer for the King and his Family and the Parliament. His views were conservative, his manner gracious and at all times tolerant, rather than resentful of the Governor's edicts and continuous imposts.

My father often said,

"Mr. Crane will never be disposed to make the Society of the least service to us for fear of offending the Governor."

So at our annual election, he proposed a change in the Chairman. The members divided on this and split into two camps. The result was that my father's contingent won, and a more liberal man was elected Chairman who more nearly represented the interest of the Society. This occasioned a commotion in the Colony and several counties were inclined to see in our action disloyalty and rebellion. My association with the Militia had been detrimental to my reputation and I was supposed to be something of an outlaw. Such was the state of local patriotism in Virginia at that time. My father, a man of deep and most profound convictions, saw in all this his worst fears realized. The citizens of the county were far from having any strong urge to fight for their simplest rights. They were all, with few exceptions, younger sons of men of privilege at Home and were receiving allowances from England, only caring for their own personal comforts. The poor settler, the backbone of any country, meant less than nothing to these "Cavaliers," as they called themselves. They had enough slaves to labor for them, and often their taxes were lowered by the Governor on the excuse of their relationship to members of the House of Lords.

My father stood by his guns, and said these things openly. The new Chairman also was frank and correct in his statements of fact, which reflected on these patently pampered subjects of the King. In a short time, this all simmered down, and the only residue was a little feeling against my father and those who were of his opinion. No son of such a father could stand by unmoved when this was the daily portion of the man whom he revered and respected above all others. I was sick with the misery of it all as I saw men deride my father on the streets of the town, the very men who used to seek his advice and opinions on county matters.

My brothers were also affected. My elder brother went so far as to write a letter of remonstrance to me to the point where I called my brother to account telling him what I had in my heart. His manner was never the same to me again. No part of my future life was ever to dissipate his complete disapproval of me and my views. My father was glad of my sympathetic attitude and I am happy to say he made me his confidant. We were brothers-in-arms against the long series of Home impositions. All of our friends were dividing into the two opposite camps. We were very much in the minority and often felt the sting of ostracism to which our opponents treated us. We were drifting rapidly into sectionalism, and the enmity engendered was ready to burst into a dangerous conflict. We championed the poor landowners—our opponents, the rich ones. We had little encouragement from either the churchmen or the schoolmen. The former, of course, were on government payroll and were never inclined to speak one way or the other on the subject of the taxes. The schoolmen, supported by the State taxes, seemed to feel they would lose the patronage of the great land owners if they spoke up for the poor, so we saw that only those who suffered would be with us. The least important of the settlers were our supporters.

We became, in a few months, a sort of political party and we chose our few officials according to their sympathy or opposition to our views. All was in such a state that we finally came to outright enmity. My father had to resign from the County Board of Selectmen. I was outlawed and made to sever my connection with Mr. Collins, who knew his business would suffer if he retained me.

Such was the picture.

❀

THE RISING TIDE

DICTATED SEPTEMBER 15, 1944

WE WERE NEVER SURE of the loyalty of others, even of the members of our own party. Some who joined in their enthusiasm would cool off and then become spies for the opposition. I often found myself wondering what we were in for when I would discover one of our members hobnobbing with important members of the opposition. My father and my younger brother at home were often cautioned against some member, known to be a traitor to our cause. We lived in a ferment of doubt and suspicion. Lifelong friends and neighbors became enemies, and we had such a feeling of insecurity that life was very sad and difficult for us.

One day, while making my way on my horse to the town to make a speech to the townspeople favorable to us, I was shot at from a clump of trees, receiving a flesh wound in the upper left arm. I made an effort to staunch the blood with my handkerchief, but soon the flow began to exhaust me, and I was forced to dismount and lie down. I supposed this was the end for me. I must have been unconscious so for an hour when a passerby, a man whom I knew, saw me and came to my assistance. He staunched the blood, and within a few minutes I came to.

My acquaintance gave me some whiskey from his flask

(for all carried one in those days) and soon I was on my way to the town. My rescuer was one of us and rode behind me, my horse at a walk. Of course, I was late and the audience was in a rage at my discourtesy, but when I appeared pale from loss of blood and my voice weak, they were instantly the more intent on hearing what I had to say. I sat during my speech, and the forty-odd men crowded close to hear. Well, I was never so good at a speech as when I have had a little upset. This time, I flatter myself, I did myself full justice. The speech was, of course, an appeal to assert our rights and overthrow the present regime. We gathered all but five of those present into our "Society" or "Party." On my way home, I fainted and fell from my horse, Leather, who galloped home and when he came to the gate riderless and whinnied for help, the stable-boys ran to the house and gave the alarm. My father and brother came out, and one led Leather (who seemed to know where I was) who pulled along so that they came upon me just as I was recovering consciousness.

This episode fed the flame of indignation among our friends and those of our Party. They declared no life was now safe. Many came into the Party that had been lukewarm before. We now saw the hand of Fate in this small affair and I treasured my wound as a sign that I would be a part of the new way of life to be known in the future. Of course, I only saw it as a moral battle and never for a moment dreamed of such a thing as armed force.

We at home vowed to be avenged by carrying our cause to the Courts. We appealed to the authorities to find the would-be murderer who had attacked me. But no step was taken to discover the murderer. Such was the regime we were asked to pay to support. Nothing so far had been so drastic an example of our helplessness and want of protection from the Home Government. Many, lukewarm before, became hotheads and talked of burning down the Courthouse.

We, who were the leaders, concluded against any lawless or violent acts and made our friends see that always we must have a clean and fair record. We came out now with greater boldness, demanding a new and proper administration and the removal of the Governor from England. We would pay for what we got from Home, but that was all.

In our pamphlets and other literature we explained our reasons for demanding a change. We were loyal subjects, law-abiding and self-supporting. We would pay for any service or luxury furnished by England, but we had no means to spare to pamper the politicians, and we were weary of the regime that was destroying the prospects held out to us by the Home Office when inducing us to go to America. We looked to a very marked growth of sentiment in the near future as more details and facts were presented and the arguments we offered were unanswerable. We were appalled by the arrival of a new Governor whose first edict declared we were rebels and would be treated as such. Public meetings were forbidden and the rights of even private assemblage of more than four male persons (not of one family) was forbidden.

Men were to be hauled before the Governor, who could act as a Justice and sentence the victims to hard labor in His Majesty's sulphur mines. (Where the sulphur mines were, we had no idea, but we supposed them to be somewhere in Britain.) The prospect of being taken away to such a fate did, indeed, give us pause. Still, we were determined to resist. We met in secret in the woods, in barns, on dark nights, sometimes in small rooms in the taverns, or in private homes. We kept up each other's courage and made up our minds to keep together in close association and, when the time was ripe, to defy the Governor and defend ourselves even to the death.

Such was the situation in the Colony when I saw in a newspaper that New England was also making a demonstration against any further oppression. When an additional tax had been placed on tea (already highly taxed), they had thrown the latest cargo of tea overboard. I showed this article to our friends at our secret meetings. If the people of Massachusetts were able to resist to such a degree, we could surely do likewise. We had no difficulty in making up our minds now. We were not alone. Massachusetts was the first Colony to openly defy the Home Government.

Soon, riders were coming south with the news of the town meetings in New England and told us of the great spirit of the vote that was growing. Men who were from other Colonies who came to tidewater on business said that their Colonies were ready to follow Massachusetts in its rebellious attitude against the rapacity of England. In no Colony had the settlers suffered as did those in Virginia. It seemed to have been a target for the oppressor. We began to meet openly.

The Governor issued one proclamation after another in his endeavor to quell the rising tide—all were ignored. When his Bailiffs arrested two or three poor chaps and had them placed in the stocks in the public square, we went to the Governor's Mansion in droves to protest. He never deigned to see us, so we left, but with this warning,

"Release those citizens from the stocks or we shall do so."

No attention was being paid to our warning. A dozen of us (I was one) took our axes and freed the men. We hurried them to a good hiding place and cared for them. Their families were also looked after.

This was too much for the Governor, so that his nerves gave way, and he sailed on the first ship bound for Home.

❦

Arrest

Dictated September 15, 1944

No one who was not a part of the situation can imagine how we rejoiced when the Governor left our shores. We built bonfires and we sang, we marched, and we held meetings at which the emotions of the audience rose to so high a pitch that often the speakers were carried about on the shoulders of those who heard their words. All this made a profound impression on those citizens who were members of the aristocratic class. At one of our meetings, a little child was carried up to the platform as an example of the poverty of the poor, taxed-to-death planters. The little fellow was five years old but so small that he seemed but three. His little face was so thin that he appeared to be a small wraith of childhood. Many wept when he was asked what he got to eat, and he said,

"I eat the same as our lambs do—the grass. When I am in bed, I eat the corn husks. They're sweet. I swallow the husks, so my Papa won't know I ate them. Then, when I go to play in the woods, I look for mushrooms. They taste like meat. I love to find a nice big flat one and take it home. My mama cooks it for me. I hunt for mushrooms every day. Then, I go to the brook and find some water-weeds (cress) and eat that, but that's hard to find."

The little fellow was so clear in his speech that all heard him and many sobbed as he told of this bitter side of a child's life in our Colony. His clothing consisted of a shirt so ragged and worn that it only partly covered him, and his little legs and feet were bare. One garment, and that in tatters, was all he wore or possessed. We investigated and found that his older brothers and sisters were bound out in service in a distant county, his mother weak and ill from malnutrition, and his father obliged to work as a scavenger for the village. They lived in a lean-to outside the village. The father owned three acres of land but was too poor to get seed with which to raise a little crop. His work paid him two pounds a year. He formerly had been able to hunt and trap wild game and so was able meet his wants; but the new law now forbade him to use his gun to provide for his family, or even to trap, though the rabbits and squirrels overran the county and were becoming a menace eating up the garden crops. This child, of course, was at once cared for and a collection taken up to relieve the family.

❦

We had among us a few men who had served on the Council and, among them was my father. He was a natural leader of opinion and fearless in argument. He now became a strong advocate of a new government for our Colony, one whose officials were all elected by the settlers instead of being sent from England. No great enthusiasm was evinced for this plea but a few of our best families favored it, and that carried weight with the poorer settlers. We saw little chance of going ahead unless the taxes were taken off food, clothing, and the right to hunt wildlife restored when the mating season was over.

We had a very fine class of men who were of no opinion, who only wished to let all drift and see what would happen—these were in the majority and prevailed.

What happened next was the arrival of a new Governor of all the Colonies, and a large body of soldiers who were to keep down any sign of rebellion.

No one was surprised, and none were found who seemed happy over this circumstance. No one gave any cause for trouble at first and it was supposed by the Governor that the mere presence of force had subdued the people. Only a ripple of discontent was noted when two citizens were arrested for non-payment of the Home tax – my father and myself. We were both arrested and thrown in jail. My mother, in a panic, rushed to pay the taxes. My father begged her to take it all calmly, and make it a test before the Court of the legality of the tax under English law.

We had no counsel and spoke in our own defense. We had read the law in Blackstone pertaining to the levy and payment of taxes and knew that the Governor had no right to levy the taxes we suffered from arbitrarily, but they must be submitted to a body legally representing taxpayers. This, of course, had never been the case with the Home Government. No one concerned had raised a voice against his levy.

At the time, we were very popular. Even men who were not of our opinion respected my father and considered him one of the finest minds in the Colony. He had been sought in many cases, even by the Justice who presided over our County Court. His views were never made a subject of ridicule, even by those who were against them. In short, Augustin Washington was known for his keen intelligence as well as his probity.

My own case was different. I had friends, but they were not very influential, and having fought with the Militia was supposed to indicate low tastes and a lack of dignity. My career as a surveyor was also not to my credit, and many predicted a sad end to so fickle a son of my father whose fine qualities he had not inherited. My father, I am happy to say, thought otherwise and often said,

"George, I am proud of you because you are not afraid to speak your mind and espouse a cause."

My mother also said,

"George, my son, I feel that you can never fail for you put your heart wholly into all you believe in."

Their faith in me was my recompense and my shield and buckler.

Now, I'D LIKE TO SAY a word about my brother, Charles. He was a man who was overshadowed by my father, and later, by the part I played in events. Yet he gave such help as without it we might have failed. He gave of his means, his mind, and strength, all through these difficult times. No man was ever less concerned with fame, or to win acclaim and public favor, than Charles Washington. I love him as I never loved another man. He had a soul so pure that never could one doubt his motives. He gave of himself unstintingly in every cause that might bring benefit to his fellows.

*Charles Washington
SAR, Lexinton, KY*

Charles's death, was to me the saddest of all my life's experiences. His memory sustained me in my darkest hours and often since, here in the Realm of Spirit, when the Republic seems in grave danger, it is Charles whose warm words of encouragement sustain me and bring me comfort.

MY FATHER

DICTATED SEPTEMBER 14, 1944

EVENTUALLY THE current regime found itself being not only criticized by the Aristocrats, but discredited politically. The Governor gave his resignation to the Home Secretary and we were then in the County's own control, through the Council. Although the President was an out-and-out Tory and made no pretense of sympathy with the settlers' complaints, he was overruled by the members who had a majority on our side.

The tax on wool was left, but game hunting was permitted through the season when it was too plentiful to endanger its continuity. All was peaceful for a time, although the Crown Tax still drove out the small land owners and the many who found it burdensome.

My father became the center of attack when he declared, "These wool and game laws remitted are but a drop in the bucket. We need to be free of the Crown tax before we can hope to invite, in full honesty and moral conscience, the settlers from Home who would, if they were assured of a chance to prosper, be happy to emigrate to Virginia."

He was called a firebrand, a rebel, a man whose only pleasure was to stir up trouble in the Colony, which would ruin Virginia if he prevailed. We lived in a constant state of anxiety at home. My mother was ever fearful of an attack on my father such as I had suffered. We went to the town in pairs now, and someone stayed behind to protect our home.

Letters threatening to burn down our home and barns and to destroy our crops arrived almost weekly. At one time, my father was threatened in the street when doing business in town and asked if he was ready to make a statement of his views before the Council. He was, of course, not at that moment ready to do so, but said if the Council would give him a few days' notice, he would be happy to do so – but not unless he could say plainly, without danger to his liberty, what he had come to see was the wisest course for all the settlers to pursue if Virginia was ever to be more than an extension of the Home Country's feudal system.

He was then assured that the Council would give him its protection and permit him to speak freely.

❦

WHEN THE NOTICE was served on him to appear before the Council and explain his views, he made a vow to speak his mind, no matter what might be the consequences to himself. For twenty-six hours he was in his room writing, and praying to Almighty God for guidance and help to so present the case of the poor settlers that the head of the Council would be moved to grant them justice.

I remember his pale face and weakened voice as he finished the paper he had prepared and, as he laid it down for us to read, he said,

"My sons, you will now read all I have written and give me your opinion. If I have erred by saying aught that is not reasonable or valid, call my attention to it. If I have overstated a fact, make a mark under it and I will modify my words."

With that, he left us to go to bed, where my mother had prepared to have him served with such nourishment as was suitable after his long fast. Charles and I were astonished by the eloquence and beauty of the manner in which he had phrased his ideas. We had never thought of him as a man gifted with such a talent. Our only knowledge of him as a writer had been the half dozen letters we had received when from home. Here we read such profound and inspired words that often we were moved to tears. Charles, indeed, was obliged to stop reading and handed the paper over to me. We had thought it best to read aloud, the better to get the effect he would produce when he read his paper before the Council.

I remember well the scene: a small room where my father

kept his account books and his private papers. There were stacks of seed grains in the corners and a writing table and two chairs and a few maps on the wall. The single window was uncurtained with only a paper shade at the upper sash. Two candles and writing material were on the table and a newspaper rack stood beside it. That was all.

Charles sat at the table and I in the other chair on the opposite side. It was evening and we knew the long, twenty-six hour vigil and labor of our father had left him in collapse. We knew the hour had come when the work he had put his heart, mind, and hand to must either succeed or fail and, if the latter, we knew the fate awaiting us. His toil and my mother's had made of our estate and home a place that was often admired. His place in the community was one of dignity and his word was accepted as second to none. We faced the humiliation and, possibly, the ruin that came to those who dared to oppose the ruling powers.

We thought of all this as our father, silent and trying to recover his strength, prepared to face his ordeal which would take place in two days. Charles and I determined to both be with him at the Council meeting and we planned to have a guard of men, of whose loyalty we felt sure, to guard our home in our absence.

My mother came to us as we sat there, and said,

"My sons, you are very quiet. It is because you do not like what your father has written?"

We told her we were so overcome by the sense of our father's great mind and his ability to put into words his feelings and conviction, that we were silent because of this revelation of him. She then read it.

Again and again the tears came and, as she finished, she laid her head upon the table and sobbed aloud. We knelt on either side of her and tried in silence to make her feel our understanding and our affection. Her arms went over our shoulders as if we had been the small boys she so often held thus. I love to remember all this. It gives me renewed faith in the greatness of my father and the goodness of my mother.

ALL WAS SERENE as we three walked into the Council room, my father leading, then Charles, then I. We took our seats side by side, in the rear. My father was calm, and said before we entered,

"Now, boys, we shall prevail. Keep perfectly quiet and make no demonstration, no matter what is said or done."

The business of the meeting was soon over, and the President, in a sarcastic manner, called out,

"We shall now have the views of our friend, Mr. Augustin Washington, on the state of the Colony. Mr. Washington, you will please come forward."

My father rose and went to the platform where the Chairman continued to sit. His chair was on my father's left and, all during the reading, the so-called gentleman tried to make his facial expressions eloquent enough to counteract the statements read. That he failed even to get the Council's attention made his effort somewhat ridiculous. As my father took his place and faced the Council, a murmur went over those men facing him. His pale face showed plainly the mental strain he was under. His dark hair and eyes accentuated his pallor, and the audience could not help but note that. As he began to read, he saw the Chairman's grimaces and was all but dismayed at first, but soon he could see that this was being ignored by the others.

The reading soon held the audience spellbound. My father's voice and his clear and fine articulation, as well as his eloquence, made the listeners forget all else. It lasted fully an hour, that reading, and when he finished, the tribute of rapt attention was broken after a moment's silence by a roar of voices and loud handclaps. A few, perhaps four or five, were silent, but the majority prevailed in their applause.

Charles and I had sat there as still as two stone images doing our best to show no feeling in our faces. We did look at each other now and then to see if both noted the Chairman's antics, or when an important point was made in the speech. As Father sat down between us, we nudged him with our knees and he answered likewise. We had a sense of great exaltation and were sure that no other man there could refute what he had presented so clearly.

The Chairman, as if greatly bored by all this, asked if anyone cared to answer the charges made by Mr. Washington. One man rose and proposed that no attention should be paid to them as they were not at all important. This was immediately received with a shout of disapproval from the majority. So great a shout that no one seconded the proposal. A babble of voices rose and all that came of it was the Chairman announced that the meeting was dismissed.

One man rose and objected, saying,

"Why ask Mr. Washington to present his views if we are not able to discuss them?"

Others approved this noisily and, in the end, the Chairman was obliged to yield and continue the meeting. One man rose and, taking the platform, said in effect that he had been profoundly interested in Mr. Washington's speech and had come to see things much more clearly since listening to what was probably the finest picture of current life in Virginia ever presented. He went on to say that the arguments were irrefutable and that sound policy indicated a consideration of the facts presented, and he hoped this would be followed by appropriate action of the Council. One rose to oppose him, but his arguments were so lame and his presentation of them so inadequate that he made apparently no progress with his listeners.

My father was then asked to reply to questions. This he did easily with facts and instances. When the meeting finally closed after probably the longest session in the county's history, a crowd gathered about us to congratulate my father, one man saying,

"You should be on the Council, Washington. You would be of great help."

Others agreed. The Chairman went by with scarcely a nod of his head.

❀

ALL SEEMED TO BE working our way. Still, no action was taken by the Council to remedy the situation. After a three months' wait, our party addressed the Council, asking for several reforms. This opened the way for those who sided with Father's views. The result was the removal of the tax on wool and more liberal game laws. It also gave a reduction, by one third, of the Crown Tax. The people, as a whole, were very much disappointed that the Crown Tax had not been entirely removed. Still, we had won in some measure and the settlers were inclined to see in it a sign that, in time, a complete abolition of the Home tax would be possible. At home, we were glad of even this small advance in our cause and, for the time, rested on those sparse laurels. My father said,

"In time we shall be free. Be patient. We are now in the majority."

❀

VIRGINIA MILITIA AGAIN

DICTATED SEPTEMBER 15, 1944

SOME TIME LATER, my father realized I was in a rut and suggested my taking over the work in the matter of animal breeding. This I disliked and, rather than do it, I went to Baltimore and signed up with the militia which was then becoming a respectable service, by comparison with our old regime. My father said,

"Well, George, I am glad you have decided on your vocation. You would never make a farmer and you may carve some sort of career for yourself in the Colonial Militia."

This was the last of my hanging around. Once back with the boys, some of whom were still in the service, I found we were now old enough and, in some cases, sensible enough to behave in a manner to inspire respect. My old friend Corliss was waiting to greet me. He was a magnificent looking soldier, his lameness offset by his splendid head and shoulders. He could march with the best of them and his happy-go-lucky disposition was an inspiration to the other men. He was still a private, having no education but seemingly indifferent to the fact. We were never much together but, now and then when off duty, I would enjoy a dinner with him at a tavern and a long talk over old times. This man has always remained in my memory as one of the most beautiful human beings I was ever blessed to know.

When I got into the stride, I found I had many things to learn and some to contribute to the service. I was now a Captain, and responsible for the feeding and clothing of the Company that I commanded. We were foot soldiers, and I resented the manner in which we were shod. In the matter of economy, I could see no great saving, since it took a pair of moccasins two weeks to wear out; while boots, with care, would last six months. At last I prevailed. Another point on which I was determined to succeed was in the matter of rations. Our food – bread and fat pork when on duty – was the cause of scurvy. I wanted a bag of dried fruit or vegetables added and, after some bargaining, got it. No coffee – only a spoonful of sugar added to hot water – was our drink at meals. My father had told me of the benefit of coffee in stimulating the blood circulation, and I again made life a burden to my superiors by insisting on a tablespoon of coffee beans for breakfast. These we crushed between stones and, scraping up the bits, always with some dirt and gravel, we boiled it and found it cheered and strengthened us for the day's work.

My other achievement was not so successful. I asked for a uniform, something that would identify us as the champions of the Colony. The outfit that was given reduced us in appearance to the status of monkeys. The coat came only to the waist, and was bright red flannel braided with blue. We wore our old linsey woolsey trousers and boots. Our hats were a bright blue cap with no visor. Instead, it had a chin-strap. For warmth and protection against the weather, we had a square piece of blue flannel that had a small hole in the center where we thrust our head. This offered little protection from either rain or cold, and looked so absurd that the men simply refused to wear it. I begged for a topcoat, but that was refused. At last, we compromised by making a small blanket into a shoulder shawl. Even then, the red jacket and blue cap made the men so unhappy that I begged for our old uniforms of hunting shirt and field cap. I had made so much disturbance by this time that my popularity with the men was only exceeded by my unpopularity with my superiors. I made no more suggestions and confined myself to training and studying when I could find the time.

⚜

ALL WAS GOING well with the Company, and we were doing our work around the Fort when word came that a raid by Indians had been made upon the settlers of the western counties again. We got this message one night and, without waiting to sleep, we began to march. This was the beginning of a long campaign in the western counties. We were defeated at first and badly disseminated but, by persisting, we finally drove the Indians over the mountains with so many losses in dead and wounded that they sued for peace. Only thirty returned.

This tragedy so worked upon my feelings that I felt I could not bear to remain, and requested a furlough. This I was given and went home, where I fell ill and was confined to bed for seven weeks. Slowly recovering my strength, I finally was able to return to duty.

At this time, I was not a very gallant fellow. My work occupied me when on duty. Marriage never entered my head. I saw many attractive maids and a few of them had been very kind. One especially, a fair young lady whose first name was Sally, came to care for me and I sometimes felt she was the one who might be my choice for a wife. Still, I was far from eager to bind myself down with a family. I loved the open too well, and I was so essentially a man's man that I feared I would never make a woman happy as her husband.

One day, I was teasing Sally about her little trick of pouting when we were together, and she said,

"You ugly brute, I hate you!"

Thus ended the little romance. The last I saw of Sally, she was nursing her ninth child by a member of my regiment. Sometimes, I will admit now, I felt a twinge at the affliction that had marred my facial looks that occurred when my elder brother took me to the island of Cuba on a business trip. There I had been exposed to the dread disease, smallpox. On recovering, I was so marked that I was ever shy of making the least advance to a girl. She had to do the courting, if there was to be any. The disfigurement came upon me when I was only thirteen, an age when we should be the most charming.

At any rate, Sally's remark but confirmed me in my avoidance of women. Perhaps it was providential that women were but a minor part of my life. Also, my future would not have given me the work which it was my greatest happiness to perform. My father seemed to feel my affliction much more than I. My mother, too, was inconsolable and wept over me until I began to think I was a monster of hideousness. At any rate, my brothers, all handsome men, looked upon me as a blighted creature and, except for Charles, the youngest of us, gave me to understand that I was doomed to be a bachelor.

Charles, with me at home, made me his hero. I was to him the ideal of a man, a patriot, and a soldier. Often, I wondered at the way he would express his love and his sincere admiration for such an ordinary fellow as I. Nevertheless, his loyalty and affection made up to me, in great measure, for the coldness of my other brothers. As readers of our history know, these two were half-brothers, while Charles and I had the same mother. I have been struck by this many times – the differences in feeling where the blood is changed. Well, all my mortal life I bore those scars. I'm sorry to say they always troubled me except when I was at war. Then how could I be bothered about such a trivial scar when surrounded by men who had lost their limbs and their lives? When I was in the field, no comrade or enemy ever spoke of them. They were concerned with my other qualities, not my facial characteristics.

❦

AN ACCOUNTANT

DICTATED SEPTEMBER 16, 1944

I SEEM AT TIMES, perhaps, to be telling the story of a very different Washington than the man you know. But my intention is to speak as I knew myself to be then and share the privacy of my thoughts. I see no need to go into memories of events so well recorded by historians. My intention is to share what they could never know about me. It is customary to make of a biography the tale of nobility and exalted virtues. My life was far from exhibiting these high qualities all the time. But I was quite indifferent to the slaves we owned, which was a behavior typical of the day. Today, of course, such behavior would never come from my spirit, or from me if I were mortal again. But I must recall who I was then with honesty, and I will say I was a man of my time, of my society. Humanity continues to learn, thank heavens. My mother often said,

"George is a very strange boy. He has no idea of marrying and he has no close companions. I am sure he is very lonely."

I often heard her say this to my father, who usually replied,

"Well, Mary, George is not an average man. He is a lone wolf, and will not hunt with the pack."

Perhaps it was hearing him say this that made me further inclined to solitude, to hunting and fishing, while other young fellows were merry in the village or town. I found much to think upon especially after my dreadful Quebec experience, a military defeat and humiliation that I do not care to recount. But it was my first humiliation as a military leader and I would remember Quebec all the days of my life.

Let me just say that I saw clearly that I was sent on a mission that was intended to be a complete failure, the Governor unable to realize any way in which we could survive that terrible journey homeward with no provision made for us by him. He knew the ways of the French, and their exchanging prisoners had previously meant handing over the Indian captives in health, with well-fed bodies, to receive crippled invalids who perished before reaching home. My ignorance of this fact was providential. I knew nothing of these former blots on our history and the men who were responsible. The consequence was that I was alert to every sort of opportunity and my long years spent in the fields and woods had made me an expert at trapping and shooting, taking and making cover, and in detecting the direction of sun, moon, and stars, as well as an Indian.

Some of my companions knew this, having been with me in former years and they were always ready to follow me and obey me in all my rather extraordinary suggestions and orders. Their cooperation and unity were perhaps the greatest element in our fight for survival.

We all arrived in Richmond, except for a boy who, against my orders, swam too far out in the Hudson. The Governor did not even receive me when I reported with the men. Instead, I was handed my pay and given a receipt for the returned men. They were then taken over by an officer and marched off to the Post.

I never saw any of them, but Corliss, again. Neither did I ever again see Governor Dinwiddie. He was so chagrined at the story the men told and by the indignation aroused by his cruel indifference to their fate, that he soon sailed for Home. His successor was not appointed for several months and the Colony was administered by a Lieutenant Governor, who happened to be of a different caliber.

The historians made no mention of the prisoners and our terrible trek from Montreal to Virginia. The writers tell a perfectly false story saying that Governor Dinwiddie sent me north with an ultimatum to the Six Nations. Well, what sort of Chiefs would they be to yield to a distant governor's ultimatum when they had the backing of the French? This falsehood, given out by the Governor was to cover up the real purpose which was nothing less than to rid Virginia of some prisoners who were the sons of settlers that were against the rapacity of the Crown, and his own inadequacy as an official. My work on my land had been taken over by my father and so I had a crop to sell. This was welcome news when I returned, for now I could seek some sort of a berth in Philadelphia, where my brother Augustin was doing well with a mercantile firm.

My pay amounted to ten pounds for my several months hardships to and from Canada and, with the fifteen pounds my crops brought, I felt there was plenty to see me through whatever lay before me in Philadelphia.

I remained at home a few days to rest and recuperate and then made a pact with my father to take over my land, for what he could make of it, and apply half the procceds to paying off the ten pounds still due on it.

When I said goodbye, my father, now growing grey and beginning to see age coming on, said,

"My dear George, make this your final decision. You are now twenty-two. You have now no more time to waste. I think you are making a wise move. Be sure you take this to heart. A man must make his way before he is forty. After that it is a hard task."

My mother was, as always, ready to see in anything I did only success. What was best in me she upheld, and the rest ignored. Charles, my younger brother, too, always gave me praise and encouragement. To him, my military experiences were very fine examples of manly character and he loved me for them. My elder brother, Lawrence, was keen on my going into the Navy, for the Colonies were combined in support of that branch of Service. I could not bear the idea of confinement onboard ship and would not listen to him. That was ever a matter of dissension between us. He had no use for the State's Militia and looked upon it as a contemptible waste of time for a member of a family such as ours.

ABOUT THE AFTERLIFE

WHEN I CAME TO THIS part of my life, I was in the toils of an idea that I could make life yield to me what I wished. I tried this, and found that disaster attended every exhibition of my own will. This you readers can see for yourself. My own self-will was to make a great soldier of myself, to serve my Colony. I was in the toils of the old theology and thought that my belief in a personal God was all I needed to make my personal wishes come true, providing I harmed no one by them. My own will never got me anywhere. The same result I observe in the lives of others on Earth, which from present position I can perceive quite clearly. There is a plan for each human life; of that, I can assure you.

This was pointed out to me in Philadelphia by a friend I acquired at the warehouse where I was employed very briefly. The man was ten years older than I, married, and had three children. His name I shall not give, as he has many descendents. He has not changed since coming here, for I have often met him and he seems to be in a static condition, though he is very intelligent and quick to grasp an idea. What is holding him back? Here is a lesson I give to you now! Usually, we learn the laws here and use them to our own advantage and that of others. One of the great Etheric blessings is that we cease to think of ourselves as old. Since we feel so young and active mentally – our personality reflects that sense of youth and we take on the appearance of former years. My friend was seventy-odd at his death, and looks it now because his spirit remains so very old and bound to the memories and substance of this one incarnation. I have spoken to him about this, and he says he still feels the weight of those long hard years of his Earth life. He carries guilt, grief, and regrets that he did not live a more courageous life at a time when our Nation needed men and women of great courage – just like now. In fact, there will never be a time when America will not need its people to be courageous. My friend has never been able to get into the feeling that is needed here to make his mind his servant. I talk and labor with him, but I see he must reincarnate before he can shake off the many years of negative thought and come into his own.

To revert to our old days in our dreary warehouse, he said one day,

"Washington, what is it you believe in? You seem to have some strange secret source of power that carries you over everything."

I could not reply very cogently, since I was unaware of anything of the sort. I tried to say so, and added that I often prayed and hoped to see my prayers come to pass.

He smiled, and said in a less than respectful tone,

"Oh! So you are just a Christian. I thought you were something more enlightened."

I was daunted by his facial expression of contempt, rather than his words. I explained that my people were professed Christians, though I was not a religious man. He seemed relieved to hear that, and told me he was an atheist. I was horrified to hear such a damning thing of a man I respected. I asked him why he could not believe in a Superior Power. He was cryptic to me then,

"Because if there is, it is an evil power and I don't wish to credit such a damnable thing."

In the end, I came to value the friendship of this good man, for I saw that he depended only upon himself and tried to keep all selfishness out of his mind. He was poor and lived in the simplest way, with no pleasures save reading, walking out on Sunday with his wife, and now and then attending the theatre which he loved. I made it a practice to join him when he went up in the gallery at the play and there we saw vice punished and virtue rewarded, except in the tragedies, where Shakespeare does not stack the cards for his heroes and heroines, but deals out the truth that man lives by the cause and effect of his own mental and physical actions.

We used to read the plays before we went to see them acted, and there I found the many beautiful passages that have lived on the lips of actors for three centuries. What a joy it was to go with my friend who loved his Shakespeare better than any other, who led me through the plays with a sort of genius for making them live. These evenings in the gallery were the high spots in my otherwise dreary life at the time.

❦

Off for Boston and Meeting Sam Adams

Dictated September 19, 1944

*Sam Adams
from a portrait by
John Singleton Copley
Courtesy National Archives*

I returned to my Philadelphia warehouse and my accounting. This was a confining occupation and, after six weeks, my health began to suffer. I became ill of a strange malady that made me not only weak, but crippled my left side. My brother, whom I had seen only twice after I arrived, was notified. He at once made arrangements for my removal from my lodgings in a private home to his house, where he could in some measure look after me. I was there only two days when my father arrived and took me home.

Here again, I made a quick and complete recovery in the fresh air and under the ministrations of my mother. What a wreck I was when I arrived! At the sight of me, my mother nearly fainted and my good little cousins sent up cries of terror at my appearance. No more confinement for me! I decided to go back and play my part on my own land and see if I could make it support me. In a month or so, I was planting tobacco and cotton with a little corner saved for a few vegetables.

❦

My NEXT CROP was a failure, and I then had no money with which to make my last payment on my land. I came to see that I was never meant to be a planter, and so asked my father to buy my land at less than I had paid for it. With this money I decided to go to Boston and try my fortune there. I knew better than to coop myself up before a desk and meant to try for service in the Militia of the Colony of Massachusetts, which was always at war with the Indians. My father realized my future did not lie in farming and, with another "Godspeed," saw me off for tidewater on the coach. Once again I faced the unknown.

The experiences on the way amused and charmed me. In the coach I met fellow travelers who told tales of their own adventures and those of others. All seemed to feel that our great land was a place where fortune was a gamble and no one was secure. I resented this, even though so far my life confirmed this idea. One gentleman, a merchant who hailed from over the mountains, was vociferous. He was traveling to Boston to fetch his goods. Another was particularly bitter and said, in effect, that we were all a lot of fools to try to run the Country with each Colony selfishly caring only for itself with no strength to make a powerful State. Unity, he said, was all that could make the land safe or prosperous. This gentleman's name was Mr. Samuel Adams.

The idea began to obsess me. I thought upon it constantly. While the others were of various opinions as to Mr. Adams' views, we were all talking our heads off—when we suddenly found ourselves making such a clatter that the one lady passenger complained that her head was aching because of our noise. We apologized and I could but wish the lady had my mother's table bell, for soon we were going at it full-throatedly again. She finally begged to be permitted to get out and climb up beside the driver. This had the desired effect. Mr. Adams himself offered to leave his seat, as he had been one of the protagonists in the vociferous debate.

My own embarrassment was extreme, though I being younger than the others had taken the least part in the discussion.

The lady smiled at me, saying,

"Dear sir, pray forgive me if I have hurt your feelings. I did not mean you when I spoke."

This only confused me the more, as I saw the other three men exchange jocular smiles when the lady singled me out in this way. We arrived in Richmond in the evening and, as I assisted the lady to alight, she whispered,

"Dear sir, come to my home in Richmond and stay, instead of at the tavern. It would make me and my family very happy to entertain you. I know you are a gentleman."

Of course, with such an inviting prospect, I was not inclined to quarrel. The lady's home was charming and the family also. This consisted of herself, her husband, and her mother. All were very friendly, and my stay of two days waiting for the coach that would take me to tidewater at Norfolk was a delightful episode that I still recall with pleasure. I was young enough to love any new acquaintance with people and places.

My Richmond experiences hitherto had been brief and confined to duty. Here I was at leisure to inspect the city and to see and hear much that was new to me. My hosts were Mr. Carrington and Mrs. Carrington. Mr. Carrington was a banker, so the establishment was in keeping with his position. I had never before been in a city home. I had never seen such nice furnishings nor heard such topics discussed. I was shy and only spoke when addressed.

Mr. Carrington inquired the object of my journey to Boston which I, of course, told him. He was not much in the way of giving advice, but he did say,

"Be careful. Those Yankees are pretty smart and they need watching. Look out you do not get fleeced."

I marveled at this, and promised to be on the alert in my own interest.

❧

AFTER THIS LITTLE interlude, I went off happily and full of zest for what lay before me. I caught the stage only to find it full, but the seat beside the driver was the best place to be. I saw the lovely scenery and even on the second day when it rained, I was happy and content to feel the sweet air and warm raindrops on my face. We got to Norfolk in time to catch the packet for New York.

My little stateroom was only six feet long and I was six feet seven inches. I managed to get a little sleep by putting my feet up on the partition. Still, I enjoyed even that novelty and felt none the worse when two days later found us in the most glorious and unique harbor, where the Hudson runs into the ocean at the end of Manhattan Island.

I found myself wishing I had chosen this destination rather than Boston. We had a few hours ashore and I made the most of them. I was agape at the marvels before me. Such an array of buildings! They seemed to be a very beehive of business, and the fine houses and carriages that were continually to be seen made me wonder at the riches they indicated. I never, in later years, got the better of that feeling even when I occupied important posts there.

Never had I seen so many beautiful horses or women so gaily and fashionably attired. Men, too, wore the most flashy garments I had ever seen. What riches they seemed to indicate! My own appearance in my linsey woolsey coat and my military cape looked simple and almost shabby beside them.

My mother had been my tailor and her dear hands had made my shirts, stocks, and knitted my blue woolen stockings. I wondered if Boston was as extravagant a place and the people so fond of rich dress.

❧

SERVICE IN MASSACHUSETTS

DICTATED SEPTEMBER 20, 1944

WE SAILED AWAY with our cargo of human and other freight. This time, I was given a somewhat larger berth and rested well as we went along the Sound, not out at sea very far.

What lovely weather we had and what an exciting journey!

The passengers played chess and cards and even the ladies on board joined in the round games the Captain suggested in the evening. The boat was steady and we romped through a dance or two when someone played a jew's-harp, or simply sang some old tunes with a lively tempo.

I found myself looking at a very pretty girl who sat out the dances, and she smiled so sweetly that I was bold enough to ask her to dance. I had never danced with an unknown female before and found the experience very exciting. So, I imagine, did she, for her eyes were sparkling when it was over. She said in a very low tone,

"What shall we do now?"

I suggested that we take a walk around the platform of the packet among the freight. This we did, and at the corner of the main side of the saloon, I put my arm around her. At this, she made a pass at my pocket, but I caught her hand and kissed it. She pretended she had mistaken my pocket for her reticule on her arm. Of course, I saw what was up and saved her face. She then wished to return to the saloon, and presently I saw her dancing with an elderly gentleman that, some hours later, was heard bitterly lamenting the loss of his chronometer and wallet. There was no sign of his pretty little partner, who was said to be sea-sick in her stateroom. The captain, however, in a harsh voice was heard demanding that she return the lost articles. How it all ended I never knew. I was never again quite so responsive to pretty girls who smiled so sweetly on packet boats.

All was the usual hubbub when we made port at Boston. My letter of introduction to the Commander of the Post at the Battery was from a gentleman who was not in the service. Consequently, I was at some pains to find out just what sort of reception I would receive when I presented it. I learned from a sentry that this officer was a "damned old fool who ought to be taken out and drowned in the harbor."

This seemed to be confirmed by a soldier in uniform, whom I encountered eating his breakfast in the tavern near the Post. His answer to my inquiry was,

"Damn his eyes. I wish he was starving in hell!"

Not heartened by what I had learned from the private soldiers, I decided to make inquiries of the citizens. I asked the tavern-keeper what he thought of this Commanding officer and got this,

"He is an old brute who hasn't been sober in ten years."

Well, here was a fine prospect! What was I to do? I made up my mind that I must ignore all these comments and face the Commander as if they had not been made. When I presented myself at the Fort, I was made to feel a bit out of place, since I was not wearing a uniform.

The orderly looked me over and apparently decided to treat me to a bit of his wit,

"What do you want to see the Colonel for? He doesn't wish to buy any fish."

I said I had a letter to him which would explain my business, which was of a military nature. My inquisitor was not to be taken in. He said with a guffaw,

"God bless us, this is getting too much when a fish vendor brings a letter of introduction!"

I was now losing my temper, and said sharply,

"Deliver this letter at once, or I shall report you."

This seemed to only amuse him the more, and he said,

"By God, what the devil do you think a fishman's report will amount to?"

My reply was to walk away. This made him change his tune, and he called after me,

"Come back! Can't you take a joke?"

I returned in a mood to knock him down – he saw it and began to apologize. At last he disappeared with my letter of introduction, and I was presently ushered into the presence of a bloated old officer who had a nose covered with rum blossoms. His drink-ladened breath fouled the air and the whole atmosphere was blue with the smoke from his long clay pipe. He read the letter and seemed impressed. Observing my unusual height and breadth of shoulder, he said in an attempt at the humorous sally,

"You have never been in the regular service, but I see you have the physique of which good fighters are made. Take a seat, Captain Washington, and tell me something of your experience."

I was glad to find him at least willing to concede that I looked like a fighter, and so was in the mood to speak freely of my record. He watched me with a bilious eye, and then said,

"Why are you looking for service here?"

I said quite simply,

"Because I saw no future in Virginia."

He was amused at this and asked what sort of a future I expected in Massachusetts. I told him I understood they had a trained and competent army and that there was a good deal of active duty. In such a case, a man always had a chance to prove himself and gain promotion.

"I see you like fighting. Well, you will get a bellyful with us. We have a hell of a lot of it. We can offer you just what you are looking for."

I did not know what to make of this man and said no more. He stared at me for a moment, and then added,

"By God, Washington, I believe you. Most men come to this Post to get away from the bailiffs or a girl in trouble, but you seem to be a man with the real soldier mettle. I shall be happy to give you a command."

That was the best word I had yet had given to me in all my years of military service. I was given a company to command in three days and had donned the British uniform as a captain of foot soldiers. I found the men about what he had said—a lot of hangdog looking fellows who only enlisted to get away from some girl or their creditors, with a few who were looking for adventure with little sense of all to be expected of them. I was appalled at their appearance and manner, and contrasted them in my mind with the courageous comrades I had fought with. I was somewhat dashed at the prospect.

❦

RELIGIOUS AND RIOT DUTY

DICTATED SEPTEMBER 21, 1944

I WAS NOT VERY happy when I took command of this surly, ill-looking lot. They had no respect for themselves and none for an officer.

I kept them at work, drilling them in their target shooting and dagger throwing. I gave them lessons in wrestling, with an eye to not only hand-to-hand fighting—but to build them up in body and give them something of an appearance of men. They were a miserable lot physically and an Indian could make short work of any one of them.

At first, they resented my hard discipline and long stretches of target practice. I was unpopular also with my brother officers for the reason that I worked with my men instead of leaving all the hard work to the sergeant.

After two months' incessant work, there was some improvement in the work, as well as in the appearance of the company. When we were inspected, the old general was moved to say,

"By God, Captain Washington, you have really made them like soldiers."

This, I was told, was a most unusual speech from a commander who had not within memory ever paid a compliment to men or officers before. Of course, I was pleased and hoped that when the test came my men would meet it. However, I was far from confident that they would.

We were ordered off to quell a disturbance in the vicinity of the town of Salem. Our orders were to take possession of the town and put it under martial law. When we arrived, we found the trouble was a religious outburst that had culminated in the dreadful murder of several citizens who had tried to lead the people into an insurrection against a poor unfortunate man who had been told he was a prophet. He had predicted the end of the world and made enough converts so that as many as twenty men and women had been giving away their belongings and property, getting ready to meet their God.

No amount of reason could prevail upon them to resume their daily tasks and continue life as usual. Stores were closed and several people made a public bonfire of their furniture, proclaiming their freedom from all worldly belongings. The state of mind of these people was so high pitched that no amount of reasoning could affect them, and they chanted their views in the public streets and watched their hard-earned home furnishings burned as they yelled out their hymns or shouted prayers to the Almighty.

As I was not a very religious man, I had little sympathy with all this and ordered my men to arrest any citizen, man or woman, who indulged in these religious orgies.

Soon we were attacked by these hysterical creatures and had our hands full to keep them from half killing us. Women were worse than the men as they tried to scratch our eyes out and tore at our hair. However, we finally had the leaders in custody and quiet reigned in the streets. The fires were extinguished and a few things saved from the flames.

The mayor and his bailiffs came to thank us for restoring order. So far, my men had only had to defend themselves. Now, they must keep order. My own feelings were all against these zealots, but it seems some of the Company had been the sons of Anabaptists and were believers in the second coming of Christ at any time the Church leaders decided. This was a complete surprise to me, for I had never detected the least religious belief of any sort among the men, least of all that of an Anabaptist.

When quiet again prevailed, we all went on the Common where I found four of the men on their knees in prayer. Not the silent prayers of men who deeply desire Divine intervention in their affairs; they were laughing and crying and calling upon the Deity to come and save them from the wicked world and take them to their heavenly rest. They seemed demented and, when given the order to fall in and march back to the quarters established, they yelled defiance. We were at our wits' end to know how to deal with them. Finally, I ordered my sergeant to fetch some water and with a gourd we dished water from the bucket into the faces of the yelling and screaming soldiers, which had an instantaneous effect. The townspeople had gathered to watch this and we were acclaimed as saviors of a disease they called witchcraft.

A very dignified man came up to me and said,

"My friend, the devil is now making his stand in the bodies of your men. We must drive him out by prayer and fasting."

We were in no mood to listen to this counsel, as we had marched all night and had not slept and our stomachs were demanding food. My part was to try and placate the old bigot while the men got to quarters and prepared food. I was all but in a faint when, after two hours of walking with this man around the town, he himself fainted on the roadway. I pulled him to a safe spot on the footpath and left him to go to my quarters in the mayor's home, where I was hoping to find a hot meal waiting. My heart sank when the mayor's wife said supper had been over for two hours and she could only offer me some bread and milk.

I left to try and find a tavern where a hot meal might be had, but that was a vain quest. No inn or tavern was permitted to be opened after 9 o'clock and it was now twenty minutes past that time. I sat down on the church steps and I fear my thoughts were far from devotional. Finally, I roused myself and made for the men's quarters, which were in a large warehouse near a small but clear stream. The men were asleep. My own case was so extreme that I envied them and was about to make myself a bed of straw on the dirty warehouse floor when a voice said,

"God damn you, what are you doing with my straw?"

This, from one of my own men who had been out on a debauch with a Salem wench. He had not recognized me. I made him apologize and told him my predicament. Instead of any expression of sympathy or help, he burst into such a fit of laughter that he woke several of the men. Then he told them the joke and they all roared; but no one offered to give me a bite of food, a drink from a flask, or a blanket.

I sallied into the night, going to a small shop where there

was a window filled with sweets and made such a to-do that the owner in nightcap and gown and with a candle came to the door. Peering through the window and seeing my uniform, he opened the door a little way. When I had explained my plight, he too found it amusing, but offered to sell me several of his wares, which only consisted of candy and sweetcakes. He did manage to get me a bit of cheese and a drink of milk. For these wares, he charged me triple price and refused to let me sleep on his shop bench. This was too much, and I told him I should report his refusal to the general on my return to Boston and tell him how an officer in the King's service had been treated. He became at once less hard and ended by permitting me to lie on his wooden bench, a foot too short for my length and with this I had to be content. Morning came too soon and I had to return to the mayor's house, hoping a hot breakfast would be waiting. Not at all. The mayor's wife again said,

"You are too late. Breakfast has been over for an hour."

I told her I had been fasting since the morning before and needed hot food for the day's march back to Boston. My words fell on deaf ears, and she only remarked that the Army would have to provide it for she could not. I found myself thinking of my own home and the way we fed any wayfarer who asked for shelter. Mr. Carrington's words came back to me, also. I had come to see how very true they were.

Once at the tavern, I made such a breakfast as I could out of the meager provisions they had: a sausage only two inches long, two fried eggs, a hunk of stale bread, and a tin cup of weak tea. What I thought of Salem on the march back to Boston could not be put into words. My men were not very complimentary either, and said they would be damned if they would ever go to the rescue of those townspeople again, and hoped the next time the devil got loose among them that he would do a better job and burn down the town.

My Anabaptists were quiet and looking a bit sheepish. We returned to our Post and all indulged in a twenty-four hour sleep. I reported to the General, and then fell upon my own bed in a stupor that lasted until the next day was turning into evening. We all had a nice hot meal upon awakening and one that made me feel that, after all, the spirit must wait upon the flesh.

❀

ALL OF THIS WINTER we were quiet, so far as the Indians were concerned. We gave some rowdies in Boston a taste of our quality when they rioted at the main entrance of the Town Hall protesting against a certain ordinance that was passed that forbade the sale of liquor after eight o'clock in the evening, or before nine in the morning. The mob threatened to burn every tavern in the city unless the law was rescinded so that whiskey could be purchased at the waterside taverns up to midnight and by five in the morning. This was to favor the seamen and fishermen who wished to make a tavern simply a convenience to obtain their own liquor. All were men of the sea, a very husky lot who loved a fight and stopped short of nothing when engaged in one.

My Company was ordered out to drive the rioters away from the Town Hall and to keep order on the streets nearby. We had about seventy men and the rioters were a crowd of at least three hundred—not a very equal match. We first fired a volley of blanks to show that we were ready to shoot. This was answered by a shower of stones that put five of my men in the hospital, but to their credit, I must say, they stood and fought even with their heads covered with blood.

My own great height made me a target and I was hit four times, but saw the stones coming and ducked. This was my old trick in Indian fights. I got a bash in the right jaw that dislocated it, and never was it quite in line again. Another stone caught me on the lip and hurt like the devil, but only loosened a couple of teeth. My men were so mad that they fought like tigers, and while far from giving a military account of themselves, they went at the mob with their muskets reversed and clubbed the rioters unmercifully. Fifty were left on the streets waiting to be carried home when we finally stopped. The meeting had been over for an hour before we cleared the streets. My own case was the worst, and the General sent me to hospital where I had my jaw attended to and made a recovery in short order, twenty-four hours. I never was good at staying in bed and being nursed, so I was back at the Post almost before any of the men who had been hurt.

This episode brought on an epidemic of resignations. My seventy shrank to forty-two men. The General cursed them uphill and down for their cowardice, but the men were not impressed and went their way. One chap, a little stocky fellow, was ready to make his getaway without the formality of resigning. I explained to him that he would be shot on sight as a deserter if he did that, whereupon he burst into a fit of weeping and declared he never dreamed a soldier's life could be worse than home life. So, there I was with less than half a Company. Recruiting was very difficult. The pay was wretchedly low and the living conditions poor; the food not anything to tempt even the most desperate man and there was always a menace to health and even life itself.

Even I was a bit downhearted over the way I had been again disfigured. No man can protect himself if he is a target for a mob armed with stones. My jaw was painful and not yet fully healed and my teeth had been broken off in my jaw. I was sick of this sort of service that seemed more in the line of police work than that of a soldier.

My father arrived unexpectedly after a letter I had sent him telling of my experience, and begged me to give up this wild dream of glory and a military career. I was almost ready to give in when I remembered my last period as a farmer and decided against repeating that. My father was greatly shocked at my swollen jaw and disfigured appearance. He was also angry to see how low the scale of living for an officer was in his Majesty's service. He made me see that we, as Colonists, worked hard and deserved at least decent food, quarters, and some sort of social recognition. The latter we did not receive in Massachusetts any more than we did in Virginia as Militia. When I spoke of a career, he smiled and said,

"What sort of a career? You will be a broken and pitiful figure if you keep this up much longer."

I knew he was right, yet some inner force seemed always to blind me to a full realization of how sad and miserable my lot really was. I seemed to be hypnotized by the very things that were so wrong—I loved the training which I gave the men, men who were unable to really profit by it because of their inferior physical equipment. I loved the very name of soldier, and try as I would to take a realistic view of my present situation, I only came back to the same conclusion that I was where I belonged. My father departed for home with a sad farewell and said I was again making a wreck of my life.

One small circumstance seemed to brighten my life at this time. A pretty little tavern girl said to me one day,

"Captain Washington, you are the finest soldier in the Army. We girls all say so." She was only a tavern maid and a poor judge of military matters, yet she raised my heart by her little speech and I made up my mind that I was meant to be what I was. This girl was not a sweetheart, but just a barmaid serving me.

One other incident gave me encouragement. A brother officer had said,

"Washington, we all watch you drilling your men and envy you the way you handle them. I wish I could get as good results."

Such words from chaps who seemed seriously interested in the work made me feel that I was more than a mere tyro at it. I stuck to it through another year. In that year, we were idle most of the time and were only away from the post twice. Those were both occasions when we were sent to quell a riot of citizens in a nearby settlement who were determined to establish a community of vice, with a gambling house and three houses of prostitution, to be the center of entertainment for the seafaring men when ashore.

All we had to do was arrest the owners and the girls in the bawdy houses and bring them to town for trial. These poor wretches paid a fine of six pounds or went to the work house. The latter was the enforced choice of all but one – the madam who had run the house.

Another occasion came where we broke up the same sort of enterprise by arresting all concerned and bringing them to the

Boston Court. I hated this sort of duty, it was the means of so disgusting me that I finally asked to resign, though the General said,

"By God, Captain Washington, you are all the army I've got. When you leave there will only be rabble in the King's uniform."

❦

Service in Williamsburg

Dictated September 25, 1944

My life was a bore to me, and I had to find an outlet for my energies apart from my work on the land. It was when the Colony was being governed by a native Virginian for the first time.

The way we came to get this satisfactory regime was through the efforts of our Party, which the opposition had dubbed "the Cranberry Merchants." This term indicated the poorest people in the Colony who in the season went to the marsh land, which was free public land, and picked these sour wild berries and sold them for a few pennies a bushel. Our name for the Party was the "Farmers." The word "farmer" was despised by our Aristocrats, as a farmer in England is usually a tenant of a great landowner. Our Aristocratic settlers, on the grants of land given them by the King, called themselves "Planters," and a "Farmer" was a lesser landowner with, as a rule, fewer acres and slaves. My father was the largest landowner of the Farmers' Party and led the movement. Naturally, I was deeply interested as his son, and myself a small farmer. My father was unique in this – he held a place in the rank of the opposition which he called the Aristocrats and, at the same time, led the Farmers in all their political activities. It was because of this that I came to know the inside workings of the Colonies' politics of both Parties.

We decided to make an end of an imported Governor and choose our own ruler of Virginia. The Home Office was first inclined to squelch our efforts, but finally decided that the peaceful thing was to give us our way and then we would give our Crown tax with a better grace. The man we chose was a farmer who was just as keen a partisan as my father and owned a holding of 200 acres and only a dozen slaves. We loved the man for his great courage in all matters bearing on the good of the State, as well as for his lovable and manly character.

I shall never forget the great joy I experienced in this great man's company. He was at all times a gentleman and ever an example of high and finished manners when in public office. In private, he came to be my ideal of a gentleman. I often visited him in his home, which was but seven miles from ours, and there enjoyed his hospitality which was of a gracious sort. We loved to discuss the future of the Colony and he often would say,

"We must never become slaves to the Home Government. That will serve neither the King nor the Colonies. An enlightened and free people are the greatest of all subjects. We must learn to think and act in our interests, which can never fail to be in the interest of the King."

This became the watchword with the Farmers' Party and my own fixed convictions. We were never very much of politicians, since we were already wedded to the soldier's idea of service to the State.

However, as the year came to an end, I found myself electioneering for my beloved friend and we brought him in triumphant over Lord Baltimore, the Home candidate for re-election. All was astir over this event in the Colony and even in the adjacent one of Maryland and of the Carolinas.

My own part was to make the round of the taverns and try to get the habitués to vote. This class, as a rule, were too listless in political matters to go to the polls. I made many speeches in the taverns and on the Village Common where the younger loafers practiced quoits or danced with the wilder of the girls. Of course, the Aristocrats made much of the disgrace of permitting such characters to sway the election. We knew only too well that they were right in a sense, but we also knew that without them we would never win. Here, then, perhaps was the first corrupt machine.

Here in the United States it has gone to such extremes and from above we wonder, we hope, that Americans will reclaim their free and honest elections. Everything is observed from here —there are no secrets!

We saw our candidate installed in the Governor's chair, and went home wondering why we had not made some sort of a bargain for a job in his service. The Militia was now under his jurisdiction, and I might expect some sort of promotion in the State's service under him.

Well, I took no steps to bring myself to his attention in this way, and so let the opportunity pass. My father, still in full vigor, was made a Collector of the Revenue for the State and, when he came to see how poor I was because of my low tax, he said,

"My dear George, what in God's name are you thinking of to allow yourself to sink into such a position? You are talented and have done good work for your Colony. I shall not rest until you are in a better situation."

When I had no answer for this, he said,

"For the love of God, rouse yourself and make some effort to better your condition."

This spurred me to make a journey to Williamsburg, and I asked the Governor what prospect there was in a return to my profession. He seemed to answer in a very uninterested way, and I left for home in a state of deep depression.

A few weeks later I was the recipient of a letter from the Governor asking if I would consider the post of Superintendent of Militia at a salary of one hundred pounds a year. This was such a shock of joy that I all but fainted. My answer was to take myself at once to Williamsburg and personally thank my good friend, the Governor, for his great favor. I did not return home, but had a messenger take a letter to my father and mother asking them to take on my land and dispatch my body-servant with my belongings. I was so happy that I forgot everything but the joy of planning the work ahead. The Governor had given me far more than my dream had held. I was determined to show him my gratitude by my service and I envisioned a future at the head of a Militia that would be a credit to the Colony.

All went well and I was able to show results. I had a command of some 2,000 men, who had in some instances seen a bit of Indian fighting. Among them, of course, was Corliss. He had been made a lieutenant and was a good commander, but his unfailing good nature often resulted in a lack of authority and so he never got any further promotion. One other member of that first outfit was a captain now, a chap named Stevens. This man was a bad influence in any command, as his habitual ill-nature made him seek victims to torment and his men always hated him. I saw at once the reason why Stevens' company was so disorderly and so badly in need of discipline. These two old comrades envied me my office, but each showed it in a different way. Corliss spoke his mind frankly, but remained my friend. Stevens tried to undermine me with the men and other officers, to the end that I was obliged to challenge Stevens, and in a duel wounded him in the shoulder. This was a scandal that I never was able to live down.

My office was taken from me and I was dismissed from the service by a court-martial appointed by the Governor. He was never cordial to me again, and I was forced to apologize to the Militia. Stevens was promoted to my office and, as time went on, made such a mess of the Militia that the Governor called me back in ten months to resume my place. He said, when I came before him in Williamsburg,

"Major Washington, will you kindly make your apology to me so that I can reinstate you? The Militia is now but a crowd of malcontents. You can, I know, restore them to a semblance of what we must have – a Militia that we can depend on."

Of course, I apologized for my hot-headedness and went to work. I had served six months before and made good progress. Now, ten months of Stevens had undone all my work and I had a lot of men who had neither respect for themselves, their officers, or me. It was a difficult task ahead, but somehow I managed in a few weeks to instill a new spirit. By the time six months had passed, I was proud of the showing the Militia could make. I drilled them in the use of their arms until they were experts, and I gave them a sense of dignity that soon made them a splendid looking lot on parade, and even some sense of responsibility when off duty. The latter was as astonishing to themselves as to the citizens and, most of all, the Governor. When I, at last, had the happiness of visiting my home, my father said in a voice so resonant with joy,

"By my soul, George, you have come into your own at last. Now I am at peace about you."

I wept tears of thankfulness to hear these words, for I had known that I was his one son who had disappointed him.

My brothers were also warm in their congratulations and my mother was so happy that she too wept for joy. I had been the afflicted child and therefore the nearest to her mother's heart. My young cousins were always my champions and now simply shouted their congratulations.

Mammy Banty, now obliged to have a girl slave to take on her lesser duties, came and kissed my hand with such a dear and loving expression that I kissed her old withered face and held her in my arms. Faithful friend that she always had been! The other slaves were jubilant and simply showered their hymns of praise.

All this but showed me not only their love, but how well they had known my failures in past years. The whole plantation seemed to ring with joy that the one who had always before come home in defeat had, at last, come with at least a good report and a sign of a future in which there was promise.

When I returned to Williamsburg I began to consider once more the matter of taking a wife. None of this was on my mind when I was training the men and planning the future of my work. I only thought of it when out in the social world or when I saw the happy homes of my fellow men about me.

Even the Governor asked me why I had not married. I frankly told him that I had not been able to support a home, for one thing, and my facial disfigurement made me shy of making any advances to a girl.

He pooh-poohed this, saying, "Women like men who are

strong and who have ability. A handsome man is usually shunned by them as a husband. They fear for his faithfulness."

This was a new idea to me and gave me a little more courage with women. I had come to believe I would never be able to win the love of a woman. This I now felt might not after all be true.

George Washington
by Gilbert Stuart
Courtesy National Archives

CHAPTER FOUR

FULL GROWTH

Superintendent of Virginia Militia

DICTATED SEPTEMBER 26, 1944

BY THE TIME I was in my thirties, I had my full powers of body and mind. That is, I had command of them, and my physical health and strength had never been so vigorous. I was still in Richmond and the Superintendent of the Virginia Militia. My salary had been increased to six hundred pounds a year, and I was considered a fairly prosperous bachelor. My father had been able to draw on me when his crops failed, and it was my great happiness to offer him assistance. My mother was not yet able to consider me as a perfect man, since I was still unmarried and showed little sign of ever taking a wife. Life in Williamsburg was gay, and I met many delightful young women but never fell in love with one of them.

One evening, while dining with the Governor, he said, "George, can't you find a girl you would like to marry?"

My answer was that I saw many who were lovely and desirable, but none had moved my desire to possess them.

"By the Almighty, you should have been a monk," he blurted out.

I confided to him my whole romantic experience, including Elizabeth, my quadroon mistress, and Sally. Also, I told him of my mother's diligence in the matter of keeping our neighbors' daughters as guests in the house and her disappointment that I was immune to all their charms, so far as desiring to want to marry one of them.

The Governor was nonplussed and said,

"I believe you are destined to meet someone yet who will give you a run."

He was really concerned and said many mothers had spoken to him about my strange course and were somewhat inclined to put a wrong construction on my single state. My own amusement offset any embarrassment I might have felt at the Governor's words, and I think I said something to the effect that I was as immune to the opinion of those matchmaking mothers as to their daughter's charms. At any rate, I was not to be shoved into matrimony to silence gossiping matrons and went my way in the little social swim of Williamsburg as gaily as ever. But all this did disturb me, and I had been very lonely at times and wished I had a sweet lady companion to take into my deepest confidence. I drank more than I should in order to dull these pangs of loneliness somewhat and gambled a bit, as well as making my love for wrestling, riding, and hunting a good part of my life in the hours of leisure.

My troops were well trained and I had made good progress in my military studies. We were now a formidable little army. I was proud of the men and they appeared to like me and my way of training them. I had one or two enemies among the officers who were older than I who desired my post of Superintendent of all the State Militia. The others appeared to be really attached to me and I was very happy in working with them.

I SAW ONE DAY in the morning sunlight a fair lady tripping across a muddy street, her dainty shoes sinking ankle deep in the mud. Without a moment's hesitation, I picked her up and lifted her over the remainder of the mud and then, setting her down on the sidewalk, apologized. The lady was pretty and she laughed gaily as she thanked me and said,

"Major Washington, I shall be forever your admiring servant for rescuing me."

We walked a way together and when she arrived at her door, she asked me to enter and join her in a warm drink. This was an act of hospitality that few young women would dare offer a bachelor. I accepted. She was largely the cause of my contentment with single life. For three years, this gay and pretty woman surreptitiously received me as a lover. I am sure I was at least for a time, her only guest who received her favors. My subsequent visits to her home were always by invitation and we were very much in love.

This I record to make myself quite clear as to the side of my life which has for stupid and puritanical reasons been ignored by my biographers. My life was an open book, and most of my contemporaries knew these facts and seemed ashamed to speak of them. I feel no shame myself and consider my life comparable to that of most men of the world to which I belonged. I was never a seducer, and in the instance of my Williamsburg lady friend it was a case of mutual desire. She was not a woman to receive a man she did not herself desire. She was of independent means and a woman of thirty-four when we met. So, I owe no apology to the world's opinion. I never seduced a girl or failed in my respect to a virtuous woman. I had no desire to poach on the happiness of another man. Let this be clear.

❧

As TIME WENT ON, the Colony was being settled and business in many places sprang up to make Virginia prosperous.

We were proud of this and all citizens seemed content—even the Aristocrats.

My father, now beginning to feel his years, seemed to be the one that most of our neighbors looked to in deciding questions pertaining to the welfare of Westmoreland County. We were always the most forward looking County in the Colony, this owing to my father's leadership. When I would be home on a furlough, he would talk over County business with me. I was keen at all times to discuss all matters when it came to Westmoreland. One matter he was greatly perturbed over was the long and bitter fight over the Crown Tax. He often said,

"We must be free of this tax before the Colony can be fully settled. No settler can afford the double tax. I am sure no court of law would find it legal."

My views were colored by these talks. I often thought how easily we could fill up the Colony with good citizens, if we only did not carry the burden of the Crown Tax. I spoke of this to the Governor once and his reply I never forgot,

"My son and heir will not pay that tax. A new generation will refuse to be taxed by a distant sovereign who has never set foot on this continent and who uses our labor to provide the extravagances of his court."

My father had said as much but, somehow, the Governor seemed to make it all clear in my mind. When I was at home, we used to discuss this, but never was a prophecy made that the Colony would rebel. Here was a new idea to me. When, how, and who would lead such a rebellion? My mind kept running on this theme and soon I began to make plans as to how it might be started, feeling that it was indeed destined to come in my time.

I never imagined my own part in this. I expected the first uprising to come in New England where, indeed, it did come. I knew that section was far more disaffected than Virginia, and their taxes much more than ours in aggregate. I never pictured myself as more than a simple member of the Militia that, in case of our being faced with British troops, would bear their share in whatever fighting might eventuate. All my dreams were so nebulous that I was not a participant at all.

My own part, as it came about, was so purely accidental that I never had the sense of being one destined or marked by Fate. When we used to talk about what might come, I saw always a horde of soldiers, my own among them and older officers commanding them. I imagined men I knew by sight and name.

Well, those were days and nights in Williamsburg when we danced and dined and drank toasts to the King, and felt in the case of most men that it was a fairly fine world we lived in and any change in it would lie in a future so distant as to be scarce even imagined.

❧

MEN OF VIRGINIA

DICTATED SEPTEMBER 27, 1944

No TIME NEED be lost by any reader of history who pores over the doctored records of the British officials, who were instructed to send reports always favorable to the Crown and the Parliament. A Governor-in-Chief was always appointed just for, what you moderns may call very aptly, "window-dressing." The State of Virginia was the first Colony to refuse to permit the Crown-appointed Governor to enforce the laws we were not in favor of. Virginia also was the first Colony to make a stand against the Crown pacts and its perfectly absurd system of assessment. Virginia was the first State to give to the other Colonies the object lesson that the poor landowners counted as citizens equally with the Aristocrats. True, we were of the party that had no access to the records that were, at all times, kept in the custody of the British officials. Even the House of Burgesses was, in the main, composed of Aristocrats who allowed no ordinary citizen to question any of the procedures, much less examine the records.

We were often astonished at the way in which the public

was informed of the deliberations of the House of Burgesses. We got nowhere if we protested and so we were largely spoon-fed as to what went on.

It was at the County meeting that we worked and there we learned to make decisions that bore on our welfare. The House of Burgesses, up to the Revolution, was quite a distant and mysterious parliament to the average settler. Only when a man with a fine brain like Patrick Henry made a speech that so roused the opposition of the Aristocrats that they were impelled to discredit him by outside vilification did we get a hint of the way things went on in the House of Burgesses.

Still, we knew that the future of the Colony was discussed there and laws under which we all must live, work, and try to develop the new lands. Many tried to go to Williamsburg during the session and hear what was done. Few had the means or could afford the time from their tasks to do this. So we were usually in the dark as to what was being done for or against our interests in Williamsburg.

James Monroe, in his statement in the House of Burgesses when he asked for a new and fairer tax law, was all but ostracized by his fellow-members. I recall that I had many times, as a youth and later, spoken

James Monroe
by Gilbert Stuart
Courtesy National Archives

against the British tax outrage, but it took years before we dared to put the case before our State legislature. Such was the power that the Aristocrats wielded. My own feeling is that the many years of toil and self-suffering endured by the poor settlers of our Colony sapped their energies, and their descendents show a loss of vitality that is the result.

THE FOLLOWING EPISODE occurred during the time when I was stationed in Williamsburg. This was the occasion of my birthday, and my father and mother had asked me to come home, if possible, to celebrate it along with their wedding anniversary which occurred the next day.

I may say here that my birthday was November 14th, and I have never wished to disturb the American people in their very gracious habit of remembering me on February 22nd. This error was brought about by the fact that my mother recorded my birth in Alexandria on February 22nd, 1732, and did not realize that this would be considered my birthdate. Our family Bible was correct in the record of the family, but this was ignored by the British official who made up the matter for my biography that seems to have been a concoction of misstatements on many cardinal points.

I was very much in the way of making my duty a stern matter and hesitated to take a furlough, but my mother's letter was so very touching in her plea that I asked for two weeks' furlough and was granted three. I remember well the journey home. I had a very fine horse and went by way of the old trail that rarely was used by travelers going west from Richmond. This took me through the counties of more than usual beauty and I loitered on the way, enjoying the lovely season of autumn which is so perfect in its expression in Virginia.

My horse was spirited and I had difficulty in keeping him in an even pace. He seemed to sense the sweetness of the earth and was unusually excited when I came to a ploughed field of lush meadow. All I had to do was say,

"Go slow now, Danger," and he would stop his cavorting and walk. My eyes were suddenly surprised by the sight of two men lying in the shrubbery near the trail. I saw that they were watching me as if they had been posted there. I dismounted and went over to them. They rose and one of them asked if I was Major Washington. I said I was, and the other man then asked if I had any recollection of him.

I saw a bearded and shabby individual of about forty-five and could not recollect having met him before. He then told me that he had been one of the boys in our company that tasted Indian warfare for the first time. He gave me his name, and I dimly remembered him. It seemed he had learned that I had stopped at a roadside inn for a meal and had hoped to see me as I went on my way.

"Can't you do something for my friend here? He needs a situation and he is a good shot. He has a family and wishes to join the Militia."

I told him that he might be recruited, but must go to Williamsburg and pass an examination before the recruiting official there. This seemed to dash their spirits. However, I gave the poor fellow a piece of advice,

"Don't waylay travelers, or you will get into trouble."

At that, the first speaker was at my throat and threw me backward on the ground. I managed to turn as we fell and had him under me. My horse was now in the field feeding and I saw if I did not soon get him, he would be in a clump of woods and difficult to catch. I called to him as I was falling. He was trained to come at my call and bounded over the road to me.

My assailant was now ready to cut my throat and rob me, but my faithful Danger was at my side. I held the man down with my right hand, I caught the horse's bridle and pulled him to me until he was near enough. Then, I let go of the man and leaped into the saddle just as he rose and drew his knife. The other chap was standing with his knife out, but behind the other fellow. I simply put my heels to Danger and he was off and away like a flash. The men yelled with rage and tried to follow, but Danger soon left them behind.

My own good fortune held until I reached my home. I said nothing of my near escape, and all was joy and happy reunion.

Mary Ball Washington
Courtesy Mary Ball Washington Museum, Lancaster, Va.

MY MOTHER, I FELT, was now grown into old age. Her whitening hair and sad lines of care in her face made me think of the time when she would no longer be there to advise and make me her confidanté. It was with a pang that I saw how she was slipping away from us. I loved her with such a passionate affection that a world without her did not seem possible. I had always made her the center of my small universe. I loved my father as a man and a wise counselor, but she had been the very soul of home and to her I could say what I never confided to another.

My brother Charles, now the head of the plantation, was so concerned that he told me she was really slipping out of life and I might not see her again. This agonizing thought I put from me and determined not to harbor it. She was now sixty and that was old age in those days when women had no care beyond what they could do for themselves as they carried on their heavy tasks.

My mother and I had many talks over family matters, and among them we spoke of our mutual desire to see slavery ended. I had realized for some time what a wrong institution slavery was. I came away with the fixed determination to free the ones I owned as soon as possible. My mother had given them all lessons in reading, spelling, writing, and the simple rules of arithmetic. They had as good an education as any of the white farmers except, of course, the rich planters and their children.

The whole question of slavery now took on a different aspect, and I found myself thinking upon it constantly. It had been abolished in England. Could it be done away with here in the Colonies?

I had no solution in my mind, but I was not happy when

I thought upon this thing that had been the darkest page in our brief history.

My mother never ceased to bewail and deplore the fact that the institution was wrong and would only bring harm to both master and slave in the end.

All this I set down because the exact truth about my own conflict with slavery is seldom told. But perhaps that is because the conflict was not obvious to my friends, or to my biographers. Certainly, because I owned so many slaves by the time of my death, who would imagine that I thought slavery an evil? But I eventually came to realize that it was very much an evil and would always be a blot against the history of this Nation.

❦

GENERAL FORSYTH

DICTATED SEPTEMBER 28, 1944

MY CHIEF WAS General Forsyth, a man who had been trained to fight Indians in the early days of the Colony. He was a real soldier and demanded discipline as well as courage and training. The men thought him a bit too harsh, but to my mind he was an ideal commander.

One characteristic of the General was a love of the wines that he imported from France, and his cellar was a joy for any wine lover to behold. It was the General's boast that he was able to test the age of a vintage by its odor. Port was his usual habit, but sherry and the light wines had their place at his dinner table. He seemed to me to be as sober after a quart as after the first small glass. He had the ruddiness of a port drinker but no paunch or jowls. His tall, spare frame was as agile as any man of forty, though he must have been sixty-odd years old. He lived in his quarters alone, except for a very old slave woman, called Tessie, who performed such fantasies of cookery as to remain a dream to any guest who partook with the General! Tessie acted as butler, serving the wine as well as the food. She was a large and handsome woman of at least fifty and when she served us wore a long dress with a white lace fichu and a lace cap on her wavy hair. The General never said anything of a rude nature, as men will when together, until Tessie had placed the wine on the table and retired. Though he never spoke of her, I knew he loved her and that probably she was the cause of his never having married.

When I was honored by an invitation to dine or sup with the General, he usually made an excuse of some business connected with our work. However, as soon as that was disposed of (and it rarely amounted to anything serious), he would begin to tell stories of his youth and the hard way of life in that period. I was always fascinated and enjoyed every detail of those times. He especially loved to dwell upon the way the settlers were obliged to make a home secure against a sudden raid of the Indians. Some of the tribes were friendly, and most helpful to the settlers in matters that had to do with the raising of tobacco, the trapping of small animals, and the method used in woodcraft of all kinds.

He said that friendly Indians would often give warnings when a raid was to be made by the savage tribes. My favorite of all his stories was one that concerned the Chief Powhatan, the father-in-law of John Smith, one of the pioneer settlers of Virginia. This story I often asked him to recount, as I wanted to get every detail in my mind. The tale was simple enough, but it showed clearly the constant vigilance required of the men and women who first dared to settle in our Colony.

It seems that Powhatan was a real Chief, not simply a brave man who was a good fighter. He was a very intelligent and cultured Indian. He had been at pains to learn from the white man to read and write their English language in order that he could deal with the treaties intelligently. He also was a powerful man with his weapons, the bow and arrow, the tomahawk and knife. Powhatan also had a deep spiritual nature and was clairvoyant as well as clairaudient. He spoke with the spirits of his ancestors and listened to much that was unheard by the others of the tribe. His advice was always of paramount importance when a treaty was made. He would see that justice was done to both parties.

When his daughter, Pocahontas, was a child, he saw as in a vision the coming of the white man and that she would love and marry one of that strange and, to him at that time, unknown race. He used to say to his daughter,

"Pocahontas, be sure you love the white brave who will come here, for he will take you for his squaw. He is not a very big man, but he is brave, and he has knowledge that will teach you many fine things."

The little girl would cry out,

"My father, I do not wish to be the squaw of a white man. He is a sick man. I do not like to see men with pale faces. They are sick men. Save me from this paleface man."

The father said it was only when the palefaces came and settled among them that Pocahontas learned to believe they were strong and well. She came to love John Smith, as we all know, but her father was the man who, above all others, made it possible for the settlers to occupy the land. Powhatan said,

"This land is for all men. I see it in a dream. They will come from all points in the great boats and they will make of our land the richest and most powerful land in all the world. We must be happy to help them do this. We are brothers, and we are all children of the Great Spirit."

When the General would retell this story, I seemed to feel it was the full truth of what was to be. My mind would conjure up scene after scene in which I, too, saw the peoples of the earth converging on this beautiful land I had come to love beyond all else in life. General Forsyth was also sure that this would come to pass, and he said one evening,

"Major Washington, you may live to see this vision of Powhatan realized. I shall not, but I know it will surely be."

A fine example of the General's ability to see what a recruit was worth was in his manner of examining an applicant. He would conduct the examination personally. His first question was,

"What kind of lice have you, gray or white?"

Usually the answer was,

"White."

"All right. When do you make a raid on them?"

"Once in a while."

Or, perhaps the answer would be,

"When I can get time."

Once, he said to a chap after this reply,

"You are a lazy good-for-nothing and I wouldn't let you louse up my post. Go home and clean your head and body of lice and then come back. If you can make the Sergeant believe you can learn to fight, then come and see me again."

The General often said to me,

"A man who has lice will never make a soldier. The lice show that he has no fight in him."

Not a very pretty sort of a conversation, but the General knew what he had to deal with and he had convictions in the matter. Nonetheless, I had a deep affection for this soldier. He had served his people since his fifteenth year. He never seemed to wish to enter the social life of Williamsburg and was called by many a perfect old curmudgeon. To my mind, he was a fine and wise soldier and a man of deep spirituality. He had been in service all his life and he was a most accomplished chess-player. I was his pet opponent and we had many a bout over chessmen. One of his main diversions was trapshooting. I used to set the clay pigeons on the spring and then watch the perfection of his instantaneous and unerring aim. He often said to me, in confidential mood,

"My dear Washington, you must make yourself a judge of men. You are destined to lead them and you have little experience in the world. Make it a rule to size up a man when you meet him. Soon you will learn to see through them."

This advice seemed to me too far-fetched to be taken seriously. However, I made a sort of game of trying to see through the men I came in contact with. This became a habit after a time, and in later years, I found it a help in my work in both war and peace.

Many of the men I met were like myself, with well-to-do

parents, very well mannered, and with fine ideas as to the future they meant to create. Some of them even were bold enough to aspire to become important leaders of opinion. These were apt to be lawyers and political aspirants. My own military profession was not conducive to political mindedness, and I never had any desire to hold office.

The General was loud in his opinion that I was a born soldier. This pleased me, but I realized that there was small chance of distinguishing oneself in any career the Militia could offer. The General would often say,

"Go to France and join their Army. They are always in need of talent and always at war. The pay is poor but they have a fine Army and they appreciate good men."

I was not able to feel any desire to go to France and fight. I loved Virginia and wished only to serve her interests. When the General died, not long after this talk, I was conscious of a deep sense of loss. He had made himself an integral part of my life, and I could not bear to think of the Army without his leadership. General Forsyth has never been honored by history, and seldom mentioned. I wish to make this belated testimonial to him.

He was a skilled campaigner, a great leader and one who inspired his officers as well as the men in the ranks. He had a sure sense of what men he could rely on and never seemed to fail in any undertaking. He was loyal to his Country and to those serving under him. He spent money and time in the study of his profession and was always abreast of the times. He gave to our Militia the dignity of a regular Army and was at all times trying to improve their status as well as the fitness. My own memory of General Forsyth is of a man who was never to have a successor so able and so unappreciated.

Dismissed for Dueling

Dictated September 29, 1944

At thirty-two, I was still a bachelor and having a mighty good time in Williamsburg. I loved my work, and I had a deep appreciation for my superior officer, General Forsyth. At home my family was prospering and my slaves were placed in my father's care. My land paid for their keep and gave them a bit of spending money.

Meanwhile, I took life as it came. I loved the life I lived. I was popular with the officers and the men respected me. I had a very comfortable room in the barracks and I had the run of the commissary. I lived from day to day in the hope that we would eventually be free from the Home domination. This gave me a feeling of a future where I might be of service.

My reading was entirely on the subjects bearing on my profession: history, biographies, and the arts. Our library in the barracks was limited, but I had access to General Forsyth's, who was a collector of serious works. My leisure was spent in the hunting field, and a fine gymnasium in the barracks offered me opportunity to indulge in my favorite sport, wrestling. I had few superiors in that field at that time.

As for love and the ladies, I was well content with the sweetheart I had. She was four years older than I, but still beautiful and a most ardent lover who could be as amusing as any woman in Williamsburg. Her home, where our meetings were, had all the refinements of life and made a charming setting for romance. This lady defied all convention and never attempted to social climb. Her father had left her a large estate and she found her happiness in running it and her own personal life. The women of Richmond were horrified at her bold stand and ostracized her to such an extent that she never was received in any home. She made light of this, but her wit was bitter against the Richmond women. She had never married because she had not found the man she felt any lasting passion for. Her code was a loose one, but she paid the harsh penalty.

I loved her honesty and way of making her life to suit herself. Naturally, I was happy to be her lover. I was true to her and adored her. Many arrows were aimed at me for this companionship, but I paid no attention to them. I was not a marrying man, and the matrons of the town called me some pretty hard names. This only served to make me treasure the more my lovely mistress.

One day, I was riding along a lonely road and saw my lady in a very hot embrace as she stood by the wayside, in the arms of one of my younger officers. I rode on as if I had not seen them. The lady was in a dither over it, and wrote a note asking me to sup with her that evening. I sent an excuse and supped at home instead. Later in the evening, I received another note from her asking for a liaison that night. I went to her home and was astonished when she said,

"Darling, you saw me today and you think me false to you, isn't it so?"

I admitted that what I saw indicated something of the sort. She burst into tears and declared she never loved any man as she had me. She hated herself for yielding to a momentary impulse in accepting the advances of the young captain, in whose arms I had seen her that day. I was quite wrought up and told her I was not a cuckold, that she was a free woman and had the right to bestow her favors where she chose. She became hysterical and begged me to forgive her. I told her there was nothing to forgive. She had yielded because she was impelled by her own feeling. This being so, she should be true to herself and to the man who inspired it.

What a scene! I remember at last she swooned and I carried her to her bedroom and left after sending her maid up to attend her. This act, she said later, showed her my love was gone. This was true. We had no tie but love, and no responsibility to anything but our true feelings. That being so, we could only part.

Once more I saw her and this time I realized that she had suffered, as I had, in our separation. She was with the younger officer and he was glowering at me. The occasion was a race meeting and I was riding in it as was he. We were all standing about the paddock and many of the best of Richmond's citizens were present.

My first feeling was to ignore the two of them. I felt ashamed of myself and doffed my cap to them. My horse won the first heat. His, the second. In the third, we were neck and neck when he lashed my horse over his eyes. This so blinded him for a moment that he stumbled and threw me. I landed on my head and lay unconscious for a moment. When I rose to my feet, I found my collar-bone was broken and I went back to the stables in great pain.

A surgeon was called and set the bone. I was in such a state of agony that I swore like any old sergeant. My lady was present and said,

"George, for God's sake, be a gentleman before all these people."

I was too hurt to care about the people and said,

"I'll not take any more from you, so kindly leave me alone."

I never saw her again, for she left Williamsburg shortly afterward.

I was in such a rage over the cruel blow my horse had received that, when my collar-bone was again whole, I sent a challenge to the Captain and we met the next day. I wounded him in his arm and he caught me on my shoulder. Neither wound was serious, but the affair caused a great deal of unfavorable comment. Dueling was not allowed in the Army. I had to resign my Post and was in bad odor with my old friend, General Forsyth. What a fool I was to do such a thing, when I knew it was against the Army rules.

SERVICE IN PENNSYLVANIA

DICTATED SEPTEMBER 30, 1944

NOT SO VERY long after my dismissal from the Militia, I received a letter from the Colony of Pennsylvania asking if I would accept a commission as Superintendent of the Militia of the Colony. This was a very great compliment to come from a Quaker State to a man court-martialed for dueling. I accepted, and was given the rank of Major and a salary of one thousand pounds a year. This was indeed good fortune and I set off for Philadelphia at once in great fettle.

I found an excellent prospect arriving at the Quaker city. The quarters were far better than those at Richmond, the commissary excellent, and the men were trained and in fine health. My commanding officer, General Braddock was a very sensitive man when it came to the question of authority, and I saw I must be careful never to overstep my own official rank in the least way. We were never really friends, though we respected one another and were at all times able to work together in harmony.

At this time my social life was very dull, and I fear I went too often for companionship to places that were far from reputable, such as taverns and racing stables, gambling rooms, and even less savory resorts. My only friend was a young Captain Hawkins. This officer had formerly been in Virginia's service. We used to meet in the evening and find a place to play cards or perhaps take a ride in the outlying districts. Once, we were attacked by robbers and I lost my wallet containing thirty pounds, my chronometer, and a small pocket piece of gold that my late sweetheart had given me. Captain Hawkins was more fortunate. His wallet contained only two pounds and he did not happen to be wearing his chronometer. We put up a fight, but we were two against six, and we were unhorsed and our pockets rifled by these men who were of great strength.

My only possession that I mourned was my little gold luck piece. It was all that was left of a love that had given me two years of real happiness. Hawkins mourned the loss of his sweetheart's picture, a miniature in a gold frame. The frame was the robbers' object in filching it.

I enjoy telling these little tales of my youth for they prove that I was a man and no historical records exist of such personal dramas. But this is precisely why I share them. I had a youth, by God, and I enjoyed it as a man should. We had a rendezvous one evening at a tavern where there was a lovely pair of barmaids, and we sought to make love to them when the bar closed. My girl was pure and chaste, so I simply took her for a stroll in the moonlight and returned her in her virginly state. Hawkins' girl however was far more familiar with the ways of the world and teased him about the way that he made love. In the end, he lost his temper and gave her a piece of his mind as to her impertinence. This so enraged her that she reported him to General Braddock. She declared he had seduced her. This was a flagrant case for dismissal at that Post, and Hawkins was court-martialed and dismissed.

I was less unlucky with my tavern maid, but later she became so cunning that I had to leave her to herself and make my evenings less boresome at another tavern. Well, hell is supposed to be inhabited by furies that are unable to be as potent as a woman mortal who thinks she is scorned. My erstwhile girl came to find out my new loafing place and one evening she appeared in her best finery and said she was quitting her old place and coming to this tavern on the following day. Here I was already in debt to the landlord and could not settle with him until the quarterly pay day arrived. The robbers had made away with my usual monthly allowance for personal expenditures. What to do?

I called up the paymaster and asked him for an advance, but it was refused. Then I pawned my best uniform for enough to pay my bill, and got the landlord's promise to keep the girl from annoying me.

Well, sure enough she was a determined minx and had made up her mind to marry me. I had to tell her I should never marry and begged her to seek a husband elsewhere. Undaunted, she went to the general and complained of my coldness. This, of course, was not of any concern to the General and he begged her to excuse him. She had asked him to intercede in her behalf and get me to marry her.

"My God!" was his only reply and he left her. This she blabbed to the wife of one of my sergeants with unpleasant embellishments, and so the story went the rounds of the barracks. My Orderly was often seen grinning as I left my quarters in the evening. My own feelings were not pleasant, but I ignored the whole matter and decided against any further adventures with tavern maids.

❦

AT TIMES, WE soldiers were an idle lot, and I often wondered that the tax-payers did not rebel at the cost of our keep. The State was always at peace with the Indians and no riots had ever taken place in that Colony. We were, of course, a well-drilled and capable force and in any danger could be counted on to aid the citizens should danger arise. The men, mostly Quakers, were sober and well conducted.

I had been in the service of Pennsylvania for three months when an occasion arose that we were called to quell. Spring rains caused the river to overflow and the villages and farms along the banks were inundated. This was a great calamity in the Susquehanna Valley.

We were of service in rescuing the people and their cattle and horses. I swam out twenty-three times in the night to bring the people and animals to land. We had to make camps and succor the wounded and ill from exposure.

All was confusion until we arrived. We had no experience in this sort of emergency, but we were able to improvise relief and administer it capably. Our men were splendid in their bodily risks they took in helping the victims as well as their mental alertness in each case. I was proud of them and made an address to that effect when, after a week, we returned to Philadelphia.

❦

FORT PITT

DICTATED OCTOBER 1, 1944

THE MEMORY OF Fort Pitt is not an easy one and I must tell it like a mortal – the man I was, as I experienced then – for you to feel what I felt. Naturally, today I would talk to you about the foolishness of all wars and to say as so many others have, that wars solve nothing. They merely lead to more wars. But I must tell you my story as I lived my story. Here on this side, we who fought each other at these battles, who thought of each other as savages and enemies, are now companions of the soul and of the same era of history.

Again we were idle for six months. The call came then to march westward to meet a force of Indians who had raided Fort Pitt and were burning the homes and were scalping the men and the women, too. Here was a real battle facing us. General Braddock was a very religious man and had often told us, in his rare addresses to the troops, that the Indians were our brothers and we must love them and respect them, and they would never molest us. He seemed upset over the situation and said to me,

"Major Washington, do you understand the methods of Indian warfare?"

I told him of my Virginia, Maryland, New York, and Massachusetts experiences. He confessed he had never met an Indian who was not peaceful. I gave him some pointers as to the best way to work in Indian warfare at which he was horrified. The dagger was not a weapon used under him. He despised the use of anything but firearms. The hunting knife, even, he was against using, save as a last resort. This left our men at the mercy of the savages. I told him so in plain terms. He was not a man to listen to a subordinate and this made him feel a dislike for me that he took no pains to conceal, even before the men. I then went to the quartermaster and asked if he were not bringing rations to relieve the Fort Pitt garrison. The answer he gave was,

"No, we got orders to supply our own men for fifteen days' march and back, and we will have to forage for game where we can."

I went to General Braddock and laid the matter before him. He only smiled and said,

"Major Washington, don't imagine you are going on a long campaign."

It was no use trying to make headway with such a stubborn officer and I had to desist. We were only three days at the Fort when the sentries gave warning that the enemy was upon us. All was confusion in a moment. The women screamed and wept. The men who were refugees asked to be of service. General Braddock seemed to be incapable of planning his defense and kept telling the men to be simply on the lookout. With that he sat down and took a nap in his chair. I was terrified at this and, calling my subordinate officers together, gave them what instructions I could. I wanted, if possible, to save their lives and keep them from exposing themselves. Most of them had never seen an Indian. I explained Indian attack and what they might expect in case of close fighting. This terrified them and they were already to make a bolt for the woods. I said in effect,

"My lads, you can't expect to survive except by getting the best of the enemy. You must kill him, or he will kill you. Get out your hunting knife when you see him coming and meet him with it. Get your left arm under his and throw him down. You must gain the advantage."

A yell of horror went up, and they all but fainted. We waited until dawn. No sign of Indians all night, but as the gray morning came, a yell such as those Quaker boys had never heard rent the air. Soon we were firing into the warriors who were crowding up to the stockade with lighted torches to burn us out. One Indian climbed to the top and tried to climb over into the fort.

I shot him with my musket and he fell with a yell. Another was at once up in sight, and I leaped up and stabbed him. As I fell, I sprained my ankle. This was indeed bad fortune. However, by now the Indian warriors were swarming over the stockade and using their tomahawks. The women and children were killed first, twenty women and fifty children by count lay dead in half an hour. The others, about twenty women and as many children, were carried off. We were outnumbered four to one, and General Braddock was killed as he stood shouting,

"Friends, brothers! Do not harm us. We are your brothers."

A tomahawk silenced him as his skull was split. The men were now in such a rage and terror that they simply begged for mercy. They got none. A few of the officers defended themselves, but most of the men died like sheep at a slaughter with a little prayer or a cry for mercy.

My part was to defend the Post and make as good a showing as I could. I knew I was never very agile, but with a sprained ankle I simply stood and fought off the Indians with my back to the stockade. Once I fell, and a warrior raised his tomahawk. I caught his foot and threw him down so that he lay on his tomahawk. I then gave it to him in the back with my hunting knife. My old wrestling training again saved my life.

We were two hours in this horror and, when we were counted, only ten men survived. The Indians were gleefully leading out the horses and taking what ammunition they found, along with such things as blankets and supplies of tinware. We were not able to stop them and they only wished to get away with their loot.

My disgust and horror at this bloody spectacle cannot be put into words. We had nothing left to fight with, to eat, or to sleep on. The dead lay about us and we had no way of digging the graves. Every shovel and tool of every sort had been taken and we had but our knives left. Night came and we had made only one grave, digging with our hands. All night we labored, and still we could only bury five men in this grave – and no more.

At last, we saw the sun rise as we put the last of the victims in a grave with no blanket or other covering than the garments they wore. It was a day of such suffering that we simply lay and wept as we tried to pray for those poor souls. No food, no weapons, and no blankets. All we could do was sleep.

All the following day we sat and waited for another attack. None came. We had no food and I began to think we were to be starved out. One chap had a loose buckle on his leggings. I asked if I could use it as a bait-hook. He, of course, cut if off and I tried to make a trap for a rabbit, using a bit of the skin for bait.

Soon, we heard a yell. Indians!

No, it was relief at last. One of our survivors had gone for help when night fell and had been able to find a company of hunters. They had come to aid us. The yell was their way of seeing if Indians or white men were in the Fort. We were three weeks getting to Philadelphia and when we arrived, we were a sorry looking lot. The tragedy of Fort Pitt has been called "Braddock's Defeat." Braddock was never defeated, for he never fought. It was a sheer massacre.

WHEN WE FINALLY got back to Philadelphia, we were but eight, for two men died of their wounds on the march back.

All of us who survived were half-starved and scarcely able to walk. My ankle, though bandaged, gave me no peace and I had to make my way with a crutch, a rude one I had made myself from a crotched limb and a bit of cloth. One poor fellow had two of these, which he whittled into a pair of crutches and swung his way back on one foot. All were shadows of themselves as we got to Philadelphia, where the news of General Braddock's death had been given out and he was honored in churches and in public speeches, as well as in the newspapers. The seventy or more officers and men who were also massacred were barely mentioned.

One man fainted from exhaustion in the street, and a kind old farmer took him and all of us in his wagon to our barracks. Arriving, we found no preparations for us. We were supposed to all be prisoners of the Indians. The Commissary Department Head even said,

"We haven't any beds ready and our supplies are not

enough to feed you. Better go to the Quartermaster."

Wearily, we went to his quarters, only to find him absent. I was in command and so I ordered the officer there to prepare beds and food immediately for my men. This was done but with no alacrity, the idea being that we were a nuisance and only a burden.

My temper was up and I stormed over to the General's quarters where he was enjoying his supper in a nice, well-heated room. I told him of the shameful way we had been received and of the terrible march homeward. He was man enough to be horrified and said,

"My God! This Post is going to be made over. I will see, myself, to your men. You remain here and eat my food."

I declined with thanks and said,

"I prefer, with your permission, to eat my meal with my poor comrades. We have been through too much together for me to think of being away from them now."

He wept as he put his hand on my shoulder, and said,

"Major Washington, you are the kind of man to lead any cause. You love your soldiers and they will follow you. God bless you, sir."

I broke down then, and wept like a child. I had been through it all so far with self-possession, but these first kind words went to my heart. Well, we had everything the Post afforded that night, and the General sent us a dozen bottles of fine port. All went to bed drunk and, for the first time in nine weeks, happy.

❦

RESIGNATION, BUT NOT MILITARY

DICTATED OCTOBER 2, 1944

ALL WENT ON AS before, until I had wearied of the monotony of the life I led. No amusement beyond a bit of gaming and what sports as were permitted such as cock fighting, racing our horses, and making a stab at wrestling. My foot never recovered its strength after that march on a sprained ankle, and I was no longer the champion I had once been. Any men of less weight could best me, though I still had unusual strength of leg, arm, and hand, and knew every trick of a wrestler. Once in a while I won a bout, but usually was defeated. This was not fun but I wished to keep in as good form as I could. One never knew when or how the wrestler's art might be the only salvation at the moment of imminent death.

I taught my men to wrestle and they were most grateful for the instruction. One chap, an officer, once told me he owed his life, in three fights, to the training I had given him in the art.

Time hung heavily on my hands in the evening. I longed to be at something worthwhile. No reading was at hand that was important, and I often wondered how I could endure another day of such a boring life.

MY TASTES WERE formed and my profession mastered so far as was possible at that time. I had no social life whatsoever. There was no recognition of a soldier by the few families who entertained in the Quaker city. No one ever invited me to a party and I believe there was no dancing permitted. No card playing was allowed even in barracks. What the devil should a young fellow do with his spare time? Make love and drink?

Yes, that's what most of us resorted to. I was of an ardent nature and loved women. I mean, I adored them as some sort of being that, like my sweet mother, made me happy to be with them. Their gentle nature and charming voices always touched me, whoever the women might be, were they young or old. Whom could I meet in Philadelphia? Barmaids? These were supposed, by the citizens of the town, to be the proper feminine associates for a soldier.

I even loved to talk to my Sergeants' wives, simple women, with little education. I loved to sit down with them at their spinning and tell them stories of old days in Virginia. They were always proud of this small attention. Some even named their new babies George, after me. I was godfather to at least a dozen before I got away from Philadelphia.

One little woman, the overworked wife of a Sergeant, said to me one day,

"Major Washington, why don't you marry? You are so kind to women. You would make a loving husband."

I told her that I had not met the right woman. She smiled and said,

"Oh God, I wish I had been a lady! I would be the one, I am sure."

This, of course, put an end to the pleasant relationship. I was upsetting that poor soul's life, so I simply made fewer calls until I ceased altogether to see her. One day, she came to my quarters and asked why I had stopped coming to see her. I told her I thought it was unwise and besides, I was now very busy. This latter was a lie, and she knew it. She mistook the whole affair, and from then on became a perfect nightmare in her boldness. It may have been silly to pay any attention to her, but she was there at hand and as she could easily call on me with some excuse or another, I became absolutely terrified of the situation. Finally, I saw no way but to ask my General for a transfer. He was wild, and said,

"What in the hell do you want? You get paid for doing nothing but train the recruits. What do you want anyway? A Generalship? Go to the devil!"

This I promptly did, so far as my career was concerned and threw up my commission. I decided to use some of my savings and purchase more land. This, the histories have called "land speculation," as if I gambled in the purchases. I bought thirty-five acres adjoining the thirty I already owned. This was wild land that would take years of work to make profitable. I was ten years working it for good cotton producing. All this time, I had to pour money into machinery, service, and taxes.

My father was so mortified to have me again out of my professional work, doing chores and tilling my land that he gave up all hope of my being anything more than a small planter, raising crops that would barely support me. My mother said,

"Well, at least, you will not be in mortal danger here at home, nor be killing your fellow men. I am not sorry to see you finally settled here, where I can have an eye on you. You are too reckless to be alone in a strange city."

Mammy Banty saw me as a returned prodigal and spoiled me for a week or so with her choicest bits in serving the meals. My little cousins, now two big youths and a shy maiden, were happy to have me home and frankly said so. Aunt Lucinda was too far gone in senility to care about anything but her food. My brothers were, as always, distant and in their letters frankly said they never expected anything but failure of me. Charles was the one who was ever faithful to his belief in my future, and said to me when we were alone,

"George, don't give up. Every time something happens to call you back to the work you love. I know you will yet be a General."

This was comforting, even though to me it seemed fantastic. I was sure of one thing, however – a decent living on my own land. I loved to be with my mother, father, young cousins and, most of all, my brother Charles. I was able to help him and my father in so many ways that their burden was made lighter with me at home. My father often said I spoiled him for work when I lived at home, and he was becoming a loafer. This was happiness for my mother, too. They were true lovers all their lives and to be together in the evening in constant companionship was their greatest joy. My lot therefore was not an unpleasant one.

For the next two years, my life was a quiet one. I worked hard at my land. I still loved to hunt and my horses were my chief happiness. I had been able to purchase two fine mares and a stallion and bred them successfully. One more, Cricket, was the prize winner at every fair as a saddle horse. I also had some further success as a horse breeder and reared three fine animals that won prizes whenever shown at the Horse Fair, not only Westmoreland County but the adjoining Counties. My father's early tradition that I should become a good horse-breeder was justified. I didn't like the task of breeding horses, but I adored the animals. They were, to me, like humans, and each had a temperament and disposition that was individual.

What joy to go out on a frosty winter morning on a fine, spirited horse that you loved and that also loved its rider! I never can understand men who have not ridden a horse or known the joyous companionship of one.

I had forgotten all about Elizabeth when, to my astonishment, my mother told me she still was unmarried and often inquired of me. I begged my mother to put aside all hope of Elizabeth as a daughter-in-law and to encourage no hope of my having any desire for her. She was no longer even attractive to me, and I was not a man to marry to please anyone but myself. At this, my mother would mildly expostulate with,

"My gracious, George, what kind of a man are you? Do you expect to go on like this all your life?"

I assured her that if I ever came to love a woman so deeply that she seemed necessary to my happiness, I would marry. Otherwise, I meant to take what liberties the social code permitted a bachelor, and stay free.

This was a sad and even tragic situation to my poor mother. She knew that a single man of my age was considered by most people to be either incapable of wedded life or a libertine. The latter, she knew to be my present reputation in the County. My father, less censorious yet wishing I would settle down with a wife, simply said when goaded by my mother,

"My darling, George knows his own mind. He is as stubborn as you and I shan't attempt to persuade him against his will."

All this amused me and my brother Charles, who was the anchorite of the family. He had loved a very sweet girl, the daughter of a neighbor but she died before he had even become engaged. His own feelings were too deep for him to even seek out another love, and so he lived the life of constant physical toil and gave his energies to working the plantation. If he had a mistress, I never knew it. His very mild and thoughtful nature aided him to live this way. He was a scholarly and studious fellow, who made his life up with work and mental exercise. Such men have made the martyrs of old, and the guardians of learning and the arts in the old monasteries.

My brother Charles would have been a replica of my father had he married. He lived to be the guardian of his father and mother. Beloved as few, he gave out love in return, and so his gentle soul was never troubled by those difficulties and anxieties that beset most men. I had a dear and close friend as long as he lived. His death made the world to me a much harder place, for no one ever came into my life who was so clear and dear a man.

❀

A STORY OF SOUL wisdom from personal experience.

In this time when I was making a living from my land and, after I had gone to Philadelphia, I had an experience that made a deep and lasting impression on me. This was about the time when I was studying in nautical books and thinking of getting away to tidewater, or somewhere that my failure in life would not be a source of constant remark by my neighbors.

It was on a very pleasant day and I had given my animals their food for their evening meal. The sun was setting in a beautiful sky of pink, and I was standing at the door of one of the stables and drinking in the wonder and beauty of that glorious day, when I suddenly saw – as in a vision – a small but perfect figure of a man. This was no vision but a flesh and blood youth of perhaps twenty or more, with a delightful expression of mischief on his face. He did not speak and so I also was silent. I stared at him, and then he suddenly burst into loud laughter and finally said,

"Major Washington, you big fool, don't you know me?"

I replied that I did not, upon which the little fellow's face suddenly became grave and he spoke in a lower tone, saying,

"My God, have I changed so much? I was in the Militia with you in Philadelphia. I was your Orderly and I know why you left us."

At that I too smiled, for he did seem to resemble my Orderly but was a much smaller and apparently younger fellow. I was not amused at his remark, and asked why he had called on me.

"To give you a big surprise. I am going to be the next man in command at the Post. How do you like that?"

I was not convinced as he was not even in uniform, but wore a linsey woolsey coat and a coonskin cap, a very hot headgear for the season. As I could not credit his words, I said, in as good-natured tone as I could,

"You are a bit young for a command."

At that, he flew into such a fit of temper that I saw the poor fellow was not in his right mind, and so tried to calm him by saying I would be glad if it were so. This placated him, and he was then very affable. He told me he had been looking for me for a long time and wished to have instruction in my technique in training men, as he knew I was a crack officer at getting results from the stupidest of recruits. This flattery was not lost on me and I became more puzzled than ever about the identity of this strange visitor.

I then asked if he would like to come in the house and talk this over. He said, in a terrified tone,

"No, no! I never go in a house. They lock you up if they catch you."

Of course, I knew then that the poor boy was an escaped lunatic. His little face was pitiful as he said this. Then, I asked him how he came to be at my place.

"Oh, I ran away and got into the wagon of a farmer. He brought me to Alexandria. From there I walked because I knew God would bring me to you. I pray all the time to see you, and now here I am."

This was too much to credit, but I told him I would prefer

to sit down and talk things over. We went out to the bench against the stable, which was then unoccupied by the stable boys, who were having their evening meal in the kitchen. We sat down. He was not more than five feet two or three in height, and a feather-weight, but with very fine features and a delightful smile. I then asked him his name. To this, he became angry and said in a furious tone,

"No, sir! I don't tell that to anybody. I am going to be another person and never use my own name again."

Well, we sat there talking for two hours, and all I could learn of him was that he was of a family who never would let him be a soldier and that he had run away and joined the Militia in Philadelphia the previous year. He had a bad fall from one of the windows and was in the hospital for three weeks. When he recovered and was released, they told him to go home and rest. He did go and his people, Quakers, were furious at having to keep him and so they put him in the Poor House in the insane ward. This almost unhinged his mind and he finally decided to run away and find me.

This was all because the story of my persecution by the wife of one of the sergeants had become a classic at the Post and he had heard it. Also, it seems, I was supposed to be the great and masterful officer with the men and got from them more than any other man in the way of discipline and training. The poor boy had brooded on all this and had the idea that if he could learn to train men he could become an officer and head men at the Post. I am not sure even now that the boy was insane, but was merely ignorant with a fixed idea in his head.

It was a sad and hard business to make him see how long it takes to acquire the knowledge and all that goes into the making of an efficient officer. He was too weary to understand even, and I asked him how he meant to live. He told me that he had begged food and slept in the fields. I then asked him if he would care to sleep in the barn and have his supper there. He was pleased at that, but was sure he would not care to have a bath in my room.

I had a strange bathtub, even for those days. My room

was on the ground floor, what is now the last room on the west side of the hall. I built it myself and it made a regular bachelor's den with only a camp bed, my weapons and books, a large kitchen table for a desk, two small chairs and an arm chair, a good big fireplace, and on one side of the room, two sawhorses that held a canoe of bark that I had bought off an Indian. This was my bath tub. I had a large kettle for heating water and would dip out the water into the canoe; cool it from a pail of water, fresh from the well, and lo, I had a bath that I could submerge in. After the bath, I lifted the canoe to the window sill and tilted the water out. Not a bad contrivance on the whole.

This my mother thought barbaric, since we had a bathroom with pumps and a fireplace for heating the water, a long tub with a plug and a pipe running down under the house, carrying the water down a slope. Still, I preferred my canoe and the idea that I was not dependent on any particular time, but could bathe when I chose.

To return to my poor little soldier. He refused to bathe and I tried to persuade him of the danger of illness and vermin unless he kept his body and his clothing clean. He finally yielded and I took him to my room. There he was happy and when he saw my canoe, he roared with laughter and enjoyed his bath hugely. I persuaded him to put on a pair of my drawers, socks and an undershirt and to wash out his own things. He was quite lost in my garments, but obeyed me in a very happy mood. When this was all accomplished, I asked him to let me bring his food on a tray and eat in my room. He would not do that. He said, in a shy way,

"I eat like a pig. I'd hate to have you see me. I haven't had any victuals for three days."

This was too dreadful and I begged him to let me leave him alone in my room so he could eat in private. So it was. Later when I returned, he was asleep on the floor and I did not wake him. My mother came in and looked at the poor boy,

"He is so little. How can he ever be a soldier?"

I told her that Napoleon was only five feet three and he

was something of a soldier. Our little guest remained with us for a week. Then, I bade him well and strong and able to assist me with my work. I offered to give him a sum of money for this, but he refused it, saying,

"No, I am glad to help you to pay for my victuals, but I can't take any money. I shall go now and get into the Militia again."

This he did, and I am happy to say he became a Lieutenant. His name I never knew, but he wrote me from time to time and told me of his joy at doing the work he loved. I could never reply, for I did not know his name. My mother always said she found him a little strange, but he was ever a gentleman and she believed he concealed his name because his parents were possibly gentle people. I record this to show how this boy was a natural born soldier, and nothing stopped him from following the career he craved. It was too much like my own case for me to ever forget it.

I beg all parents to be careful how they frustrate these deep and instinctive desires of their sons to follow a certain profession or craft.

❀

A Prophecy

Dictated October 5, 1944

What joy I felt as I followed my plow and once again realized that I stood in the furrows of my own acres – mine in perpetuity.

Spanish rule I had seen, and looked upon the forbidding scene the Great River presented. I had been in close contact with some of the citizens along that river and in the Western reaches of Virginia. I was now satisfied to remain in Westmoreland County and to fight for it.

When I told my story to my family, my mother all but swooned at the narrowness of my escape from death, either by violence or privation. She begged me to forego any further adventure in wild districts and make up my mind to settle down. Charles also had a word with me in private, and said in his gentle way,

"My God, George, can't you ever give up your hankering for adventure? I think you are too great to waste yourself on such foolishness."

I was amazed at his using such a word as 'great'. I was the ne'er-do-well, the odd man out of the family, and a person of small achievement except in my brief military period – and that meant little now that I had retired from the Army. I had no sort of following now as we had been growing stronger in our Party, and better men were leading in all matters affecting the County's welfare. I simply stared at Charles. Was he making game of me? I knew him too well to believe that. I began to wonder what he saw in me or my life that could prompt him to use such a word in association with me. I even tried to express this to him. He smiled his slow, sweet smile and said,

"By the time you are sixty, you will be the head of a nation. I have seen it in dream."

I was too materialistic to understand that Charles was one of the rare souls gifted with second sight, even though he saw frequently and was able to predict coming events. I simply put it down to coincidence and a highly developed mentality that could argue from cause to effect. But here was something that was so ridiculous, so out of all sense, that I was alarmed for his reason. I explained this to Charles, and he only said in reply,

"I am only telling you what I know is to be. You will have the title of President, and make the Colonies a nation to be called the United States of America. I have seen it three times now, and I want you to understand that you must now prepare yourself to carry the burden of Government and not waste yourself in anything that is of less importance."

We did not continue further. I was too overwhelmed to even speak. I went out to the barn, and with my horse saddled and bridled rode slowly in the morning sunshine as if in a dream

myself. I saw no sign of any mortal that morning and was alone
with the terrible, yet glorious words of my brother. I kept saying
to myself,

"What is going to happen?

"How can such a strange thing come about?

"When is all this going to take place?

"Who will be with me in such tremendous happenings?

"Can I ever make myself worthy of such a high position?

"Who will be the one to guide me in such dreadful
responsibility?"

I asked these and many more questions of myself, and
to none of them came to my mind an answer. Among all our
friends and acquaintances there was but one man to whom I dared
speak of this. I had the bad fortune to believe that preachers were
closer to Divinity than were common men, such as I. Parson
Mason Weems was stopping as our guest at this time. He was an
amiable and rather amusing old fool, and I gave him credit for an
intelligence that later I was horrified to find did not exist. He was
profoundly moved when I told him of my brother's words, and
said in his drawling voice,

"What a divine message! You are now in direct contact
with God. Pray unceasingly."

Which I did, but with no apparent results. I was simply a
small planter living a lonely and narrow life, with not even access
to a library from which I might learn something that would fit me
to govern. I woke up in a few weeks and said to myself, "Tomorrow
never comes. I must live today."

So, with that sensible thought I set to work to improve my
speech and my appearance.

I wore no longer the soiled clothing after work was done,
and asked my mother to make me some new neckcloths and
waistcoats. In short, I dressed for the evening meal. At that time,
I wore only linsey woolsey to beat the cloth merchants. Now I got
out my old uniform, brushed, and cleaned it and came to the table
looking like Major Washington instead of a weary farm laborer. I
began to watch my speech, and cull from it all bad habits of slip-

shod grammar and faultily pronounced words. In short, I really was quite a snob and was on my way to becoming a prig as well when my father, remarking all this, gave forth the following,

"My dear George, you are really becoming something of a bore with all this high falutin' style of speech. What is it you're trying to accomplish? I am not up to such an elevated style of conversation."

My mother, ever my champion, was quick to say,

"George is trying to speak correctly. What is wrong with that?"

The answer came pat,

"He is imitating a false model. These affectations weaken his arguments. He should speak correctly, but in only the simple words of current speech if he wishes to make an impression or carry conviction."

I roared with laughter. Charles, who alone had guessed what was at the bottom of my sudden leap from my usual way of speaking, simply looked at me with a grin and said nothing. All the time, I was happy to note that my father had no sort of rebuke beyond that of the questionable taste of my choice and pronunciation of words. The thoughts I had expressed, he seemed always to concur in.

One little incident made me feel as if I were making myself ridiculous in the eyes of even of my mother. I had donned a new white lawn shirt and was ready to sit down to supper when she exclaimed,

"George! My conscience! You are wearing your new shirt. What is going to happen this evening! Are you going out courting?"

I made a lame excuse that I wore it because I was so weary of the cotton ones. She raised her eyebrows, and that was all. I got her thought, "He may be caught by the next woman he meets if only she flatters him. I will be on the watch, for he is now at the danger age when he will stumble into marriage with the first woman who will pay him compliments."

I could see by her expression these thoughts passing

through her mind. I wonder if they were truly prophetic.

Well, life went on, and by the time my mother had made me three shirts of linen, I had again reverted to my cotton ones and showed no further indication of becoming a grand seignior or a dandy.

❦

My Double

Dictated October 6, 1944

One day as I was sitting on a log in the forest after an hour of wielding my axe, I pondered on the strange dream of my brother Charles. I knew of his pre-vision through recurrent dreams, and that always they had seemed to accurately foretell a coming event or condition. My mind ran over the years of my life and the strange way in which I seemed always to meet only disappointed hopes and frustrated efforts. I was sad and more than skeptical that this time Charles was not seeing anything, but the picturing of his own high hopes and wishes for my success. I was in a sense dreaming myself, seeing as in a moving picture the events of my life passing before my mind's eye. I then passed into a deep and dreamless state. I fell over sidewise and lay along the split log at full length. I must have slept for an hour, for the sun was low when I woke and I feared I had alarmed my family by staying out in the woods past the time for supper.

It was when I tried to rise that I became conscious that I was not alone. Before me stood a tall and fine looking man who seemed amused at my situation, for he was smiling. He was garbed in a linsey woolsey coat and trousers and his neckcloth was of fine linen and his buckles ornamented expensive shoes. He wore a hat of dark blue felt with three sides turned up and, at the left, a white cockade. His ruffles were immaculate, and on his right hand on the little finger he wore a fine looking seal ring. His hair was brown and worn in the conventional loose braid tied with a black ribbon. The man seemed to be myself, for I saw his great height and even the pock-marks on his face. The ring was a seal ring of my father's. He had given it to me as a birthday gift.

I saw how I looked to others for the first time. My feeling was that the figure was good, and the smile warm and friendly. I did not even resent my disfigured face, but felt satisfied that I looked manly and with a frank and honest expression. All this came to me in a flash. I dared not speak, and I only moved to sit up. The figure spoke,

"I am the same George Washington as you, only I am able to leave your body and roam at will. You will now be convinced because I am coming back into your mortal body."

At that he drew close to me, and I seemed to see him disappear into me. I was at that time unaware of the astral or etheric body, and so I was a little terrified by such an experience. When I came home, I asked Charles if he knew what had happened. He said he did, and explained how often he had the same experience. I was amazed that he had never spoken of it to me. He said that unless you have the thing happen to you, it is not believable. He added that it was a common thing for him to go great distances, and return to his body whenever he had been thinking deeply of any faraway place. When I spoke of the cockade on my hat, he saw it in an insignia to be worn by me at some future time. This was to be the sign of our Revolution, a white cockade on a three-cornered blue felt hat. I never designed that. It was the idea of a hatter in Boston by the name of Peter Salisbury. I saw it, liked the design and gave it to our troops.

❀

FIRST PSYCHIC EXPERIENCE

DICTATED OCTOBER 7, 1944

I WISH TO SPEAK about something that happened when I was about eighteen years old, if I remember correctly. I had my first personal experience in the field of psychic phenomena. We did not have those words in use then and, to me, it was just a case of "Spirits."

I was spending the evening at a neighbor's home with a dozen other young fellows. It was the occasion of a birthday party for Elizabeth, the girl I first fell in love with. We had been dancing out on the lawn to the tune of a jew's harp, and when the dance ended, Elizabeth, who was my partner in the dance just ended, suggested a stroll over to a clump of trees, where a rustic seat stood. We sat down, and had been chatting for perhaps two minutes when I felt a cold chill on my face and neck, and so did Elizabeth. We wondered what this could be, as the night was warm. It was summertime. Presently, as I spoke of the cold air, a dim figure was outlined before me, as Elizabeth exclaimed,

"George, do you see that? What is it?"

I did see it, and said so. It was the figure of a tall woman. We saw her clearly and even caught a glimpse of her face. It was a lovely girl of about seventeen and her hair was done in the fashion of the early eighteenth century, curls down her back and a broad ribbon bound them. She seemed to be smiling at us, and so I smiled back. At that, she said in a voice that sounded like my mother's,

"George, I am happy that you see me. I am your mother's mother, Fanny Ball, and I am here always in this neighborhood, so I came to the party also. Elizabeth, you must be very happy to have such a fine celebration of your eighteenth birthday."

At that, she seemed to fade out. I turned to Elizabeth, and she seemed not to have heard the voice. When I asked her, she said she only saw the lovely girl and did not hear her speak, but she seemed to understand what was said somehow because before I told her what I had heard, she said,

"I thought she wished to say I should be happy over my party."

Well, this I was too amazed over to even speak of, but I went to my mother and asked about my grandmother Ball, whom I had never seen and when she died I did not know. My mother said it was her birth that caused Frances Ball's death at eighteen, and that her aunt had told her Frances was a beauty and a great belle in the County.

This was such a confirmation as admitted of no doubt. From that time, I gave heed when I seemed to hear a voice from an unseen source speaking to me. Twice, Fanny Ball came again, but I did not see her and only heard her voice. She came at the time when I was kneeling in the furrows, praying that I might be able to marry Elizabeth. That time, she gave her name and said,

"Do not be surprised if Elizabeth should not return your love. She is not your true mate." That was all. I was cast down, but when I next called on Elizabeth, as I have written elsewhere, she revealed a nature that repelled me.

The last communication from my lovely grandmother came at Valley Forge.

❧

THE STUART BUST

DICTATED OCTOBER 8, 1944

I AM, PERHAPS, not writing as serious a biography as might be expected from a man that the public has been made to believe was a cross between a stick of wood and a high-minded materialist.

My nature was rather of an impulsive and simple sort in all my dealings with my troops and, later, with my Cabinet. I made no effort to be other than my natural self.

I had a sense of humor, though, that too seems to have been denied me by the historians. State papers or letters pertaining to war or statecraft are no place for that most human of qualities. Still, my contemporaries were aware of my fondness for a good story, a jest, and a comic slant on the strange epic we call life.

My mother, too, had a delightful way of turning a phrase to give it an unexpected, but definite humorous implication. My father was never so much at ease as when a funny story paved the way. My brother, Charles, was ever the most happy when we were at each other in a contest of wits. My two elder brothers were not so much inclined to the lighter way of looking at personas and events. The cousins even, who were from my father's side of the house, were young devils for fun, and made our house gay with laughter as long as they were with us. We missed them sadly when the boys went off to the City of New York to enter commercial occupations, and our pretty Lucretia married a fine fellow from Baltimore and went there to live.

I wish to say this also – I am not the plaster saint with the iron jaw that Stuart made me. My sittings with him were a bore, but the day I saw the finished result I gave an inner groan – for I saw my fate, so far as posterity was concerned.

There is but one portrait that I found resembled the reflection that I saw in my shaving glass or when arranging my stock and fall. This is the Gilbert's full length one, painted when I was still campaigning.

I had no idea what a painter could do to destroy you until that popular assassin, Stuart, made me his victim. My wife also has been quite destroyed by him and, when these two death-heads are hung on a wall side by side, I wonder the Republic does not fall. Martha was never painted again, and often said she was happy that her children were old enough to remember her as she was.

❀

DOWNHILL

DICTATED OCTOBER 10, 1944

ON SATURDAY EVENINGS, I would mount Prancer and cover the road to town at a good speed. There, at Timothy's Tavern would be cheer and, above all, Timothy himself.

Timothy had been a seaman. A man now some sixty-odd

years, he had gone to sea when a lad at the age of twelve, and so his speech had the saltiness of his sailor's lingo. This was always a delight to me. After the other patrons had departed we would sit by the fire with our whiskey. Finding my path, my destiny, was not an easy road. Partly, this was because I was too blind to see that every day was a part of my destiny, even my early, often confusing military career. But the seeds of my destiny were there, for I loved the military from the moment I saw a soldier in uniform. Still, as a young mortal man, I did not know what lay ahead for me. I did not anticipate the Revolution and Presidency – so there were many times when I was indeed lost and I would find pleasure in his fascinating tales of those early days on whalers and such adventures as he had on merchant vessels and in strange ports all over the world. It almost persuaded me that I had been wrong not to follow the advice of my brother, Lawrence, and go into the Navy.

Timothy's stories inspired me to send for several nautical books, and in the winter evenings to study them in a vague hope that I might still make another start, perhaps in some employment connected with seagoing. I loved those hours with Timothy. He wove an enchantment that gave me a sense of being transported to the strange lands and scenes he painted in his sailor way. I am ever grateful to that good old sea dog for the time he spent after long weary hours serving his patrons, opening his mind and his memory to give me the cullings of his colorful life experience.

In the years that followed, he grew feeble and unable to walk, but I made it a point to sit with him awhile in our old companionship when I was at home, though I chose the hours to suit our more temperate habits.

Timothy was a friend in my hour of need. God bless him!

※

ONE EARLY DAWN on Sunday morning, while half asleep in my saddle as my horse, Prancer, carefully moseyed along the road, fearing I might in my half stupor fall from my saddle, we almost rode down a man. He accosted me, inquiring the way to town.

This was a small man, and he looked very weary and walked with the rolling gait of a seaman. I found he was bound for Timothy's Tavern, but he had never been to Alexandria and was walking in the wrong direction. It seems he was weary of seafaring life and hoped his old shipmate, Timothy, might help him with advice as to how to set up a tavern. He had about twenty pounds saved up, and thought he could start a small business with it. I did not discourage him as to the poor prospect of success on such small capital, but suggested he come home with me, have a bath and breakfast, after which I would talk with him. At the moment, I was too hazy to get a clear idea of what all this meant.

He was a cheerful chap of about forty and with the same sailor lingo that I found so amusing in old Timothy. I had him clean and looking fit by the time breakfast was ready, for on Sundays, we were a bit indolent and were never at the table before eight o'clock.

In the end, this chap stayed with me as a helper for about a month. As a farmer, he was about as useful as a field mouse. He liked to be outdoors and looking at the things I did, but he was utterly useless on a plowed field. He feared a horse, a sheep even, and begged to be let off from going near them. The most congenial task he found was polishing the andirons and any bit of brass he could find. He kept my room in perfect order, and was as neat a fellow as I ever knew. Still, he was not happy on a farm and marveled how I bore such a lonely life.

At last, he went off to Alexandria where Timothy gave him work as a waiter. There he spent the remainder of his life. The plentiful food which he enjoyed and gorged himself with soon put such fat on his small bones that Timothy named him *the porpoise,* and *the porpoise* was his name to all the habitués of the Tavern.

I set this down, because I am not able to forget the man and his pitiful little figure in the pea jacket on that lonely road, seeking to begin life over, when I myself was pondering the same question. He found a safe harbor, and never complained of his fate as a waiter. He was always true to who he was, no matter land or sea. I was not to be so easily adjusted to the years that lay ahead.

❧

BITTER YEARS

DICTATED OCTOBER 11, 1944

IN THOSE BITTER years when making believe I was a planter, I made up in the depths of my mind a picture of what Charles had seen in his vision of me. I often knelt in my fields and prayed that I should be led to that great and high work, and perform it well. When alone, I would sit and picture this again, and so perhaps I made progress toward its realization. There was never a day that passed that I did not see and think upon that great and inspiring vision.

My own persistent scene of what my brother dreamt sustained me in my most despairing moods and kept alive my faith in my own power to live a useful and perhaps important life. This all was utterly without the vanity and egotism I displayed at first so absurdly. I was now Life's most humble servant. I only wished to be of use in some way to my beloved Virginia. My thoughts never reached beyond the border of my Colony, and I would have been astounded if I had known what a small world that was in proportion to the vast Continental reaches that were to become the Country, over which I was to preside in time to come!

A dreamer ever, I now became almost insane from my melancholy introspective habits. In the morning, I would rise with the sun in the summer, and after my breakfast, go out to my animals. When I had fed them and cared for their comfort, I would go to my own field and there sit down to an hour of meditation on my poor showing so far. No amount of self-praise for my work in the Militia or in politics could gloss over the apparent waste I was making of my life. When aroused by the sound of some nearby whistling of a bird or the mooing of a cow, I would rise and go about the field work of the farmer.

When the time came to return to my father's house for lunch, I was in a silent mood that only depressed my father and mother. I would then try to lift my spirit by forced gaiety, and in some instances may have been rather amusing, but my mother's sad eyes usually spoke to me of her complete understanding that this was a display of mood I was far from feeling. Sometimes I would sit in silence, and in the midst of the meal excuse myself and go to the barn, where I was free from company except my dear friends, the horses.

Often I laid my head against theirs, and wept. They always gave me tender sympathy in their gentle whinnies and nuzzling against my face. No man can fail to believe in the love and sweet sympathy of a horse, who has ever made it his companion in suffering.

All this I put down as a part of what was the man, George Washington, a part never shown to the world, yet far more important in the summing up of the character of that man than the events recorded by historians and biographers. No man can call himself perfect, and I least of all. I was made up of such stuff as all men are, and have no other power than they. I simply was a man who had suffered so much frustration that when I came to act, it was with a verve and energy that may have seemed unnatural to men whose nature was not so pent up.

God knows, I had no illusions about myself. I knew I was but a very ordinary son of a most extraordinary father. The contrast was ever present in my mind. My mother, too, seemed to me of so much greater worth than I, that to me, she seemed made of far finer stuff and ever beyond my level. This I say in all honesty and not to assume a false humility, for humility was never one of my characteristics. My limited qualities I valued at their worth, and may even have over-valued them. I had more courage, both physical and mental, than most men. I had a fine and powerful body, and a will that I could count on to carry me through any situation. These were my few virtues.

On the other side of the ledger were to be put down my

hot temper when angry, my impatience if things went wrong, my complete disregard of the opinion of those who were in a position of authority, except in military matters – and even then I had too much temerity with my superiors. I had far too much of the man in me not to love the joys of male companionship and enough of the male instinct to give me the passion we feel for a woman if we are normal beings.

All to me was bleak and dark at this point in my life. I was in my mid-twenties as I recall. I had no glimmer of light on my path, and no hope of any being shed on it in the time to come. It came to the day when I said to myself,

"George Washington, you are a disgrace to your parents and a torment to yourself. Why do you go on? Why not cleverly step out of all this and become a wanderer in strange scenes? There, at least, you can make your way unobserved by those you know are in a constant state of concern for you."

These ideas sometimes fascinated me. A man with my health and strength and whatever I had of education, could usually find in a nomad's life some interest in the great world. Still, the impulse was lacking to make me take the course and I simply plodded on, one month duller than the last.

My one release was drink. On Saturday nights, I would get on my horse and go into town. My friend Timothy was always there with a good story and a hearty welcome. I drank whiskey straight, and in an hour was free from my haunting thoughts, so that my spirits would rise and I often joined in the songs of the town boys, who also sought freedom from the week's cares on a Saturday night.

I hated myself for all this. I knew it was an attempt to stifle the longing for worthier things. Still, it was an escape for a few hours, and so I let myself go as wildly as a youth of twenty.

My First Visions of My Destiny

Dictated October 12, 1944

When I was twenty-six, I said to myself:

"Now, I am at the height of life. From now on, I shall go downhill in mind and body."

I sat on my horse on that birthday and looked in the sun. I wrestled with a younger man and bested him. Those feats gave me heart.

What came over me to do it I'll never know, but I challenged the champion wrestler of the County and was victorious. All this may have come from a false strength, partly of the spirit. At any rate, I ended it by going home in a drunken stupor.

What my parents thought, I dared not face in my thoughts. My father was now growing old and his face was heavily lined, as was my mother's. How much was due to my conduct, I dared not think. They never reproached me, or even mentioned what must have been clear to them – that I was becoming a drunkard.

It was now my habit to keep a jug of whiskey in the barn, and twice each day to take a good swig of it. My father had often said in my hearing as a boy,

"No drunkard can ever hope to carry responsibility. He has forfeited his right to confidence." I remembered this, and every time I took a drink it seemed to ring in my ears.

What was to be the end? I was attracted to drink; of that there was no doubt. What would I be in ten years?

One morning as I raised the jug to my lips I saw, as clearly as I ever had seen anything, myself as I appeared that day in the woods with the three-cornered hat on my head, bearing a white cockade. This time, I seemed to be also wearing a uniform with white shoulder straps, and I carried a musket. At the belt was my flask of powder. As I looked in astonishment, I seemed to hear these words:

"Washington, if you cannot control your appetite for drink, you can never again command a regiment."

I was so dumbfounded that I dropped the jug where it lay on the barn floor with the contents flowing out of it. The figure remained, it seemed, for two minutes and spoke again, saying:

"I am your Soul, and I am sorrowful to see you betraying me. You were destined for service to your Country, but now you shall be compelled to go down in a drunkard's grave. Can't you rouse yourself and be a man once more? Do so, and you will be the man to take the foremost place in your Countrymen's hearts."

This was all, and the figure disappeared or faded out. It was so awe-inspiring, I stood in my tracks for some time, staring at the spot where it had been.

My first thought was to tell Charles. Then, I decided to say nothing, but to make an effort to break the habit that now had gripped me firmly.

It was a difficult and nerve-wracking battle. My will was not so strong as I thought, and the craving for whiskey at times seemed more than I could bear. My mother sensed what was going on with me, and kept pressing me. My father, too, seemed to be taking an unusual interest in talking to me of his affairs. Even Charles made extra effort to interest me in going for a fishing or hunting trip with him to the next county where he had made several trips. I accepted all this knowing what prompted it. They never spoke of the change in me, but were ever ready to take me to their hearts when I would let them. So passed the year, but at its close I was now my own man.

MANY LITTLE HAPPENINGS, of no consequence in themselves, seem to hang in my mind because they have a peculiar meaning for me in my development of purpose and character. One such happening occurred when I came to town one day, and met a man on the street I had often seen at the tavern I frequented, but had never spoken to. This was a citizen of some importance, a doctor, and a man whose family was considered among Alexandria's best and most interesting people. His name was Carlisle. He was a handsome and amiable man, about fifty at this time.

As I dismounted from my horse, he stopped on his way and saluted me. I responded, and he introduced himself. I was surprised when he said,

"Major Washington, I have long wished to make your acquaintance, but we have no mutual friends present whenever I see you at Timothy's Tavern."

I was happy to make his acquaintance, and we strolled on to Timothy's and had a drink together.

I found Dr. Carlisle to be a very amusing as well as a scholarly man, and from that day on we were happy in each other's company and, as I was a regular Saturday night patron, the doctor made it a point to spend an hour or so with me in the early part of the evening. When the time came for him to leave, he always said goodnight with the parting remark,

"My boy, give me a chance to help you. I see you are making duck and drakes of your splendid constitution."

I knew what he meant. I was drinking too much, and making of my fine physique and muscular power a sad wreck. Still, I never called on him for help when I made the decision to fight my appetite for alcohol. I record this to show how kind life was always to me and how, ever at hand, there was help if only I would accept it. Dr. Carlisle came to me later, after I conquered my weakness, and congratulated me. Then he opened up, and told me how he himself had gone through the same experience, and owed his reformation to the old family physician, whose pupil he was.

We never know what is the reason for these trials, and some men do not appear able to conquer when they once give in to habitual intoxication; yet the help is there within them and all about them, if they will but accept it.

REDEMPTION AND THE FREEMASONS

DICTATED OCTOBER 15, 1944

I CELEBRATED IN solitude my next birthday, thinking with some gratification of the way I had conquered a terrible weakness, and I was just thinking what it might have been had I not been able to do so. I was looking over my past years, and I suddenly came to the realization that there had been a divine power ever at my call, and that in extreme circumstances it even manifested itself by my spiritual body taking charge of this mechanism of flesh, as in the two instances I have mentioned.

All day I was idle, and quietly reflecting upon on my years of life in a mood not exactly happy, but with a profound sense of the importance of this last year's battle to preserve my health, my will, and my reputation as a man.

Then at the evening meal, my father said,

"My dear George, I am happy to see you so well and so restored on this your birthday."

I was silent for the reason that my throat swelled and tears were near. My mother then spoke, saying,

"George, darling, I think I never was so happy in my life as I am today. You are the cause. My darling, be sure you can now conquer anything."

This broke me down completely. I went to her and, kneeling beside her, laid my head on her shoulder and wept. Charles, ever delicate, quietly left the room and the servants tiptoed out to the kitchen. I think those next few moments were the most meaningful of my life. I realized how deeply my nearest and dearest had been suffering because of me. My father left his place and, coming to Mother's side, knelt opposite me and gripped my hand in such a way that I felt his heart beat. It was such a union of hearts, minds, and souls as few ever experience. We were silent. Words could not express what each of us knew the other was thinking. At last I kissed my mother's cheek and hand, and rose to my feet in such a mood of thankfulness and joy, that before

I knew what I really was about I had gone to the woods and to the fallen log, where I first saw my other self.

As I sat there in a sort of happy daze, I saw myself again as I appeared that day in the barn. I was smiling this time and spoke, saying,

"Now I am once again myself, and so are you. We shall be ready when the time comes to play our part in the events that will make the name of Washington immortal. This Country is to be free because of you. Keep the faith, and all will be as I see it now."

At that moment, I was so illumined that my face seemed to throw off a white light. I was dazzled and as I closed my eyes, the voice continued,

"Go to the best city, learn military strategy and the science of war and study for three months. Take note of all that is happening in the other Colonies and realize that Virginia is only a part of the great Country that will be called America. Make your plans immediately. You are also to meet the woman who is to be your wife. She is now a widow. Listen to my words and obey them, and you will do the work you are meant for. Be sure to obey, and all will be well for you and your wife as you work. *If you do not make the mistake of many and set up your will in opposition to Divine law, you will fulfill that high destiny for which you were chosen. Farewell."*

The figure gradually faded out. I sat there and went over his words again and again, trying to burn them into my brain.

It was evening, and the stars were out before I rose from the log. I was as if hypnotized by the vision and the message. If I obeyed, all was to be well. That was the gist of it all. Well, I would obey.

I decided to leave and go to Boston, where I had learned a course of strategy could be taken at Harvard College. This I did and found it, too, was simply the classic course and bore no relation to conditions in our Country. I stayed very briefly, indeed. By this time, my money had been spent and I felt let down. I was about to return home when my instructor said,

"Washington, why are you even thinking about taking this course? You are an old hand at war. Don't waste your time, but go to the fountainhead which is in all the records of our wars with Britain, France, and Spain. Read history which is the proper textbook for a military career."

Well, here was a bit of advice that I could take and make use of. I returned home and when I recounted my experience to my father, he was very disappointed and made me promise I would try to get some of the books of which I had a list. By now, it was plowing time and I had to drop everything to get in my crop seed. When that was done and I had leisure to read, I had received seven volumes that I hoped would give me the information needed. It proved to be quite the contrary. The strategy was overlooked in order to glorify the victors and damn the defeated. No movements of troops were described, and my money and time had been spent for nothing.

By this time, I was completely discouraged and hoped only that by autumn I might again take a course somewhere and make better progress. In August, I received a letter from the professor who had been so kind as to advise me, and in it he gave me a list of the works he thought would make up a course in strategy. This proved to be just what I needed. It was a list of seven works by Granville, a writer who was himself a soldier, and a General at that. He was none other than an officer in the Indian wars here in these Colonies. His book was for the British but, as he was dealing the American scene, they were as valuable to me as to any British officer on duty here in our Country.

All was now clear.

I was diligent and made copious notes as I read. Also, I drew maps and made calculations in the matter of supplies and transportation. Here my nautical studies came in handy, for I saw how valuable water transport was along our coasts and inland water ways. What a saving of horsepower and supplies.

All this time, I was keeping my stock in good condition. I saw I must depend upon my animal breeding to provide me with funds. Now for the first time, I considered seriously the multiplying of the sheep and cows.

All became quiet within me. I somehow came to feel that I was doing what was intended, and in due time I would be given further directions as to the next step to be taken. When I spoke of this to my father, he said in his quiet way,

"All is well."

That little phrase of three words has become my slogan, even my catchword. In my most desperate moments, I have said it aloud, again and again, and it seemed to make the path clear before me.

All is well.

No words ever served me so well. My troops used to say,

"Washington says 'all is well.' Hellfire! Just what does he call 'well'?"

Yet they too would gain a lift from the words, and endure all the better for their influence. In my darkest hours at Valley Forge I would say, even as I wept for my suffering men, "All is well."

❀

ON NOVEMBER 4, 1752, I was initiated into the Order of Masons. My only hesitation at this venture was overcome by my determination to seek all the knowledge the Masons have treasured and which, even today, in the higher degrees, make clear the laws of life that govern humanity, both in the mortal and astral body.

In time, that is within a few months, I had gone through the degrees. I then wished to take an examination for the rest. This was a record, it seems, and my Grand Master assured me I need not rush through the degrees so hastily. I had a feeling that I must work up while I was still free to study and told him so. His reply I never forgot,

"Washington, you are never to fail in what you once put your whole heart and hand to. You are one of the old Masons of ancient times and you are here to perform a duty. Never forget that."

George Washington as a Freemason

I found his words staggering and, in some way, seemed to feel that they were prophetic. All now was study and my thoughts centered upon going through the degrees as rapidly as possible. When I had taken the degrees, I was in despair of ever mastering the deep and profound truths that are set forth so cryptically in Masonic literature. Only my firm determination to solve the meaning of every sentence held me to the task. As I sat one evening deep in my study of a lesson, I looked up and there I was again, standing before me, now smiling and nodding as if in encouragement. I did not speak but stared at the figure, and when it spoke I could see how much I had missed of the inner significance of what I was studying.

I set this down to encourage all who have been through the bafflement and discouragement while preparing to go forward in the study of Masonry. I also set this down here to encourage those who, in and out of Masonry, are now determined to make huanity aware how close the world of spirit is to their own. It is the same world, the same planet. The only change is in the degree of vibration.

While on earth, we are encased in a body of chemicals drawn from the food and drink that come from the earth. When we are in our astral body, we are free and composed of the small cells so incalculably infinitesimal that we speak of them as vibration. Our minds, in which we live, move, and have our being on all planes, are more active than when in mortal bodies. Also, we are immortals, or deathless beings, and the laws of incarnation are the key to much that makes for our progress.

The modern who cries down immortality little guesses that he is uttering the lie that is destroying all the courage, hope, and ambition natural to a man who knows he is on his path of evolution, and that the laws of eternal life are his to use. To ignore them is to step backward inertly and sustain a loss of mental and spiritual courage. Without these, man is doomed to blindly and falteringly misuse his present span of life.

Benjamin Franklin was a great and profound student of the occult and was himself a Provincial Grand Master in Pennsylvania. The Order was small in Virginia, but in its membership were several distinguished men, such as William Pinckney and William Claiborne. I was only too proud to be one of an Order that could boast such mentalities and characters as these great men. Our Grand Master was also a gentleman of distinuished mental attainments and a lawyer of considerable reputation in Virginia. Few men were endowed with more wit, and his professional knowledge made him an authority often sought by other men of the legal profession.

I wish to ask my readers to refrain from judging Masonry by present day Masons. Many of them joined the order for commercial reasons only and have little conception of what Masonry is. They take the few early degrees and then boast of their Masonic standing. They are so ignorant and Masonically illiterate that they should be made to leave the Order after a probationary period. If, at the end of three years, they have not mastered all the degrees, they should be deprived of their rights and privileges as Masons. All here who have been true Masons agree that this should become the law and operative in all lodges.

To return to my own case. I was so happy to have made my degrees so rapidly that I sat down then to go over the whole course once more to make sure I had understood it all clearly. Since then, it has been my habit to go over each degree in my mind every year. The benefit has been so great in all ways that I recommend this to all Masons. You are then at all times master of yourself, which means you are master of your fate.

❀

MARTHA

DICTATED OCTOBER 14, 1944

Martha Washington
Courtesy National Archives

WHEN AGAIN THE SPRING came, I felt restless and like a lover. I went to town and purchased a fine coat and a fall of lace. My hair was beginning to show a few white hairs among the dark ones, and I saw myself as a very dignified figure. While in the shop of the mercer selecting the cloth for my coat, I was struck by the voice of a pretty young woman standing near me, looking at a piece of brocade.

"My conscience! Why do you expect me to purchase such wild looking pattern as that?"

The merchant said it was the very latest pattern in London. Whereupon the lady ordered a length of it and said, with a laugh,

"Well, one might as well be dead as not in the fashion."

She turned her pretty face toward me, and I smiled back. At that, the little lady said,

"Isn't this Major Washington of Mount Vernon?"

When I replied that it was, she went on to say she was our new neighbor, Mrs. Custis, and she was not long in residence on her estate, but had recently purchased the plantation. It seemed she was a widow with two small children. I observed that she was only in the colors of half-mourning, and was about to discard them for the gaily-colored brocade she had just selected.

When she left the shop, I escorted her to her carriage, which was at the door. Her driver was in a very smart livery, and beside him sat a boy of six or seven and on the seat with a maid was a sweet little golden-haired girl of about three. Before driving off, Mrs. Custis invited me to call on her, and I made a note that she seemed to really desire a further acquaintance. Her day at home, she told me, was Thursday and she would be happy to receive me any time between one and six o'clock. I was not going to call until I had made myself look presentable, so it was six weeks before I had my new outfit and felt in the mood to pay that visit.

When the day came, I had a strange premonition that this was a fateful occasion. I was right, for after three more calls, I was in love with Martha Custis and after the sixth call made her a proposal of marriage. She seemed at first hesitant, but soon relaxed into a receptive mood and I left her home that day as her betrothed husband.

We were not very happy in our selection of a wedding day, for on the following sixth of January, 1759, it was very cold and wet. Few guests could survive the downpour of sleet at times, and the roads became impassable. Only half a dozen friends attended, besides my mother and Charles. My own friends were astonished that at last I had been caught. The air was filled with cries of wonderment that I had succumbed to Martha.

❦

WE WERE LIVING in her house, and I rode to my place each day and continued working my land. I did not wish to be a burden on my wife's estate. Her means were ample for herself and her children. I hoped in time to be able to justify her choice by making some further contribution.

Martha was not a very happy woman when she found me so determined to go on with my own farm and to continue my studies of military science. She occasionally upbraided me for my preoccupation, but then she would tell me,

"My love, you are the man of my heart, and I will do as you think best."

No woman could put up with such an oaf as I often seemed and not complain. Martha hated my seriousness at times and my devotion to study. Nevertheless, we were happy and I became attached deeply to her charming children. I came to love them as if they had been of my own blood. My little step-daughter, Mary, seemed to me a little angel, and she was soon wont to nestle in my lap as naturally as if it had been her father's. The boy, Frederick, was also soon riding with me, and when in the hour before bed, he would say "Tell me a story, Major," I would give him some of my adventures. He became a dear son to me, and one I came to love with a life-long devotion.

Only happy things came of my marriage. I thank God for the impulse that led me to purchase the new coat, and to discover my lady among the flowering silks. From the day I met Martha, no other woman has ever laid in my arms. All through the Revolution and until my death, she and she alone has been the one love, the one passion, and the one desired woman.

❦

CONSTITUTIONAL ERRORS

DICTATED OCTOBER 20, 1944

WHAT CAN I SAY that will adequately pay my debt to that great and distinguished man, Benjamin Franklin? In the years after my marriage I was a devoted reader of his paper, and all of his speeches in the Philadelphia public meetings I made my study.

I thought, and still think that Franklin was the greatest mind of our time. *Poor Richard's Almanac* was my daily companion, and started off the morning after family prayers. His deep and profound wisdom – as well as a delightful humor – pervaded every sentence that he wrote.

In our times, no American equaled Franklin as a writer on life and affairs. When I began to study him, I felt like a schoolboy with a beloved master, from whom I could accept ideas almost whole, without reasoning, for every word and idea bore the stamp of truth. My own mind was capable of understanding him; that was my happiness. No reader who has to pore over a sentence and puzzle out its meaning is on the level with the author, even though in the end he gets the meaning for his pains. Franklin had the divine gift of making a reader feel that he was reading to him his own unspoken, informed convictions.

When I later came to know Benjamin Franklin, I was even more impressed by the greatness of the man and the power of his intellect. He is undoubtedly one of the most gifted intellects we in America produced during this era. Franklin is still here in the Spirit World, the thinker and the prophet to us who love him, and frequently seek him to ask advice and counsel. We watch and observe carefully this Nation we worked and fought so bravely to found. Some of us realized we had incarnated together to give birth to America, not in the beginning of the Revolution, but as the battle wore on. You may not be aware that those you call the "Founding Fathers" still carry the sense of responsibility they felt when administering the affairs of the Republic. All we can say in praise of Franklin is poor and inadequate to express the values we place upon this great Soul.

Well, I cannot but wish we had made him our first President. I feel that the two mistakes we made would then have been avoided.

The first was making the suffrage too easy for a newcomer to possess; and the second was the way in which we made the Executive the Commander-in-Chief in the time of war. Both these errors Franklin pointed out and warned us about. My own weight of opinion was with him, and he often said,

"George Washington, you and I know that these are terrible and tragic errors. You will never succeed with your Dream unless these two weaknesses are corrected." Too much power in the hands of one man was always to be avoided in America's Government.

He was my friend and counselor. Much of my accredited wisdom was due to his counsel. In no case has Franklin been proven wrong in his advice to me, in all the time since I adopted it. These two all but fatal errors in our Constitution are there because of the stupid – and all but tragic worship – my beloved Countrymen bestowed upon me. They seemed to think I was possessed of some God-like power that transcended the common man. Also, they were determined to make me a ruler for life. This, of course, I never listened to. Franklin said at the time,

"George, you see they don't want a Republic. They don't really understand the vision or significance of this Republic yet. They won't shoulder the responsibility of thinking for themselves."

All I could say – and I said it often and loudly enough – was useless when I came to try to formulate a Constitution. I debated with the best minds in the Continental Congress on the subject of suffrage. I could see Franklin was correct. A cheap suffrage would mean a cheap electorate. We argued with the men who were with us in the debates and in private conversations, but they were motivated largely by the commercial interests who wanted a quick growth of population drawn from abroad, in order to create great markets for their products. The settlers and planters also were against us. Business, money, and politics are evil bedfellows and always will be.

In the matter of making the President the Commander-in-Chief of all military forces in time of war, it was folly of the first order and I said so. The records, I am sure, must show this unless they were destroyed.

All my life since the Republic was founded, I have feared the very thing that has come upon us: an electorate polluted by members who come to this Country for no other reason than to make money – who care nothing for the principles of the Republic, who talk patriotism from the housetops and then sell out to the highest bidder. *An enlightened suffrage is important for both men and women. No amount of freedom can benefit a society that uses that freedom to lower the political and social level of the Nation.*

My observation extends over nearly a century and a half from this vantage point. We in the World of Spirit are in the same world as you. This planet is our home. The old theology that pictured heaven as a locality was put in its place by Jesus when he said,

"The Kingdom of Heaven is within you."

All is a state of consciousness. We are Earth creatures, and here is all we can know. In the Realm of Spirit, we have powers that are not possible when in the body of flesh, and we are not limited by time and space as you are. We can cover more ground and see and hear more of the world's affairs in embassies, ministries, its counsels and courts, than is possible to mortals. Because of this, my own experience has been a vast one.

I am accepted in Europe and Asia and in the Spirit Realm as the Founder of the United States. Often, I confer with them. They, too, have come to view the mistakes they made when governing their people in their earthly lives. I am asked frequently for counsel, and to give my opinion even by those who in my mortal life despised me as a military adventurer. These great men now see that the principles of the Republic were sound and that the only errors we made were the two I have mentioned, and which I now appeal to you to correct.

Benjamin Franklin would have made the correction or advocated them in such a way as to prevail upon the Congress had he been our second President. Unfortunately, he felt too infirm to then undertake the task. Adams was, above all, the next best and safest man. He said to me, as I congratulated him as President,

"My dear Washington, I am terrified at the responsibility. I pray to God that I shall be inspired to make my administration a capable one." Adams was ever a patriot, and a man of deep and sincere convictions, as was his wife, Abigail, a forthright force in the birthing of this nation.

George Washington at Dorchester Heights
Painting by Gilbert Stuart
Courtesy National Archives

CHAPTER FIVE

THE REVOLUTION

IT WAS A RAINY MORNING in the autumn of 1772 that I laid my paper, the *Pennsylvania Gazette*, on the table and remarked to Martha:

"Darling, we seem to be going along too well to worry about trouble with Home. I believe it will all come out well for us, without a resort to arms."

She was pleased at this thought and so we went along, lulled into a peaceful mood with the rather stupid complacency that humanity always tries to indulge itself in, and is so dangerous as an invitation to an enemy. I had no suspicion that in New England, they were making up their minds to end the bond that held them to Britain. I was quite set on the idea of greater liberty, but hoped it might be granted by Home voluntarily.

Martha was usually optimistic, but she always said,

"I feel there will yet have to be war to gain anything from Home. It is now all too difficult for us." One day in the following winter, I was in town and met a traveler who said he was on his way to Boston to join in a movement to free the Colonies. This, of course, came as a shock, but naturally I was immediately interested.

The stranger's name was Benjamin Franklin. He had just been on a tour through western Virginia, what is now Kentucky and Tennessee.

He was convinced of the intention of the Home Offices to make a military move against us, and try to make us realize our helplessness in the face of the military power sent to impress us. Of course, this all seemed very far-fetched indeed to me, and I was not very much impressed with its probability. However, I was impressed by the fine intelligence of this gentleman, and showed it. He took me into his confidence then, and said in effect,

"Major Washington, you are one of our best and ablest soldiers. I know your resourcefulness and valor, and I hope to see you take an important part in the coming conflict."

I could only respond affirmatively to this fine tribute and sincerely, for I was now afire with the old urge for action. When we parted, I begged for his counsel and advice, and told him my situation and convictions. His response was characteristic,

"Take my newspaper, the *Pennsylvania Gazette,* and I will keep you well informed. Also, if I have a chance, I shall visit you one day soon, and we will go into the matter with greater detail. My encounter with you today was no accident, I am sure, and I shall give myself the pleasure of accepting your hospitality."

So ended my first conversation with the man I believe to have been the Father of the Revolution.

When I reached home and told Martha of this encounter, she was greatly impressed with the importance of it, and hoped we would soon have the pleasure of entertaining Mr. Franklin.

I already took the *Pennsylvania Gazette* and pored over its editorials. You very likely can even now read them for yourself. They gave in great detail the wrongs and outrages that he had personally discovered against the people in his journey about the Colonies. He suggested in bold words that the time had come to throw off the yoke that was nothing but a tyranny that would never be yielded up, so long as we made no effort to rid ourselves of it. All this sunk in to my mind, and I saw how truly he had estimated our situation. I soon came to the conclusion that I must be ready when the time came to take my part in what lay ahead.

All this I wish to make clear. Benjamin Franklin roused the Colonies to action. Of course, Thomas Paine was a mighty force and a brilliant thinker, and Thomas Jefferson a man of unusual genius. Such great souls as never before gathered together for the talk of bringing the vision of this Nation into being. These are but some of the great men who sowed the seeds, and who made clear to the people all the issues that must enter this vital question, "Should we make a fight for freedom from the Home Government?"

I now put my affairs in such a state of order that I could turn them over to Martha, my overseer, and my brother Charles at any time.

❀

FRANKLIN

DICTATED OCTOBER 28, 1944

Benjamin Franklin
from a painting by Duplessis
Courtesy National Archives

IT WAS EARLY IN the month of May, just as the crops were in full flower that I received a letter from Franklin saying that he was coming to Alexandria in a week or two, and would be pleased to have me call upon him at the tavern where I had met him. Naturally, I was delighted and immediately replied, and stressed the great pleasure it would afford Mrs. Washington and myself if he could spend some time with us at our home. Martha, who had also been a devotee of Franklin's writings, was in quite a state of dither over the matter, and had one of our guest rooms torn up, cleaned, and resettled as if royalty was to be entertained.

It was a great day when we received an acceptance that was followed shortly by Franklin's arrival in Alexandria, where we met him with our carriage, both Martha and myself.

Following dinner, Franklin went into detail as to the situation in Philadelphia and Boston. These were headquarters for the States of Pennsylvania and Massachusetts. There, the people were in a fury at the various outrages their Crown officials had committed, and were determined to follow Virginia's example: out the Crown Governor and make one of their own native men the head of the State.

I recounted in detail our long and discouraging fight, and the acts which led to the final victory. I said we had no way of making the Home Office take notice of us until we wrote to the Prime Minister and the Archbishop of Canterbury as well as the King and Parliament. I cited my father's letter as being the item which had brought the Home Secretary to his knees. William Pitt, I felt sure, was the key to their situation as he had been to ours. Franklin did not think his people would wait to go through such a long and tedious process. He said,

"Our people are Quakers and will not fight, but Massachusetts is different. They are ready to make any gesture that will show the Home Secretary that they are through with Crown Government in local affairs. They will pay a small tax, but the poor people must be entirely exempt. Your experience is valuable to us in Pennsylvania, but New England will not be so patient."

Franklin was with us for a week, and we went into the details of my military service in Philadelphia, and my conclusions as to the great need of a philosophy that would prevent such a tragedy as the Fort Pitt massacre. I recounted to him the unfortunate way in which General Braddock had rejected all my attempts to warn him as to what Indian warfare was like; also, his complete disregard of the fundamental needs of the men when on duty away from their Post. I cited instances of neglect leading to illnesses and even deaths of men who were simply victims of his Quaker beliefs and were made to suffer needlessly in the cases where they survived.

Franklin, ever a realist and a man of supreme wisdom with the faculty of seeing into the heart of any problem, gave me his word that he would take up these things in his newspaper and even in his *Poor Richard's Almanac*. He would try to awaken a more matter-of-fact realization among his readers of what an army really meant.

The days flew by in the company of this charming and amazing man. It is quite understandable that the French came to accept and love him in the years when he was our minister, living in Paris. Martha and I were so carried away with his delightful company that when he left us, we were in a saddened and lonely mood. Here, I may say that as long as he lived, he was the closest man to my heart next to my father and my brother Charles. Not that we were ever so very intimate in our relations for both of us were the servants of our people and our duty, and neither of us had the leisure to indulge in the joy that we found in each other's company.

One thing was left clearly impressed on my mind: Franklin was a visionary, and what he had told me of the situation in his State and Massachusetts was the simple truth, and could be counted upon. I foresaw the clouds gathering still blacker, and the time not far distant when the Crown Governors of those two Colonies could no longer prevent the storm from bursting into violence. I felt I must be ready for action, and so in my mind I began to work out the small details of our plantation, and classify and arrange them under the plan of making it all possible for Charles to supervise.

❦

MY MOTHER'S DEATH

MY MOTHER'S DEATH had occurred two years before this, and I have not cared to dwell at length on the great vacancy this left in our lives. To the last, she had been the great consolation in trouble and the smiling and happy confidante of all we enjoyed.

The children were devoted to her. Martha found in her the mother she had lost so early. My own sense of loss, I do not care to speak of. Those who have read this far may imagine how crippled life seemed to me when she was gone.

Mary Ball Washington is here, and knows well that I regard her life and deeds, her great wisdom and sensitive care for others as the purest and most vital influence of my life, and that of all others within her orbit. Her like I have not met since, even with my wide and varied opportunities of knowing human character. There is no record of her life in detail. There could not be, for it was made up of a hundred good thoughts and acts each day. Her dignity forbade her ever making herself the topic of conversation and few, outside the family, know how even my father went to her as the court of last resort when dismayed or confused.

I know how highly American men place their women, especially their mothers, in their estimate and love. Still, I have every reason to know that love; and that even beyond my own comprehension and that even of my father, she lived a secret life of such high thought that it ever strengthened and held her to her course, no matter what tragedy startled her, or what desperate events confronted her and those she loved. Her brooding care extended to every servant, every neighbor, every wayfarer, and every animal that she came upon. Her vision went out and brooded upon humanity as a whole, and when she thought upon the future, she craved nothing for her own that she did not desire for all.

If the capacity to love my Colony, my Country, and my People has been credited to me, it is because I am the son of Mary Ball. My father gave me the strength to fight as he, Augustin Washington, fought for justice for his fellow men. It was Mary Ball who gave me my love for them.

❦

THE AMERICAN REVOLUTION

DICTATED NOVEMBER 2, 1944

I SHALL NOW GIVE A rather long account of my time
before the Revolution. It is difficult to say quite where or when
the Revolution actually began. For me, it began when I was a
youth. It seems to have been all the time seething and ready to
come alive during the years from 1747 and 1775. A quarter of a
century of bitter and resentful emotion had worked on the people's
thoughts, until here and there it would move them to action, as
it did us in Virginia, when we rebelled against a Crown official
being the arbiter of our lives. In Massachusetts, what is called
the Boston Tea Party gave warning of the state of mind of the
citizens there. In New York, no sign appeared. The Dutch were
like British traders, and were making that their main objective. In
Maryland, the citizens were prosperous and content, for they had
such a coastline that the sea and the tidewater commerce gave
them all they desired.

It was the Colonies of Delaware, Maryland, Rhode
Island, and North Carolina that were largely against any sort of
rebellion. Many felt that they cared nothing for the future of
the Country, which would depend upon the spread of population
into the interior. The people as a whole were as always, and in all
places, too focused on their own survival to grasp the essentials of
either the present or the future status of the American Colonies.
All were willing to take any benefit arising from the action of
other States, but were too inert to come to grips with a situation
themselves. Such men as Franklin, Jefferson, Adams, Tom Paine,
and my father could plainly see that no future beyond the strip of
Atlantic coast would be possible for men taking up land. The trade
was all there was to look to, and that was already controlled by the
Crown and the large ship owners of the coastal towns. No great
rise in immigration was to be expected, and the mounting cost to

each State of the poor farmers and pauper shelters was a problem. Men came to America, and the town taxes made their land but a challenge, and frequently a penalty.

❀

WHEN I CAME TO think over my recent visit to Boston and New York, I saw plainly what was in the minds of those men who were making a Cause of their wrongs. They wanted not a liberal status under Britain: what they wanted was absolute freedom and to live as independent States, each with its own laws and flag. I could only envision confusion and failure in such a situation.

My experience in the Colonies I had visited showed me how diverse their customs and ways of thought were. I felt there would be no binding them together in a single ideal, with a practical cooperative political code that would satisfy each and all. My conclusion was that any rebellion against present Crown injustice must have a concrete and definite purpose that could, and would, attract all the Colonies to it. No such thing seemed to be in the making, so far as I could perceive.

All the time these thoughts surged through my mind, I had the settled conviction that the time was near when the whole question would be solved. How, I could not imagine; yet I was sure it would be the very wisest and best for all.

❀

NO AMOUNT OF THINKING and conjecturing seemed to solve this burning question in my own mind, and so in the end I decided to do as before and be ready if I was needed, and in the meantime carry on my own business as diligently as possible.

Martha was so happy to have me at home and to see Frederick regaining his strength, that she put all else from her mind and gave herself up to the joy of the moment. She was ever one to make the most of the blessings she saw in her life, and never complained of anything unless it was of a serious nature. She now was coming to middle life, and was really settling down into a state of profound peace and contentment. I rejoiced over this, for I saw that nothing could come now to shake the foundation of our lives.

Our property was all under cultivation. I had now been able to save something like twelve thousand pounds by dint of my work with the land, and my investments that I had made in Martha's name. These were small loans at 2% to young men trying to take up land. In every case, they had paid their interest and, in all but one instance, returned the loan. This exception is the one I have related of the western relative's betrayal. I could rest easy in case I should be called to service, and Charles would be in full charge of our estate.

Mary was now a sweet young girl on the threshold of puberty. Martha had trained her in needlework and cookery so that she was now, young as she was, taking charge of our home in order to see how well she could run it. Her success was immediate and gave Martha much time for relaxation and visiting. This holiday, so long overdue, was really a boon. I needed to devote myself to work and study, so she was free to ride or drive to town, or entertain at home and make the most of those free and merry days.

❦

Meanwhile, I had asked Franklin to send me any and all maps of the Colonies that he could lay his hands on. I also wished for County maps of Massachusetts and New York, as well as New Jersey and Maryland. These kept arriving and, at night, I would pore over them, making notes and calculations. The many water routes lying about New York gave me the idea that this would be the center of the enemy's plans, should war come. I wished to know every body of water and every roadway, hill, and village. This seems to have been providential, for I found my notes and my knowledge of the topography of New York, Long Island, Staten Island, the Jersey shore and the coastline of Massachusetts and New Jersey, the most valued of any of my studies.

I was also keen to know what reserves of ammunition were at hand in each Colony. Also, what the state of mind was in the rural districts as to feeding an army. I asked Franklin to estimate the cost of equipping a regiment, and where arms and ammunition were obtained now. This data he furnished me and, I must say in praise of it, that I could not have had a more accurate and authentic report. All I needed to do was to master these details and study my maps.

When finally in the autumn of 1774 I received a visit from my old friend Franklin, he said to me quite simply,

"Now, Washington, you can go to work."

I gasped.

"Where?" I managed to say.

"Wherever you think it best to start. We are not ready, and somebody must make us ready. You must do that."

I stared in complete astonishment at this calm statement. In a flash, I saw a picture of myself drilling men and commanding what seemed to be an army. I said, when it had faded,

"Where does all this begin?"

"In New York, I suppose," was his reply.

Well, I was no man to try to raise a scare in New York, and said so. Franklin was not of my opinion. He tried to persuade me to go to New York, see the officials there, and make them realize what had to come. I was set against this, and forced to decline such a plan. In the end, we compromised. I was willing to go to New York if sent for, but I would not be the one to start the thing. So Franklin said, as he left us,

"My friend, you are destined to be our leader. It is my place to see that you do so. John Adams is in equal agreement, as are others I shall not mention at this time."

I could not share this feeling. I wished to aid, but I did not feel competent to lead. When Franklin had been back in Philadelphia a week, I got a letter from him saying he was running a series of articles in his paper on the need of a military leader to prepare us for the conflict that all could plainly see was coming. I read these articles, and realized he was feeling the public's mood on this. A few letters in rebuttal of his idea were published, and many from readers who supported him. It was still, however, nothing to count on, and I simply went on as usual with my work and my study.

One day late in September, a message came from him saying he was arriving the following week with a definite plan of action. This, he said, would be laid before me for my approval. It turned out to be nothing less than a recruiting plan of larger scope than usual. He said he felt a new sense of danger was coming over the officials, and he had taken pains to foster it in his paper. He also saw the Mayor and City Council, and they were all for a strong and capable military force that could be relied upon in case of emergency.

I was not keen to again visit or work in the city of Philadelphia, and gave my reasons, recounting in detail my experience there and my reason for leaving. Naturally, he roared at the matter, though he was in complete sympathy. I was sure no change had come to make the life of a soldier any more attractive or sensible. Franklin then declared he, himself, would go after the people and try and to make them see how immoral their attitude to the soldier was.

In the following weeks, his paper was hot with his stories of the wretched treatment accorded soldiers who were under the ban of Quakerism. All were of a nature to cast ridicule on the authorities for permitting such a state of affairs, and warning them that the time would come when no men would enlist in Pennsylvania.

Well, in about two months the city was buzzing with talk, and the City Council passed a resolution in condemnation of the way the Quakers had jeopardized the lives and morals of the men who served in defense of the State. Once I saw the trend was strong, I wrote a letter setting forth the cause of the Braddock massacre and spared no details. I espoused Franklin's attitude, and suggested that either the Quakers abolish all military defense or else treat a soldier like a human being.

This letter, it appears, gave the city a real sensation, for I omitted no part of the horror of our experience at Fort Pitt, nor Braddock's conduct before the event. Neither did I spare them the lack of any recognition by the citizens of the martyrs at Fort Pitt. I also paid my compliments to the Quartermaster for his conduct. Be sure I did not omit giving a full meed of praise to General Sterling for his manly and soldierly conduct in succoring our poor, neglected and suffering men who had survived the pitiful sight of the seventy who marched to Fort Pitt.

My God, what a sensation that caused when Franklin set it up in larger type than the usual articles, and on the front page of the *Gazette!* No wonder we had the town in an uproar. I had attacked their hero, Braddock, and then made an appeal to recognize their own miserable failure.

"This man, Washington, is a liar. He has tried to dishonor the memory of a man who died a martyr."

The crowd seemed to feel this was true, and went to the *Gazette* office and demanded Franklin's denial of this. He was not to be intimidated, and said,

"You know you are trying to cover up your own conscience by attacking the man who was the savior of all the men who survived, the man who marched across the State on a crutch, and who served his men as few officers have been called upon to do! Shame upon you! I shall now put your conduct before the people, and let them decide the matter."

This he did. In the end, he won, but no action was taken. Poor Franklin, who had labored so long and so diligently, saw that what I had told him was true. Pennsylvania had no public spirit, and no love of Country. That was the curse of Quakerism, or so it looked to us at the time, which otherwise is a fine and noble religious sect.

When I heard all the story, I begged Franklin to desist and never make another effort in the *Gazette.* But to do what he must do to save his paper and himself and privately, under a pseudonym, write the New York and Boston papers in the vein he felt was needed. This he began to do. One article in a New York paper, signed Christopher Mores, aroused so much comment that the City Council held a special meeting to discuss the propriety of increasing the militia and arming them with more modern weapons. Another paper attacked the article, but got nowhere. One result was the casting of several new cannon and of creating a cavalry troop.

My own feelings were then in a ferment, for I could not see what part I could play in all this. My poor brain was tormented with ideas that seemed valuable, but there was no outlet for them. It was not until the year 1775 when I made up my mind to leave home, go to New York, and offer my services, that I got a moment's peace. We were now at the seething point in our relations with the Home Government. Mobs had stoned the windows of the Governor's Mansion in the city of Boston, and British sailors were attacked on the streets of New York. A bevy of girls had been seen trying to tear down the British flag on the Custom House at the Battery, and boys openly hooted at the Governor when he rode or drove through the streets of New York. Such were the surface signs of the feelings the people had toward the British.

Once I had decided, I lost no time and was soon in New York, where I presented myself at the Post on Staten Island and offered my services. The Commanding officer was a rather young and raw Lieutenant. He referred me to the Captain, who was not much older or apparently more experienced. The young gentleman was quite upset when he was faced with such an old campaigner. In the end, of course, I saw the General in Command and then explained my errand. He said, with a grin,

"Major Washington, you have been out of service for some time. What do you expect me to say?"

I retorted that though I had been out of service for a few years, I had been in it for twenty years. That brought him to his senses, and he asked me to sit down and go into full details as to my reasons for wishing, at my age, to resume a military life. I did so at length, and the old boy opened his eyes.

It was four hours later when I left him, with my commission and the rank of Colonel. I was installed in quarters on Pine Street, and the Quartermaster received an order to outfit me with three uniforms. Within a week, I was in command of three regiments of infantry.

The men were not especially notable for either their drill or their marksmanship. At once, I ordered a system of daily practice at target shooting, as well as a physical examination of the men and a program of gymnastics that, in a month, made them into something I could be ready to take on parade.

My General, who was aged and weary, was not even interested in reviewing the men. However, my junior Officers were fine fellows, and really were delighted at what had been accomplished. I made a game of wrestling and held contests in the gymnasium. I taught them several tricks for use in hand-to-hand fighting, and this they seemed to think great fun.

In another month, the old General came out and reviewed us. He was kind enough to say that he had no idea I could accomplish such results with the mean-looking lot who had been, in his mind, a set of riff-raff. Soon, he was coming to our wrestling games and target shooting. The old chap became enthusiastic, and said one evening,

"Colonel Washington, I believe you could make a soldier out of a straw man."

This, I repeat to show how small a thing a soldier was in those days, and how little faith the old officers had in them.

My time was fully taken up with my work and writing letters home. No time was there for any social life or amusements. Still, I was happy. I was cresting fine defenders for the Country, if they were needed, and I loved the training of the men. They seemed to like me, and so all was well.

❧

THE BRITISH ARRIVE

DICTATED NOVEMBER 3, 1944

ALL THIS TIME, I was receiving letters from Franklin. He was ready to quit the city of Philadelphia and move his paper to New York. None of the journals there were writing on the critical situation, and Franklin felt it would be the first scene of attack when war broke out.

To me, it was a mistake for him to change his base, and I wrote him so. This he regarded as a sign he should stay where he was, though he was irked continually by the indifference of the people there.

We would occasionally meet, Franklin and I. All we could think of was the coming conflict, and so we were always in a stew about arms, ammunition, and food for troops. Pennsylvania was the logical food storehouse, but the farmers showed no real interest in making an effort to provide a reserve supply. We wrote to many men who were wholesale grocers and butchers, to commission merchants and to the weigh masters for lists of their sales and amount of their storage. These they supplied us, but this only showed how terrible the situation would be if war came.

All I could do was to make estimates of what would be needed in food, clothing, blankets, weapons and ammunition and to supply the wagons and horses with harness and fodder. All this was published by Franklin, in the hope that a fire would be lit under some of the readers, and a movement started to prepare to defend the Country and supply its armies.

All in vain!

It was six months after I had taken up my profession and was in the midst of the work of planning for emergencies, when Franklin came to New York with a message to me from a former Governor of Pennsylvania. This was Callander, who had been retired to private life years previous, and was now a leading financier in Philadelphia. He was interested in the Franklin effort, and saw plainly the drift of events. Callander was shrewd enough to see that money would be made in war contracts, and was forming a group to make weapons in case war loomed. We, of course, saw his motive, but welcomed his attitude. I was pleased to receive Franklin's news, and a few days later Callander called on me. I was, of course, not in a position to do more than offer suggestions as to the type of weapon we would need, and to coach him in the way best calculated to gain further information from the General in command.

We were but two days conferring on the subject – Franklin, Callander, and I – when we were suddenly stunned by the appearance in the harbor of a British war vessel, and the debarkation of a regiment of British soldiers. Our barracks were at the corner of Broadway and we could see the men coming ashore, and their supplies being tossed out the hold to the gangplanks.

I went at once to the General's quarters and reported it. I found the old chap dozing over his luncheon, and he woke with an oath at this disturbing of his daily habit. I then gave him the news, at which he calmly remarked,

"Well, she is welcome, that ship. I think a touch of Home discipline will be good for these lazy, good-for-nothing soldiers."

I was too astonished to reply, and asked what he supposed was the reason for the presence of these British troops, who came with no warning. He was not ready with an answer, and I went on to say that we might expect trouble if the citizens did not favor this action. The General, ever a compromiser, was not going to go into that, and merely dismissed me with,

"Colonel Washington, you are simply anticipating something that will never happen. I shall expect you to keep your men quietly in barracks and make no trouble."

These were his orders and, of course, I obeyed them. The men were all excited and wished to go out and see all that was going on, but I said they must obey and remain in barracks until further orders. One young officer came to me and with a grin, remarked,

"I believe this order is not from you, sir."

I told him it was, and must be obeyed.

Franklin rushed over to see me within an hour of the landing of the British troops. I told him our orders, and he stared at me incredulously. Callander then came to talk it over, and I only could give him the same answer to his question, "What will our troops do?"

Well, all was quiet for two days. The citizens were agog and very serious in the main. The British were quartered by billeting, and the officers were busy calling on the householders to provide them accommodations. Two warehouses were converted for their men and the contents ordered removed. This was such an outrage, that the owners rushed to our General and demanded protection of their property. The Mayor was also requested to make his authority felt. In the end, the owners got only the meager satisfaction of seeing their clients' goods piled on the docks, and the guard of British soldiers to protect them.

In my quarters were several maps of the adjacent islands and territory. I was quite aware that they were not a necessity in my present work, but I hung them where I could frequently study them at odd moments. Now, I took them down and placed them in a chest. I felt no sign should be visible that I had knowledge, or means of study that showed any anticipation of war on my part.

It was not more than a week after these events when I was called by Franklin to come to his tavern when off duty that evening, to meet several of the most public-spirited citizens of New York. Of course I went, and was pleased to see there more than twenty of New York's most influential business and professional men. One in particular struck me as being the most daring and capable of the group. This gentleman was named Crane, and he was an old-time settler who had seen the Colonies in their early struggles.

He was keen to demand an apology from the King for sending to a peaceful community a body of armed men, and then billeting them on the city. That is just what had happened. The order was posted that the people of New York City were thenceforth commanded to furnish housing and food gratis to three regiments of British foot-soldiers and their officers. Also, a tax was levied by the Commanding British officer who furnished the men their pay. A howl did go up at that, and the newspapers were very outspoken in their resentment at the uncalled-for action. Crane wished to know what could be done to overthrow the British rule and get going on our own, each Colony for itself. I was in no position to counsel resistance, having nothing to resist with. I did, however, say it was all up to the people and, if they would hold meetings to protest and issue proclamations, it would show the British that the Colony was aroused and resentful. This, he declared, was not enough. We must have immediate action, so in the end nothing was done, and the people paid the tax and supported the officers and men. My own disgust was profound and I was tempted to throw up my commission and go home, washing my hands of it all. One thing only prevented me, and this was the affection I had come to feel for the men and my subordinate officers. We were a united body, and the military spirit of all made a command I was proud of.

When the British held a review, I asked my men to watch them and judge for themselves which were the best trained—they or us. Of course, they were eager to find merit in their comrades, but even discounting this very human consideration, we could make in drill, on march, or at target practice a far better showing.

❧

WE WERE NOT HAPPY as the months passed, and the British swaggered about the town. They were a good lot of men as individuals, but their insolence and condescending manner, which was true of both officers and men, began to make both my command and the citizens think them a nuisance. We were often invited to parties where I met the British officers, and in all instances their insufferable attitude was enough to spoil the evening.

I remember one instance, when attending a very charming party with dinner and dancing at the home of a leading citizen. The supper had been a very excellent one and the punch bowl kept filled. My hostess had said to me, in confidence, that she hoped the British officers would be discreet in their libations.

The truth was they all became intoxicated and made unpleasant remarks to me, as well as to my officers present. In deference to our host, we let them pass. However, when I was about to pay my adieus to my hostess, a young British captain, quite drunk, came up and with his face thrust up toward mine, said in a drawl,

"My good friend, you should not show yourself in public with such a pocked face. You scare the ladies."

My hostess flared up and rebuked him, but he persisted in his insulting remarks so that I said goodnight and left, but waited until the officers reeled out of the house. Then, I went up to him and his fellow officer who was trying to keep him on his legs. I simply wrenched him from his friend's hold and then said,

"An apology, sir, and at once."

He was too far gone to understand what I said, and muttered a few curses. I then asked his name, and he could remember that. It was Captain Loud, one of the Fusiliers. I sent my card to him the next morning, and said that I would be happy to receive his apology for his insult of the previous night. No reply was vouchsafed, so I called on the Colonel of his regiment and gave him the story. Naturally, he was upset and himself apologized, and said he would see that Captain Loud did the same. I came away still in a rage, and only by walking ten miles into the country did I again find calmness.

What a cad!

Was that the conduct of "an officer and a gentleman" of which the military caste of Britain so loudly boasted? I seemed once more to be the butt of a fate so difficult to bear, that I refused all invitations from that time.

My young officers also complained of the conduct of the British at any affairs where they met them. I spoke to our General, but that old fool worshipped the British Army since he had received his training there.

❦

WE BORE THE PRESENCE of these foreign invaders for three months. At the end of that period, a recall came from Home. We cheered as they embarked and gave the salute of three rounds from our muskets. This was reported to the General, who called me up on the carpet for it. I gladly took a dressing-down. We now knew we had no friend in the General. He would turn us over to the British in a moment if we ever came to grips. We were all Colonials and, all but myself, natives of New York State. Dutch, as well as English, a few Scottish and Irish and Welsh and three Germans, were their racial strains. We were Americans all, and that fast gave us unity.

❦

IT WAS NOT VERY long before we again saw a warship unloading British troops on the Battery. We realized, then, that this was to be a permanent policy of the Home Secretary. This time, the people demurred and refused to house the officers. The warehouse owners asked the Mayor for police protection of their property but, naturally, he dared not furnish it. The meetings now began to be held almost nightly, where speakers proclaimed the injustice of making them support all these soldiers, who were neither needed nor desired in a peaceful and law-abiding community. I attended a few of these meetings in my civilian clothes and learned the mood of the people.

Two men appeared to be the leaders of these gatherings of protests. They were simple and quite without influence in the matter of either political or financial importance, but they were fine specimens of manly and intelligent citizens. All this, I reported to Franklin.

We were only now coming to see how far the people would go in their own interest. It was not long until letters were appearing in the newspapers protesting against the state of things. I remember one that said, among many other things in the same vein:

"If I must carry a soldier on my back, I shall find means to throw him off before he breaks it."

Torch-light processions were then coming to the fore, and one was formed that carried transparencies bearing such slogans as "Take away your Redcoats, King George," and others of the same sort.

The City Council now took notice of the way things were going and began to hold special meetings. The Council was divided, but the majority were for making a stand against supporting the British troops, or even letting them stay to create all this friction and discontent.

At last, an incident occurred that was a spark to the timber of the people's emotions, the public demanded action by the Mayor and Council. This was a small thing, but it was enough.

A Colonial soldier in uniform was standing by the door of a shop when a British officer came out. As he passed, he spat in the face of the Colonial private. This he reported to me. I sent the man to identify the officer the next day when the British were having their drill. I accosted this officer and requested his name—it was Lieutenant Manning. I thanked him, and then again called on the British Colonel in command and asked a public apology for the insult. This was refused. I then said that I could not be responsible for anything that might follow, as the comrades of the man who had been spat upon regarded it as a reflection upon themselves as well. This seemed only to amuse the Colonel, and he offered the following remark,

"Since when does an officer have to apologize to a private?"

My reply was that in our Country, a man has personal

dignity whether an officer or a private, which, so long as he conducts himself properly, is to be respected.

"Well, your ideas here need to be changed if you are to be taken seriously."

I then left and went to our General, though with faint hope of any action from him. To my surprise, he did flare up with,

"By God, this is too damn much. I shall myself take up the matter! Colonel Washington, make a report of this in full, and I shall send it to the Home Office."

This I did. However, all this circumlocution was no satisfaction to the private who had been spat upon, and he and a few of his comrades lay in wait for this young whippersnapper and gave him a good beating. Of course, it was then the British Colonel's turn to call on me, which he did. I explained that all this the Lieutenant had brought upon himself, and that the whole matter was now on its way to the Home Secretary. This dashed the Colonel somewhat and he left in a rather chastened mood. I cautioned my men against any further revenge and all was quiet for three days until a British officer, on meeting a Colonial officer, gave him a cut across the neck with his walking stick.

This man turned and caught the stick, jerked it away, and gave the Britisher a cut across his own neck and, throwing the cane to the sidewalk, went on his way. This, too, was a cause for another call on the Colonel by myself. This time he gave in, and said:

"Colonel Washington, I will ask this officer to call on you today at 5 o'clock to apologize. Have your man there to receive the apology."

Of course, when the British officer apologized, he did so with a sneering smile, but as his words were correct as an apology, the incident ended.

Many such clashes began to take place, until the British and Colonial officers and men could not meet in a shop, theatre, or even on the street without trouble. No reply was received from the Home Office by the General. He now saw that he had been a miscalculator as to the position he was in. He became in a few weeks a rabid anti-Britisher, and was as good a Colonial as the best of us. This gave me the heart to continue at my Post and certainly to face what lay ahead.

❧

FRICTION

DICTATED NOVEMBER 4, 1944

WE WERE IDLING ALONG, making a show of work by holding target shooting matches, the usual forced marches to the Catskills and back, wrestling to keep in shape, going to the most popular taverns on Saturday, with a poor attendance at chapel on Sunday. The General seldom appeared, and I only saw him when I went to report.

All the time, I was keeping in touch with Franklin, and he was writing the articles that fired the spirit of the people. Still, no sign was seen of a rebellion against the present regime and high taxation. I became quite pessimistic about any change, and began to consider making up my mind to resign and forever quit worrying about the less fortunate than myself. I was now able to bank a hundred pounds a year from my salary in addition to the profit Martha would have from our joint plantations, which amounted to three hundred pounds annually. So, all was prosperous with us. I need no longer feel ashamed of my part of the bargain, for I had now managed to put, as my share, into the bank, two thousand pounds in case I died. I had also managed to bank, in all, five thousand pounds in her name. This was a fortune in those days, and she could thus endow her children and have plenty for her own use as long as she lived.

My own satisfaction in the matter was that I had been accused of marrying to better myself, and had been instead the one to increase Martha's modest estate left by her husband.

❧

ALL WAS SERENE AT the Post in September of 1774. I had been there a year nearly, and had made the three regiments under my command a really fine line of soldiers. All was harmony, and I felt a sense of deep satisfaction as I watched the men drill. They had come to be as fine a looking outfit as any I had ever seen.

I was lonely for Martha and Charles and the children, but I passed my evenings in reading or at the theatre. The troupe from Philadelphia were giving a season of drama at a fairly good theatre, and I loved the drama and the art of the actors. They took one into a realm of the make-believe that left one refreshed and stimulated. What I saw I do not now recall, except for one very bombastic play called *Balthesar* in which the hero was a very much persecuted Jew, who was as rich as Shylock and far more inclined to usury. He was in the end found to be a fine young Christian masquerading as a money lender, so that he might tempt the enemy of the King to such perfidy as would destroy him. All came out as planned, and everyone felt happy over the young patriot's cleverness. The words and situations were aimed at the cheap seats, and their occupants responded with such stompings, clappings and cheerings that I feared the ceiling would come down. Those were the days when naturalism was sacrificed to declamation, and noise was considered a vocal necessity in the case of an actor who was cast in a heroic role. Balthesar rose to such vocal heights as to all but deafen us. Still, he managed to win the love of the very handsome daughter of his sovereign and came to be a power in the land. I was amused at the audience as well as at the players, for they were so partisan as to make more noise than the hero when the evil ones of the play were exposed. Our evenings went by in those rather primitive amusements, and what with letters to be written home and to Franklin, the hours were filled between supper and bedtime.

ALL WAS QUIET, UNTIL the word came suddenly of another shipload of British soldiers to be added to those companies already in New York Town. No word in advance was sent to the officials, and there was a riot on the docks when the General ordered two more warehouses to be vacated and used as barracks for his fresh troops. The rioters were the riff-raff, but all the same, they represented the attitude of the citizens. My own observation of the riot was merely what could be seen and heard from my own quarters. Our men were itching to be called out and join in the fray, but we were ordered to stay in barracks by our own General. However, I called on him to ask his views on the situation and he was only ready to make a stand when appealed to by the city officials. I knew this would never happen. The Civic Council and the Mayor had shown no spirit of resentment at the way the Home government was imposing on the people of the city.

A few days later, we were having a review on the plaza of the Battery when an orderly from the British General came up to me with a note, which proved to be a request that no reviews should in future take place near the Battery. I finished the work and then reported this to my General. Well, the old boy did make a few hot remarks, but said finally that we must obey the British orders. I tried to make him see what an absurdity it was to allow a foreign contingent to banish us from our own special drill ground. I had no success and was pretty sore at heart when I left him. My junior officers were ready to make a demonstration to him, but I persuaded them it would only get them in trouble and change nothing.

We marched to a spot near the place where now the City Hall stands, and there held our next review. A number of British privates had tagged along with the usual crowd of onlookers. When we were making a sudden about-face, one Redcoat shouted,

"C'an yer poor mackerel, yer don't know yer left foot from yer right."

A boy nearby heard him and shouted,

"Yer filthy British. Go jump off the dock."

The urchins loved our troops, and were not inclined to

listen to any criticism of them. The British soldier started for the boy, who ran back of our line, followed by about five other street boys and two or three men. This interfered with the completion of the maneuver, and I called a halt. We came to rest and the soldier was caught between us and the crowd of boys. He called out to me,

"Get yer Goddamned rookies out of my way!"

I saw my Sergeant go up to the man and feared a rumpus. Then, I made a sign to my Captain to march the men to barracks. The order cracked out, and the Sergeant stopped and went into his position. We marched past this Redcoat without looking at him. I reported the incident to the General and asked him to make a complaint to the British Commander. He said he could not be bothered with such trifles and that ended the matter for a time.

My men were not so easily placated. They were full of fight and looking for trouble. I spoke to them about being careful never to give offense and set an example of good manners to the British and, also, to keep the citizens on their side in case trouble arose.

However, it was but three days before we were in a melee with a squad of Redcoats who came marching down in front of our barracks and held their drill there. My men were leaning out the windows and spoofing them when I came in and ordered them out of sight. The Sergeant of the squad came to see me with his complaint and I apologized for the men. He was a fine old soldier and knew his job, so he accepted my apologies and left. We learned later that the men wanted to break ranks and beat up some of our fellows that night, but the Sergeant ordered them to behave on penalty of guard house.

We had no peace when out of barracks, for now there were six companies of the British in the town, and every inn, tavern, theater, cock fight, or billiard room was a rendezvous for them, as for us. Ladies on the street were amazed by their rude remarks, and we were finally asked to patrol the sidewalks in front of the shops where their shopping was done. This naturally led to clashes and a few broken heads. My men had been admonished to keep quiet and ignore the British soldiers, unless the latter were creating a disturbance or addressing women shoppers. We made some arrests the first day. We had ten on the second and on the third, a body of Redcoats came down ready to take our own patrol district. I had expected this and saw them leave their barracks. I then went over to the Colonial quarters and ordered a squad of twenty men with both Sergeants and Lieutenants to go to the district and support our patrol. They left on the double quick and arrived as soon as the British. Our men on patrol were keen for a fracas, and were getting ready for it when our squad arrived. They were disappointed to have to forego a fight they had been itching for and begged our Lieutenant to let them fight it out themselves. Of course, we could not have that and so all passed off as though both squads were merely exercising.

Our Redcoat prisoners, seventeen, were released after I had given them a stiff talk on street behavior, and reminded them that they were guests in the city and must conduct themselves of such. One prisoner piped up:

"Guests? Hell, we're the owners. Yer only Colonists."

I gave that fellow a lecture on Colonists, and I fancy he never forgot it. The average British soldier of that time was arrogant and far less acquainted with good manners. We had no more trouble, and for a month we were unmolested in our drills. I made the mistake, however, of looking on this as permanent.

A man came to see me who said his wife had been assaulted and raped by a British soldier when she had gone to see her mother in the evening. On her way home, she had been forcibly taken from the sidewalk to a nearby clump of shrubbery and there knocked down and her clothing torn from her, and the outrage committed. He had gone to the Mayor, but got no satisfaction; then to a Judge, who said he must produce witnesses. I told him he was now in the right place and I would take the matter up with my General, and see if he would call on the Mayor about it. All this, I put in a report and sent to the General. To my surprise, he merely laughed and said:

"Boys will be boys."

I had no idea that a man would feel no shame at such a thing, and this was my crowning disillusionment with Army life.

I had been with rough, rude boys in many a tavern, but no decent woman had I ever known them to insult, much less approach.

"We must be very kind to women, especially those who have no escort." This I had taught my men. Here was a commanding officer who only thought the horrid incident amusing. I went back to the husband of this victim, and apologized for my own General. He was then ready to fight. He said:

"Colonel Washington, I won't rest until I have had revenge on that dog. I shall take the matter in my own hands."

The next day, he went to the British barracks where the men were, and under pretense of selling a dog, was able to pick out the man as his wife had described him. He made a pretense of offering the dog and, when the soldier turned to him, he drew a dagger and slashed the soldier in the face, cutting his chin open. He then threw down the dog, and stood off the men who rushed at him. He told them he was there to avenge the rape of his wife. This stopped the crowd, and the wounded soldier cried out,

"I didn't touch her. The slut tried to rape me."

At that, the husband threw himself upon the soldier and they went down in a flash, where on the floor the husband beat the soldier to a pulp. Then, he marched out and came over to me. I was horrified, and also sympathetic, but I feared for the man and told him so. He was poor and, also a foreigner. I asked him to go at once to his priest and lay the matter before him. In the end, the case got into the papers. The citizens raised a purse for the man, and the judge bound him over to keep the peace. The soldier was sent to guard house for six months. The woman was ill, and lost the child she was carrying.

This incident became a public scandal, and no woman felt safe on the streets unaccompanied. We, in our barracks, saw the British soldiers keeping watch on us, and so we were careful to pay more than our usual attention to our conduct in public. All this to say that the citizens of New York had enough of the

Home treatment through the forcing of British troops on them to support. Later, it bore strange fruit.

※

ORDERED TO BOSTON

DICTATED NOVEMBER 5, 1944

THIS LONG (PERHAPS TOO LONG) account of my two years' experience with the New York Militia is set down to give you a picture of the contempt the British soldier had for the native troops, and how the people bore the cost of those troublemaking Redcoats, who performed no service whatsoever to the Colony and were a constant source of trouble.

My men were loyal to the King, and had no idea of making him a subject of criticism for the conduct and attitude of his army toward them. When we had settled down to a sort of truce, the next thing that arose was a request for our barracks to house the British troops. This was a long, two-story frame building on the Battery that had once been a warehouse, but its conversion into barracks had been made to conform to military needs some years previous. We, however, had the good fortune to be given a long, two-story stone building a mile northward that would be a far more comfortable place, and away from the continual sight and sound of the British. True, we loved our old home and the handy drill and parade ground of the Battery, but I found an excellent location but half a mile north of our new barracks, and so in the end we were to a man well content. Your City Hall now stands on the site of that old building and we drilled in a field now occupied by the buildings north of it about half a mile and near the East River.

We were a merry lot on moving day, and our songs and laughter made it clear to the watching British that we were happy to leave. My own quarters were better located, as my sitting room was on a corner, and gave me a view in two directions, so that

I could better observe the men. Soldiers are like children and always a watchful eye must be kept, for their idle hours are apt to be filled with harmless mischief.

We were soon settled and at home in the new barracks. All was quiet when one day, a week later, I had a call from a farmer asking remuneration for the apples my men had stolen from his orchard. I was, of course, glad to settle for them at his own price, for I as well as the men suffered from the lack of fruit and vegetables in our diet. I had asked the General for more variety, including fruit or vegetables, and he consented to add them, but only when we had used up our present supplies and new ones were ordered. I saw no hope of relief from scurvy for three months in that case and told the men to save some of their pay to buy fruit and garden crops, such as cabbage and turnip, and drink less whiskey. This the older men did, but the younger men were not so wise.

🌸

WE HAD TWO MONTHS of peace when we were notified by our General that he had a request from the Governor of Massachusetts to send a regiment of Militia to Boston at once to reinforce their own troops, who were only two thousand strong. Trouble had broken out between the British soldiers, forced on the Colony, and the citizens of Lexington. We were en route for Boston in twenty-four hours, but we could only procure three stage coaches and five wagons for arms and luggage. We packed ourselves eleven in each coach, the rest clinging to the top of the luggage vans. This was too much for the horses, and for us. We began to drop out and march afoot in relays, so that we managed to make the journey in five days.

Arriving in Boston, we found the town in a state of the most intense excitement over the clash between the British troops then quartered in the vicinity. The population was aroused over the many depravations and impositions of the British, and were arming themselves with shotguns, scythes, and whatever weapon they possessed. They were gathering in groups all around the

State, preparing to expel the King's soldiers from the Colony. We found no official or military officer at the coach station outside the town, so I ordered the men to remain there while I rode into the city to see the Mayor. I had my mare, Chancey, and had given her a hard journey, though I walked fully half the way, but the roads were heavy and tiring.

At the city offices, I found a crowd of frenzied women clamoring for the Mayor to defend their homes. One elderly woman said to me,

"I am a grandmother, but I can shoot. Give us guns and ammunition and let us fight with you."

I asked her name. I never forgot it. It was Jane Leavitt. I hope her descendents have some of her fine spirit in their veins. A girl was heard to say while she stormed at the way they had borne the insults, as well as the expense of the British troops,

"By the Almighty, I can march with any man and shoot as well. Put me in a uniform and let me fight for our rights."

Her name was Kate Lawrence, a pretty lass no more than fifteen, with fair hair and shining blue eyes. I remember those two, though every woman there had come to offer her life and strength to defend her homeland against tyranny.

When I saw the Mayor, I was shocked to see a small and weary old man of seventy. For forty-eight hours he had been at his post but still stood up when I saluted, and offered me a chair with perfect calmness and courtesy.

We were called for the purpose of keeping order in Boston and would be quartered in the barracks of their own Militia, now on active duty outside the city. I asked the necessary questions, and was given to each a practical and fair reply. Our status was to be that of a sort of auxiliary force to maintain order. Our General had not come with us, so I was in complete command and had full responsibility. Mayor Howell, if I remember, was the name of this fine old patriotic official, and I revere him now as I did then. Would to God we had his like in such posts now.

We were well bestowed in Boston's barracks by noon; our patrols were keeping the street quiet, and forbidding any crowds to gather. I instructed my men to always salute a citizen when requesting, politely and with a smile, that they aid in the safety of the city by not loitering or assembling to talk of the grave situation. No citizen resisted, and all gave hearty thanks for the order kept. It went on for two days with no incident to disturb us. Then word came that the farmers were marching from all directions and would converge on Boston. This was too serious to be permitted, so I called on the Mayor and begged him to issue a proclamation asking all the people to remain in their homes, and in no wise add to the confusion; to request the taverns and shops to close at 6 o'clock in the evening and not open until noon, and also to beg those men arriving in the city to come to the City Hall and there arrangements would be made, as far as possible, to care for them. When this was issued and posted in windows and on boardings, the people at once obeyed, and there was no single instance of anyone ignoring the requests of the Mayor. By nightfall, the city was quiet and our patrol and the watchmen met no loungers on the streets. Such a thing was a tribute both to the Mayor and the fine citizenry. Even the children went quietly to and from school and were not seen on the streets again.

By the next day, many men were pouring in to Boston from the nearby towns, villages, and farms. Arrangements had been made by a committee, appointed by the Mayor, to list the houses where the incoming patriots could be billeted. It seemed almost incredible the way in which the strangers were at once taken into shelter, and given food and attention. The food was now the critical question. How to get supplies to feed the incoming men?

The Mayor called upon all those who knew the surrounding farmers to ride out to their districts and contract for any available livestock, eggs, and other produce. The millers were asked to grind flour up to full capacity. The butchers were organized to care for the livestock driven in, and the tanners to take over the hides. No such thing as a refusal to cooperate was heard. All worked at whatever task was given them. In three days, every warehouse was full and requisitions were made for space in barns and even attics and cellars in private homes.

Women met in churches and made shoulder straps, leggings, and white cockades. All cloth was purchased and wool was taken over by the Colony at market price. Massachusetts set a pattern, never before seen in the world, of unity and work for a common cause that has never been equaled in all history.

The housewives searched their homes for linen to tear into bandages, and scraped for lint. This work they did day and night, and brought each her supply to the town's hospital, where soon these offerings overflowed the place, and the Mayor asked the women to keep further supplies until called upon. The children, boys and girls alike, were enrolled and carried messages, as well as helping to scrape lint and roll bandages.

All this, I saw with my own eyes. There was no undue excitement, simply the quiet determination of each one to add his or her mite to the common cause. My heart would swell as I watched it all, and I prayed that these people should never know defeat. My men, also, were deeply impressed. They loved these Yankees and were happy to be among them, doing what they could to keep everything moving in orderly fashion and with as little apparent effort as need be.

❧

I NOW COME TO THE terrible debacle that was known as the Battle of Bunker Hill. I was not present, and I have only the facts as they came to me secondhand. We were all seated in our quarters at 10 o'clock on the night in June, when word came of the defeat at Breed's Hill, now called the Battle of Bunker Hill. I went at once to our General, who had only recently come to Boston and taken over the command. I asked the General what he had heard, and he only grinned and said,

"These Yankees got their belly full."

I was too disgusted to reply, and merely asked if he had any orders; upon which he said in a very loud voice,

"Yes, by God, I have, Colonel Washington. You are a traitor and a bad influence in the Militia. I hope you are not remaining in the service!"

I replied with, I dare say, equal heat,

"I am an American, loyal to my Country, and to my fellow Countrymen. My resignation will be in your hands tonight."

With that I left, went to my quarters, wrote my resignation and sent it by my orderly to the General. Needless to say, he accepted it, and I was packed and out of my quarters within the hour. I was too furious to sleep and, after engaging a room at the nearest tavern, I walked the streets until dawn. Throwing myself on the bed, I slept an hour then rose, and went to see the Mayor. I found him up and at his desk. I spoke of my resignation and my desire to aid the cause of Massachusetts, and also gave him the story of my military career. He said, in a shaking voice,

"Colonel Washington, you can never know the love our people have for you and your soldiers. They have been, I know, the reflection of their commanding officer in their considerate and sympathetic attitude since the moment of their arrival in our midst."

This was good to hear, and I then asked where I could enlist in the Army and who was the recruiting officer who might be inclined to consider my application. He referred me to the officer then stationed at Concord. The next day, I rode to Concord, and was given a very cool reception by the young Lieutenant in charge. I was not inclined to deal with him, and asked for his General. That, he seemed to think an impertinence, and evaded an answer. I laid my card on the desk and left. Apparently, the card impressed him, for his orderly came running out just as I was mounting Chancey and asked if I would come back. I thanked him, but declined. I rode a little way and then returned, my anger having cooled a bit. I went in and saw the Lieutenant, red in the face, giving the orderly a tongue lashing for I caught his words "You didn't give him my message or he would have come back" with a lot of bad language thrown in.

My presence put an end to the vituperation, and he apologized to me. He said he had not known who I was, and had orders to give the General's whereabouts to no one, but I would naturally be an exception.

I found General Craddock a very cold and distant man with a military bearing, but with very little of the customary manner of a commanding officer. He was querulous and irritable and his voice thin, but harsh. I gave him my credentials, and he said, quite brusquely,

"Why don't you stay with your own outfit?"

I then told him of my previous evening's experience and he laughingly said,

"So, you are just out of service and want a command."

I explained that I had no need of one, as I was a man of independent means. He calmed down then, and asked why I was looking for trouble. I assured him I was simply hoping to aid in what I believed to be the cause of all Americans. This he looked surprised at, and was thereafter a little more amiable in his attitude. It ended in my going over to his quarters as his guest to breakfast, for neither of us had eaten that morning, and it was now 10 o'clock.

During the meal, we talked over the situation in Massachusetts and came to an understanding. Afterward, I learned to respect and like this thorny, but skilled soldier.

❀

A Brigadier General

Dictated November 6, 1944

IT WAS NOT VERY LONG after this that I received a letter from General Craddock, asking me to dinner. I accepted, and found with him the Commander-in-Chief of all Massachusetts troops. This gentleman, General Seymore, came of a long line of British Army men and was steeped in all the traditions of that institution. Personally, he was charming, and we hit if off immediately. All went as merrily as possible until the port was on the table, when General Craddock declined to drink to the health of the King. General Seymore took umbrage at that and left, after drinking to his sovereign. I had not lifted my glass, and so knew I was out of favor with the Commander-in-Chief.

When Seymore had departed, Craddock was ready to make of me a confidante and opened his heart in a long tirade against the Crown, and its personal extravagance and indifference to its subject's well being, especially those of the American Colonies. Naturally, I was able to sympathize with his views, and from that moment he seemed to feel a warmth toward me that was quite a tribute to our mutual understanding. All the rest of the evening, he labored the subject and when we parted, he said,

"Colonel Washington, you are my very good and valued friend. I shall look to you when I come to organize the Army in a few days."

This, of course, was all I could desire and I responded heartily, and expressed my sincere feeling at his proffered friendship.

Two weeks later, I received a commission as Brigadier General. This commission was a surprise as I expected no advance in rank, as I was a very skilled trainer of troops rather than a strategist. However, I determined to act up to my new rank and study as much as possible to gain the proper outlook and knowledge that was necessary.

Only one thing troubled me. I missed my old regiment, and the officers and men I had been training for two years. I gave a dinner to the officers. Of course, the Major who was promoted to my Colonel was included, and we were together in a tavern private room from 9:00 p.m. until dawn of the next morning. I asked my successor to read to the men, when in barracks, a letter of farewell I had written. This he did, and in a note to me, he was most affectionate himself and said the men, without exception, were deeply saddened at losing me. This gave me some comfort, but I missed them and our work together.

ONE DAY, AS I WAS riding out in the country, I came upon a couple of men who were strolling along the road. When I pulled up to greet them, one of them came up and said,

"Colonel, I can't stand it now. I'm going to resign. Can't I get back under you?"

I told him what the situation was. Both men then declared they were going to enlist, and would I be so kind as to get them where they could be under my command. When I told them of my new rank and that I could not train them now, they were somewhat dashed, but still wished to come where I could take an interest in them. I valued this so highly, and was so relieved to know of their desire to be with me that I made a vow to have them in my personal entourage as orderlies.

This I was able to do. Their names were John Collins and Terrence Keating. The latter was always Terry, and the former Jack to me. They were for the next four years my almost constant companions, and were never at any time anything but my willing and loyal friends. I received them in the Executive Mansion when President, and had them as my dear and honored guests to dine. They outlived me, and here are still with me in my Spirit life.

Terry and Jack. They can never know the part they played in sustaining me in the darkest days of my life.

❀

IN A MONTH, LACKING a few days, I was on my way to survey the territory north of Boston. Already I had studied maps and tried to locate all towns, villages, and even farms in the County. I also had made a large map of all water courses and lakes, springs, and brooks. When General Craddock sent me, he said in parting,

"Keep your eye peeled for the supplies, and get some estimate of what the farmers have in reserve. Also, do all you can to make them understand that we are at war. Do not let them help the enemy with food. We need all we can get."

With Chancey under me and my pack horse along with

my luggage and weapons, I made every day count. I was really enjoying this new side of the work, and loved to make my reports as factual and exact as possible each night. Usually, I found an inn to stop at, but often one was not available and I would put up at some farm house. There, I would fraternize with the family, and I gained much valuable information as to the supplies, roadways, waterways, mills, the drinking springs, and clear waters fit for bathing. A soldier never bathes unless he knows what the water contains, so I was glad to get all the information possible as to the rivers, ponds, and lakes to be found.

On one occasion, a farmer asked me why I wished to know so much about the water to be found. I explained, and he then came out with this remark,

"My God! Do soldiers bathe? I thought they were crusted, and were not cleaned except with curry combs."

I assured him that one of the fundamental rules of a soldier's life is to keep clean. Also, to be sure his socks are washed every twenty-four hours. This becomes impossible during war, of course, but bathing was a means of preventing lice.

Then, the farmer proceeded to indite a letter to his wife, absent on a visit, in which he said,

"My dear, I shall probably enlist, for I find that soldiers are not the dirty dogs I thought but are made, under orders, to wash themselves and keep as clean as possible."

He never showed up in my command, so I do not know whether his wife was to blame for his lack of patriotic fervor or not.

☙❧

ON MY RETURN TO Boston, I was happy to have my report commended by General Craddock, and to learn that I had overlooked nothing. He did say, by way of helping me in my new office,

"You will find use for a plan to make your reports of your journeys of inspection briefer by eliminating all but the essentials."

I saw that I had overshot the mark. This, of course, was better than giving less information than was required.

My life now became a constant tour of inspection. I soon learned to make my reports compact, and yet comprehensive. Several counties were inspected and their resources tabulated.

Also, I was able now and then to take my command and train the men myself. I made a point of their physical condition and had them, in three weeks, in marching trim. They were mostly farmer lads who were strong and accustomed to hard labor, but with a poor sense of rhythm and little knowledge of firearms. Massachusetts was not like Virginia, filled with wild animals, and their shooting was mostly with rifles, and for winged game. Target practice was not especially successful, so I made a point of going to the ranges myself. I often took a hand in the work, and was able to help the men get into the work with enthusiasm, which brought good results.

My Colonel, Captains, and Junior Officers were not very expert in their work either, and it was clear that they would also need help. I asked the Colonel if he would like to spend three evenings a week as my dinner guest, when I might be able to aid him in some ways. He was too proud to accept, and later was made the victim of his ignorance to such an extent that he was hated by his Juniors and ridiculed by his men when the time came to put us all to the test.

The Juniors and Captains were delighted to come and dine, and make an evening of the discussion of the various parts of our duty. All in all, I managed to have a Brigade of fine troops, well-officered, and in good fighting trim at the end of two months' diligent and constant work.

All was in readiness for action. My Quartermaster was an old Militiaman and as experienced as I in Indian campaigning. He was a tower of strength and made my life much easier by his wise administration of his department. I was also lucky in the Sergeants who were old seasoned campaigners in the Colony. Our title was the 12th Foot.

WE WERE IN BARRACKS in the town of Cambridge when the order came to march to the aid of the troops under fire at the junction of the two rivers that converged near the highway leading out of the city, winding northward toward Cambridge.

I was ready, and so were the troops. Our supply wagons were on the road in an hour, loaded for a two weeks' campaign. We had no difficulty in locating our position after a three hours' march in the afternoon.

Well, we arrived just at sundown and bivouacked in some fields that had been cleared of their crops. All was in order and the men cooked their supper, rolled into their blankets, for the night was cool, and were soon asleep. I was not able to sleep, though Jack and Terry were snoring outside my tent in their blankets.

I took a stroll about the fields and down the road, and watched the distant stars as they seemed to be keeping watch and ward over the sleeping children of men. My thoughts, as ever, flew to Martha and Charles and home. What if I should fall on the morrow? They would grieve and feel bereft. I knew my good height, six feet seven, was always a target and I must ever be prepared for the final exit.

No man who is in combat takes thought of his life. It is in the moments when all is quiet, and he has leisure to think of those things which are the deepest in his heart and mind, that he communes with his soul. I came to a fallen tree and, as I had been walking for an hour, I sat down to rest before returning to my tent. As I sat there, silently pondering the situation, my astral self again appeared before me. This time, he was in full uniform and carried his gun on his shoulder like a private. I stared in silence and waited. Soon, the figure moved away, and pointing to the sleeping men said, in a low but clear tone,

"I shall be there on the field and you will be the life and spirit of your troops. Fear not. You are protected, and no harm can come to you. I am always ready to protect you, and so are other Souls long passed to a higher sphere. Be bold, and never think of danger. You have in the past conquered fear, and now your right to safe conduct is assured until your mission in life is finished."

I was too stunned to speak, but I knelt and made an obeisance. Then, the figure spoke again,

"George Washington, we—you and I, are one and the same. I speak as you when I say we are not meant to be independent. You will free the people of this Country, and you will be its first ruler. Give all your heart and mind to this thought, and you cannot fail."

Then he came close and I saw him no longer, for he seemed to merge into my own body.

All this I set down to be read by as skeptical and unspiritual a generation as ever the sun shone on. The Masons and the Spiritualists, the Catholics and the Theosophists, are the only ones who have the knowledge of the Astral double and understand the laws of man's being in its different manifestations in the various degrees of his consciousness, as he passes through the bands of ether surrounding this planet.

✸

WE WERE UP BEFORE dawn. I had returned to my tent and slept three hours by then. All was done quietly, and my orderlies reported no confusion or hitch in our planned arrangements. My part was now to await orders from the field of action and make ready to take our part, as directed. We were at ease, but ready to move when a rider came up with an order to go east to the town nearby, and take up our position on its south side near the river. No other orders or explanations were given. In three hours, we had done this and waited for further orders. We were there until nightfall and had a hasty meal at 7 o'clock. When the men were preparing again to sleep, an orderly rode up and declared I was not in the right position. I was too far east, and must now change and go nearer to Cambridge.

Of course, in half an hour, we were on the march, a detour of three miles. My orders were to keep near the river and be ready to meet the enemy if he tried to cross over to our side. This gave me a chance to form my lines for offense, and I made a small hill vantage point. I saw the British on the road leading toward us along our side of the river and came to the conclusion they would try to cross over on the other side by way of the bridge at Cambridge.

In twenty minutes this was evident, so I deployed a detachment under a Captain with orders to hold the bridge at our side, and I would get in between their lines and force them back. He had to hold his fire until I gave him orders.

This seemed to be a good idea, and we made a feint to attract their attention when they were nearing the bridge. As they began to turn on us, a company got in behind their front line and separated them. We then drove forward, and had them caught between our three sections. We managed to hold on until nightfall, and then I asked for help to make the action complete.

No help came, so in the morning I had no reason to keep firing and withdrew men in good order, but no prisoners were taken. A few wounded British were taken, not more than twenty. These we sent into our own field hospital, and held our other lines to wait for the British to show their intentions.

In an hour after daylight, they were ready to move against us. I foresaw we were the ones now to be squeezed, and I withdrew all troops and left the bridge undefended. This was a great disappointment, and I was disgusted that no help ever came in response to my request. I then gave orders to retreat to Cambridge and be ready to defend the town. Here, I again distributed the troops about in three sections, in case the British should cross the river. Should they do so, I could surround them and prevent a retreat. That happened, and I was glad to find we had, with only four dead and thirty wounded, taken seventy-five prisoners and found thirty-seven dead Redcoats. I reported this to the commanding General, who was then in Boston, and fifteen miles away. No reply was received, and I began to wonder what was the reason, when General Craddock himself rode up to my tent that night about ten o'clock and said,

"My dear Washington, you have spoiled all my plans. I was ready to take Cambridge myself, and now you have stolen a march on me."

I explained my previous plan, and as no response was made for help, I had to save my men in this way. He smiled, and said,

"No apologies are needed. You have done well, and I admire your resourcefulness. Your men have also been splendid. Please tell them I am proud of their fine conduct in this their first taste of action."

Well, it was all over the camp that we had stolen the prize and so, of course, even the wounded were happy. We had to make our way now to the rear of the town, where we camped for the next three weeks. All is fine in action, but the devil gets into idle soldiers, and my life was one long series of apologies to the citizens of Cambridge and the farmers nearby for the lawless way my men were acting. I paid all demands made for fruit or poultry stolen, and made such amends as I could for their rowdy conduct in taverns and on the streets of the sleepy old town. At last, we were ordered to march back to Boston to our barracks. This was good news, and we were promptly on our way in two hours. This was my first experience as a strategist, and I wondered if I could be trusted to go on with such terrible responsibility.

❀

WE WERE FIVE WEEKS in Cambridge, and I fear the inhabitants were none too happy to have our company. Our ways were not theirs, and our morals were far from the pattern they set themselves. One day, we had a preacher come and invite the men to prayer. Only ten men, myself included, responded. All the rest were looking for fun, or trouble, in town. A party of officers were making up a crowd to go to Boston to see a favorite actor in *Hamlet*, and the rest of them were lazily making the most of the Sabbath to sleep, play cards, or write home.

The men, as usual, were looking for such adventure as the inns afforded, or were in canoes on the river, or sweet-hearting in the town. The poor preacher was too disgusted to make more than a brief address, and departed as soon as possible from this godless camp. I could have warned him that soldiers in attendance at religious services were rare, but I thought he had better note that for himself.

We had no idea of what the enemy's plans were, and so kept constant watch for fear of being surprised by a flanking movement. We found, after a month, that this was indeed the intention, and so we decided to move further west in case they should attack. I held a meeting of my officers and asked them to be on their guard against sudden attack, and keep the sentries as far out as possible with but two hours duty each so that all would have their proper quota of rest.

We were now ready, with our wounded safe in Boston and the prisoners all in the military prison there, so that we could break camp in an hour and be ready for action, or to move. Our wagons were drawn up in a ring, which formed a corral for the horses. Chancey and my pack horse I kept always near me, and so I was never in doubt as to their condition. Chancey was nervous and I feared for her when it should come to a real battle. She was never in the least inclined to make a dash away from me, but I feared the gunfire would terrify her. My other horse had a more phlegmatic disposition and I was sure would make no trouble. We had the joy of their companionship in the meantime. My little orderly, Terry, was so devoted to them and loved to make them his chief care. This made me, of course, very content, as I had always been most assiduous in my own personal care of them. Chancey was my own best friend when away from home, and I dreaded anything that might make it necessary to part with her, even for a time.

All this I set down because it was to me a most important, and deeply personal matter and these conversations are meant to be about the personal recollections of my life.

The break came on a morning that was cool and frosty. We were all busy with breakfast, cleaning ourselves for the day, putting the tents in order and shaving our faces. When a sentry reported a body of British were crossing the river south of us and cutting us off from our line to Boston, I was sure we were in for a bad time.

All was confusion for ten minutes, and then we were ready to march out to meet them, along the river road to the south. We got only four or five miles when we had a volley strike us from a clump of woods at our left. We charged into the thicket, and soon it was a hand-to-hand affair. No use to recount the details, for they have already been told in the histories of the battle that the books always spoke of by a name never spoken of in my presence. I always spoke of it as the Sortie at the River. One man was injured, and two taken prisoners. We had no way of knowing what damage we caused the British, but we found three dead and two wounded. We took five prisoners. The enemy retreated in the direction of Cambridge, and we were cut off from our supplies. The enemy could now get possession of them.

All in all, it was a bad business. I tried to think out the way I should have made the attack, but never have I seen the way I could have saved our supplies. The enemy had twice the troops, and they were all old campaigners. Ours were really raw recruits, only two months in service. We had no idea who was to blame or what we called this defeat. We only knew we were surprised and that rankled. I could only think that my own fault was in never making a move, but waiting to be attacked. Since then, I have seen too much to believe I was wrong in simply holding my ground, and waiting to let the enemy take the initiative. All in all, there was no significance in this little surprise, for we won the road to Boston and lost only three men to them.

We shall not take up the reader's time to go over these small engagements, but try to show what my part was in the Revolution as I see it, and what sort of experience I got from these events.

Furlough

Dictated November 8, 1944

In this space, I shall speak of a small incident that at the time persuaded me to make a new appraisal of myself.

When we were sent out to meet the British and were considered an Army of the Colonies, I was only a raw recruit in this sort of warfare. As a strategist, I was even more inexperienced than my Sergeants. My initial success seemed to me to be pure accident, and I decided to go to General Craddock and ask him if he would let me see him in order to gain a greater understanding of the strategy he intended to employ, so that I might the better do my part to support it.

I wrote him to this effect, and he came to see me with a very dry, cryptic smile on his rather mild, but reserved countenance. I saw him in my own quarters, where I had made preparations for a little supper with a bottle of wine, and with Jack serving. When he arrived, he said, coldly,

"What's all this? I am a teetotaler."

This surprised me, as he had drunk wine at his own table when the Seymore incident occurred. However, I answered with "Take away the wine," which Jack did at once. We had no private conversation until we were alone. Then, he opened up and spoke his mind as to all he had planned. I was amazed at the daring of it, and said so. He was annoyed at my remark and came out with,

"If you are too timid to carry out this idea, I'll have to make other plans."

Of course, I assured him that I was not thinking of my part in his strategy, but of the whole picture. Also, I expressed my admiration for the boldness and courage that he had demonstrated in the whole scheme.

This mollified him somewhat, and he proceeded to turn the tables and ask me what I had been working on in my mind.

Naturally, I could only say what was true, that I was hesitant to organize any plan of action since my experience as a strategist was practically nothing. He smiled and said, to my surprise,

"I never before heard a man who was honest enough to confess his limitations. It gives me a feeling of confidence that you have a fine military conscience."

My own sense of inferiority he was unaware of, and I simply told him I could not assume anything I did not possess. He was delighted to find a pupil who was open minded and not too stupid to make intelligent use of his instruction. We talked until midnight and when he left, he said in a very warm tone,

"My dear Washington, I am confident that we can accomplish much together."

So, I was in the mood to give my loyal support to any plan that General Craddock suggested. Unfortunately, there were so many obstacles to be considered, such as the raw state of the conscripts with the barest attempt to train them, that he was never able to carry out his great and sound strategy because his troops and officers were unable to understand, much less execute it. This accounts for many of the early defeats and constant retreats by the Continentals, and the assurance by General Howe to the Home Office that there was nothing to be feared from the Colonials.

I say this here, for the reason that blame was placed on General Craddock when it was not he who failed, but he had nothing to work with that could withstand attack. Also, Craddock was hampered by the most harassing circumstances, such as the lack of ammunition and adequate food. An army does indeed "travel on its belly," and ours was empty most of the time.

All this I set down because in General Craddock, we had a wise and far-sighted soldier who knew how to win but, as yet, had no tools to work with. "Give the devil his due" is an old aphorism. Giving a military commander his due is rare.

When I went to see the General near Boston, where he was making his headquarters, he told me we must wait until spring to make any further move to oust the British. In the meantime, I was to see that my command was trained in gunnery, hand-to-hand fighting, and marching. Their health was poor, owing to scurvy. I begged him to give us some fruit and vegetables. This he did, and soon I had the men in excellent trim and able to march twenty miles a day, with but two hours rest. All that I could teach them of gunnery and close fighting, I did, and my officers also.

One man, a Captain Lemont, told me I had made him over from a very delicate-chested, semi-invalid to a robust fellow able to stand up to anything the British had to offer after that winter's work. I was happy to hear such testimony, and to know I had spent the time profitably. My own condition was poor. I was not getting the exercise or the hours in the open to which I had always been accustomed, and so I began to lose both weight and color. I asked for a two months' furlough in which to go home and see my family, and in my old environment see if I could regain my customary robust health. This was granted, and off I went on Chancey, but leaving behind my pack horse.

❀

A BRIEF VISIT HOME

NOW I WAS HAPPY. To be with my family once more, to see and hear all that there was to see and learn of what had transpired in my absence, to look upon their beloved faces and behold the scenes I had come to adore. My own Virginia was enough to put new life in me, and this it did.

By the time I reached Philadelphia, where I stopped to see Franklin, I began to feel a resurgence of vitality and strength. Franklin looked as if he, too needed a change, and I persuaded him to come to Alexandria and visit us while I was at home. We talked over the whole situation, and that wise and farsighted man, as if in a spirit of prophecy, said,

"It is to be a long and hard, bitter fight, but we shall win."

This gave me a feeling that I would perhaps not come again to my home, and I rode on my way, sad and depressed.

I found Martha quite changed. The year had been a

difficult one to bear, not only because of my absence, but because the children had now come to feel that they could be in control of their lives and had rather gotten out of hand. Frederick was a big chap. He had his father's rather heavy frame, but not a very great athlete. This made him heavier than he should have been at that age, and his mother was alarmed to see him becoming so fat. When I arrived, I was shocked to see his waistline and his jowls. So I at once put him through a hard course of training, just as if he had been a rookie. He was ever after grateful for my harshness, which seemed a bit cruel at the time.

Mary had been in great demand as a wife. Her fiancé was a fine young planter who owned an estate of sixty acres of productive land, with a pleasant house and several farm buildings. Young Bolton was a fine chap in character and the darling of most of the mothers in the vicinity. Mary, however, was his love, and we hoped all might be well with her future as Henry Bolton's wife.

As for Martha, she was the same strong and devoted woman, and a sweet and adorable lover. I made her two promises. One, that I would try to come home in six months for a furlough. The other, if this were not possible, that she should come to me for a visit of at least a month. Mary was to be married the following spring, and Frederick would be in college. She could leave home easily, as Charles would be able to oversee things as usual.

Charles, I found, was growing a bit gray now, and furrows on his face showed him careworn. I reproached myself for all the added strain I had placed upon him. He was too generous to even admit that it was a strain. We had many hours together, and they are a sacred memory. He never spoke of himself, but I seemed to know he was slipping out of life. This was such an agonizing thought as to make it insupportable. Life, without Charles and his loyal and brotherly affection, his faith and his power to inspire me, seemed to be worth far less and to make a barren prospect. He had so entered into all I knew, felt, or thought that I was, for the time being, too sad to even hide my fears.

The most happy time of my furlough was when, with my brother Charles, we rode over the countryside in the frosty winter air, and beheld the old familiar scenes of my youth. At Mount Vernon I stayed for two days, and made it a lone and secret communion with all my cherished past. No words can tell what emotions were constantly aroused by the memories of my dear parents and the days of boyhood, youth, and manhood, when Mount Vernon was the soul and center of all my days and my dreams. God forbid that I should ever come to lose those memories!

My parents and my brother are here in the world of Spirit, and we all are the same in our feeling that Mount Vernon is indeed the shrine where we can worship the Force of Life, and in that shelter live again the happiest of our memories.

I came away with Martha beside me in our carriage while Frederick, on his horse, led Chancey. The parting was not easy, but Martha was brave and smiled even through tears, which at the last moment came. We did not know that it would be two years before we next met.

❀

ARRIVING AT THE BARRACKS in Boston, I saw a great change in the attitude of the Colonel, who had been in full charge during my absence. This was not so surprising, in view of all he was obliged to shoulder. I found two of my best Sergeants had resigned, and three of my Lieutenants, also. Their places were filled by privates with little experience, and no special aptitude. My chagrin was only equaled by my irritation that such a situation should have arisen during my absence. The Colonel was, I learned, the cause of these defections because of his hard treatment of the men. I was, at first, inclined to give the Colonel a blasting, but decided that this might in the end make a bad matter worse. I gave no hint of my feelings when I invited the Colonel to dine with me in my quarters, and he seemed pleased at this attention.

All that we were able to get done in the situation was to make a new rule that a Sergeant must have had four years experience as a private or a Corporal before being given the commission; the Lieutenants to have had six years in the Militia. All this did not help my men, and I was only too sad when one chap said to Jack, my orderly,

"The Brigade went to hell when General Washington left."

Only two months, and the morale was gone. I set about to try and make the men take an interest in their work. I gave them a private talk, one squad after another. I also made it a business to personally attend drill, and to aid the new Sergeants and Lieutenants in such ways as were possible. In a month, I had confidence in the Brigade, and was not afraid to test them in the field.

Later, we got orders in April to go to the mouth of the main stream leading from Boston out into Suffolk County. This we did, only to find we were not expected, and no provision had been made for a camp there. The farmers were resentful of our presence, and I had a difficult time persuading them to even lease, for a nominal sum, a few acres of land where crops were still unsown. This was not a very good place, but we had to make the best of it. The water we drank gave the men diarrhea, and we were not able to make any progress in the matter of marching or anything, but trying to lift this disease off by means of medicine and boiling the water we drank. All of which gave me plenty of worry.

When, after six weeks, I was able to give the men marches of six miles a day, I saw a little light. We had been in camp in Suffolk six weeks when an order came to break camp and march eastward to a little town in the heart of the enemy's territory. The British had held this part of Suffolk for more than a year, and were well entrenched and able to hold out there indefinitely.

However, I gave orders that we would split into two sections and each go at them simultaneously, one on their right flank and one south of them. This would perhaps send them back into a morass of swampland, and make their movements difficult.

We tried this with considerable success, and we got to the point of making a clean sweep when I received orders to withdraw my command and march back to Boston. Why, I never learned. It was a loss of motion and of three men taken prisoners, two killed, and four wounded. We took twenty prisoners, and picked up twenty-seven wounded, and saw thirty-two killed.

My irritation at this interference at the moment when complete victory was in sight gave me the impulse to take the first opportunity to expostulate when I learned that General Craddock was removed from his Post of Commander-in-Chief, and his successor, General Leighton, had taken over full command. My own emotions were simply the anger at such a display of amateurish interference with a settled plan, already succeeding in action.

Later, I learned that the trouble was in the lack of judgment of the men of the Continental Congress, who seemed to be of the opinion that General Craddock was not going fast enough, and they chose this inopportune moment to replace him with an untried officer whose only recommendation was his good looks and flair for addressing letters to the Congress.

General Leighton's experience had been as a Colonel in the New York Militia in time of peace. He had no experience whatsoever in the field, and was given his Brigade because there were no experienced men to command it.

In justice to General Craddock I tell this, and not to discredit Leighton, though his incompetence was so evident that he also was replaced in four months, and was retired to private life after a disastrous and needless sacrifice of men and material in a silly attempt to drive the British into Massachusetts Bay. This was known as "Leighton's Folly" among us at the time, though it appears in the histories as the brave effort of a heroic commander to win the war at one swoop.

My contact with this young amateur was brief. I met him at a dinner, given by himself, to all the officers of my Brigade. It was then easy to perceive that he neither was suited to his position, or even aware of the elements of good conduct on the part of the Head of an Army. He got very drunk, and was most insulting in his remarks to myself. I overlooked them as the babblings of a man in his cups, but later called upon him for an apology. This he made in a flutter of nerves, and I left him with the feeling that his regime would be brief, which indeed it was.

Washington Taking Command of the American Army
Cambridge, Massachusetts, July 3, 1774
Courtesy National Archives

COMMANDER IN CHIEF

DICTATED NOVEMBER 9, 1944

IT WAS ONE OF THE FOULEST of rainy, cold and windy days when I was summoned before the Committee on Military Affairs in Boston.

The end was not what I expected. When the message was handed me calling me to meet with the Committee on Military Affairs at the old Market Hall, I was too dazed by it to understand what was taking place. My anger over the stupidity of General Leighton's ideas and his complete mismanagement of all the campaign details, had made me feel hopeless of ever making any success while under his command. Now I was summoned to appear before this Committee, and God only knew what I would be called upon to face. Well, I dressed and tried to put on a good

front on for the meeting. Anyway, at Market Hall, I found I had
come to the meeting too early, and so strolled about for an hour
before I again went to the meeting place. Arriving there, I was
greeted by the Committee with applause. This rather upset my
calculations. I had expected criticism, and here they were clapping
their hands when I faced them. The whole scene was like a dream
to me. I heard the chairman say,

"General Washington has been the cause of our taking
the initiative, but since he has been ordered to remain in barracks
by his Commander-in-Chief, he has now no further engagements.
We would like to have General Washington explain to us his ideas
and opinions on the present situation."

I simply stared in utter astonishment at this, and was
almost speechless. However, I managed to summon my wits;
and going to the table, I stood at its end facing the chairman and
delivered a brief talk on the present chaotic state of our Army, its
lack of coordination, and of the rudiments of a general plan for the
campaign.

This was, of course, obvious to anyone and needed no
military expertise to make it clear. I then sat down, and listened to
some very stupid and unnecessary speeches by the members of the
Committee who seemed to have no idea of what to say to remedy
matters, but were full of bombastic phrases and a lot of patriotic
balderdash. Suddenly, I heard a man say,

"Why do we go on talking? We called this meeting for a
set purpose and we are wasting time by all this talk. Ask General
Washington if he will take the Post of Commander-in-Chief.
That is what we are here for."

Applause followed. This gave me a sense of suddenly being
made a target for so much responsibility, that I all but choked with
the terror that seized me. When a man had replied by asking me
if I would take over the whole Army and dictate the strategy, I
was again in danger of collapse. Presently, my mind cleared, and I
managed to collect myself.

While I was still seated I saw, as in a vision, myself on
Chancey at the head of a vast body of troops. When it disappeared,

there was silence so impressive that I could only compare it to the great stillness that is said to be the voice of God brooding over human events.

At last, I found the strength to rise to my feet and I moved again to the table. All eyes were upon me, and I sensed what seemed to be a great and imminent crisis in their thoughts. When I opened my mouth to speak, I had no idea what I was going to say. I felt myself to be an automaton, and with no power to resist whatever it was that had me in its control. While I stood looking at the Chairman and before I had spoken a word, I saw again the vision of myself leading the great body of troops in our Continental white cross belts and three cornered hats. I saw the muskets on their shoulders, and I saw a flag that was like no other I had ever seen. It was made of equal stripes of red and white and a square of blue was in the upper left corner, in which was a ring of white stars. This flag was carried by a soldier who stood beside me on my horse, and I seemed to be saluting the flag. At that the vision was gone, and I was there mutely staring into space. I knew, however, that I had looked upon a true picture of what was to come.

My voice was low, and I had to summon all my willpower to formulate my thoughts into consecutive speech. My speech seemed a bit muffled to my ears at first, but it only took a few words for it to clear and become normal. I thanked them for their confidence and their great and, so far, unearned faith in me. I told them that lest some unlucky event should happen unfavorable to my reputation during my Command, let it be known to all present that I do not think myself equal to the Command I was so honored with. Also, I dwelt upon my inexperience as a strategist and my deep desire to serve where I was best suited. I then told them that there had been so far no really good test of the Army or its leaders, though I did not wish to appear critical of what had been done or left undone.

The result of all this was to see their faces fall. They felt I was not going to accept. This made me sure that I was perhaps destined to take over the dreadful responsibility. I told them that

I was eager to do all in my power to bring about a victory over the enemy, but that wars were not won overnight and the prospect now was dark indeed, for Britain could hold out indefinitely while we were poor, with no experience in anything but Indian warfare, and we had no riches to call upon to support a lengthy contest. Still, I knew our cause was just and, if it was their will to name me the leader, I would do all in my power to bring about victory for our side.

No applause greeted me as I sat down. A silence fell that was so impressive that I was almost expecting to see a reversal of the situation and perhaps a capitulation to Britain. Suddenly, the Chairman rose, and said in a loud and vibrant tone,

"General Washington, we thank you for your frankness and your wise and considered opinions as to the situation. We shall, however, ask you to be the leader, and to accept the position of Commander-in-Chief of all our forces in being. We wish also to ask you to formulate your plans as quickly as possible, and give them to us in order that we may be able to assist in carrying them out. Will you be ready with them tomorrow?"

I rose again and, with many qualms, accepted. Then I left, and almost leaped along the streets trying to make every second of time count in the journey to my rooms. It was but half a mile, but it felt as if it was ten times that distance before I reached my quarters.

❀

THE STRATEGY FOR THE AMERICAN REVOLUTION

I ORDERED TERRY TO MAKE some coffee and serve it to me black. I also got into my dressing gown and gave orders that no one was to disturb me. It was now noon, and I had only twenty-four hours in which to formulate a plan of campaign. I got out my maps. I was sure I knew where the enemy was, for I was always in touch with the runners who came in each day to report the whereabouts of the British. Also, I knew the number of the enemy's troops, and where they were. I had a good idea what their intentions were. My calculations had already been made as to transport and their supplies. What I now had to discover was where, when, and how to get the British into a pocket. This, I had long pondered. It was always the way I had seen the enemy defeated. So long as they were free to move, we could not hope to beat them.

My own terror was that I would get myself in a pocket with no way out, and always I had made that my prime consideration in my brief experience so far. When midnight came, I had seen what was for me a simple, but safe plan to push the British toward the coast and press them on that side. Also, to divide them, if possible, and get between them and their base of supplies, which was New York. In any case, to keep harassing them and give them no rest, and to make as much of our limited forces as possible by a sudden, swift attack where least expected, with no set battles for we had no supply of men or weapons or ammunition to make this possible.

I slept until 5 o'clock, then copied my notes, and placed them in order. I also made a careful estimate of the cost of the plan. When I met the Committee, they were all in their seats about the table waiting for me. I was greeted again with a burst of hand-slapping, and the Chairman rose and greeted me warmly. We got to my report at once. I read it, and it seemed to have merit with them. Then, I gave them my theory. Since we were poor, ill-equipped, and with few troops and arms, the whole chance of success must lie in the harassing of the enemy by surprise attacks and retreats, with great mobility of our forces and ready means of transport with a commissary that was well organized to meet these conditions.

The end of my report was greeted by a burst of applause. One man said,

"By thunder, General Washington, you are the first man we have heard from that seems to have an idea as to how to proceed. You have made a report that puts heart into us all."

Of course, I knew that he was merely being gracious, but I sensed that the whole Committee was feeling relieved that someone had at last given them some basic ideas of how to proceed.

Meanwhile, all was movement and life in my old quarters as I had my belongings ready to move to the general headquarters in Market Hall, and was given a suite of three rooms and an office. My orderlies were stowed away in one of the three rooms. I still had a bedroom and reception room. This latter I worked, ate, and received people in, for I preferred it to the larger office as a place in which to confer with the officers or other callers. It was all in order in two days, and I was ready to call a meeting of the Generals, when I had the misfortune to make a misstep on the street, and again sprained my ankle. That right one had never been strong, since I sprained it at Fort Pitt. This so upset me that I felt like canceling my appointment, for I knew the suffering I was in for and the delay it would mean. However, I called the Regimental surgeon at once, and he skillfully put it in splints so that it was almost as easy to walk as before, and I began to feel that I could proceed as planned.

When I met the Generals, they were mostly strangers to me. I had to try to size up their qualities in the first place and, in the second, draw them out so as to discover what was in their minds as to the best way to proceed. All we had to do, the most vocal of them said, was to give the British one damned good thrashing and that would end in their capitulating. I was not of this opinion, and said so. The British are of the bull-dog type who hang on, and never turn tail. This General never again addressed me in the eight years of the war and, when at the finish he was obliged with the others to congratulate me, he said with a rather sneering smile,

"General Washington, I am sorry you did not follow my idea of one big battle."

I replied that we would then have been exterminated as we had neither the arms, ammunition, or the trained Army with which to meet the Hessians and Britain's seasoned Army. He only bowed, and walked away. This man was never successful in any undertaking during the war, and at its end he joined with the British in Canada as their Chief of Militia. I often wondered how they liked him. His conceit was only equaled by his incapacity. He was the son of a very rich old Boston ship-owner, and had never seen action when he was made an officer. His experience was all in the work of drilling infantry and parading with his regiment.

To return to my first meeting with our Generals – I had no very clear idea about any of them. Four were young men, unaccustomed to military service, and only given their rank to get money from their fathers to support the war. Two were seasoned men, and it was to them I addressed myself.

When I laid my ideas before them, they saw my plan clearly and concurred in it. The young ones were silent, not knowing what to say. We had many hours together in the next few days, and I also had several sessions with the Quartermaster General and his staff. It was all clearing in my mind, and I began to see what was needed was to get our men out in the countryside while the weather admitted of it, and give the British trouble wherever we could. I made up some lists for the Quartermaster and, also, for the Ammunition Director. I sold a bill of goods to one Quartermaster myself. This was the crop of cotton that was now waiting on the docks of Baltimore from the County of Westmoreland: my own three bales of cotton, Martha's six bales, and Charles's twenty bales. This is what caused the historians to say I had profiteered in the sale of goods to the Army. Cotton was bringing in six pounds a bale at tidewater and I sold ours for five pounds a bale, taking a good sized loss to aid the war.

So goes the world. It loves to put the word "thief" on anyone who has been the recipient of either honors or rewards from his Country. The jackals are always in the lead, trying to pull down men who cannot defend themselves any longer.

Well, I managed to collect supplies and ammunition sufficient to start action. The Committee on Military Affairs helped manfully to get all possible for us.

A Personal Note of Clarification

In trying to correct the many misstatements that are also contradictory to each other, I daresay I am challenging fate, for no records were carefully kept of my Reports to the Military Affairs Committee and the Congress of Massachusetts and New York.

I wish to say here that the several leaders who commanded troops and led actions against the enemy in more distant regions were provided with support and supplies locally. They had the status of guerrillas, and were never under my command. These fighters were under the leadership of such men as Burr, Von Steuben, Gates, Moultris, Rochambeau, Ethan Allen, and the Southern leaders. The title of Commander-in-Chief given me by the Congress and the historians and biographers is a ridiculous misnomer, in fact. I shall give here only my personal experience in the Revolution and my close associates. The given chronology of the Revolution, as I have heard it read and spoken of, is quite wrong in the main. The dates are sometimes absurd. Our reports were probably destroyed to save political face for obvious reasons. No amount of whitewashing that was indulged in after the British surrender was sufficient to cover the betrayal of me and my troops. The citizens in the New Jersey Legislature were the ones who came forward with the means that made Yorktown possible. New Jersey has never received its due from the historians. I love the very name, Jersey, for its people of those years were on the whole the most humane, generous, and cooperative with their sister Colonies of any of them.

Rows

Dictated November 10, 1944

THE FIRST MOVE I MADE was to gather my forces to make a sortie on the enemy who lay in force north of Cambridge, with a strong arm of their troops extending west a distance of twenty miles, and resting on the suburbs of the town of Lynn.

I was not very keen to come to grips with the British yet, but I knew that unless I had made some sort of effort very quickly, the Committee would interfere and upset my general scheme of the campaign. I marched my forces south of Lynn, and let them rest for twenty-four hours. Then I made an attack that curved their line back to the north and occupied Lynn myself, with the enemy doubled back on Cambridge. All this was but a gesture and had no importance beyond its moral effect on my men and officers, as well as the Committee.

We held our position for two days, with the result that we had no more supplies. I had to ride to Boston and inform the Committee that if this was the way I was to be let down, I saw no chance of ever defeating the British. They seemed unaware of the needs of soldiers and thought they could fend for themselves as to food and made no attempt to furnish us with rations. This, of course, was the height of absurdity, and I made it clear that my report had specifically stated the needs of each man in the field and, also, their feeling of confidence in the arrival of supplies, if morale was to be sustained.

One man, an old-time Indian fighter, said in defense,

"We didn't have all this when we went fighting Indians."

I told him I had fought Indians, and seen my comrades die of starvation on the way back to their Post. The rest of the Committee was not belligerent, but I saw they were a lot so simple and uninformed, tackling something they had no idea of. The result was that I had to withdraw my troops from Lynn and come back to Boston, where at last supplies could be had.

One more item I made a point of in my talk with the Committee. This was the way in which they asked men to risk their lives, with no sense of obligation to them. If they wished to get rid of the British, then they must make sacrifices to do so. If they were only playing with the idea, they should take the field themselves and risk their own lives instead of a generation that had hoped to complete its own Earth life.

This put a bad taste in their mouths, and one man said in a bitter tone,

"I am not a soldier, and I would be of small use if I were to take the field."

My answer was,

"You then might aid the youths who are giving their lives up to sustain your policy. They never brought on this war, yet you expect them to win your cause, and with no trouble or expense to yourselves."

This created a scene that was far from pleasant to me. One man declared I was insulting them. I responded with equal heat that I had no intention of saying anything but the truth, and if that was an insult, I was ready to meet all comers. The Chairman appeared to be the only cool and sensible head at the table. He then spoke for the first time, and in effect said that I had told them facts needed to be taken at their face value, and I was not there to palaver or to make myself agreeable, but to give them all the information for intelligent action on their part.

What a change came over them! The old Indian fighter apologized, and the rest manifested their regrets for their words and attitudes. We then got down to business. I told them they must have my Quartermaster General at their meetings, and listen to what he said with respect, and to make arrangements to give him the power to supply our forces with all necessary food and other supplies promptly. The war could not go further until they came to the aid of the Army. I added that if they felt unable to do this, I should resign, but my successor would be in the same boat. This, the Chairman went to great pains to impress upon his members.

No war without sacrifice was possible, and the Congress must now be made to understand what was what.

I came away with the feeling that no confidence could be placed in any private citizen. They wanted the soldiers to perform a miracle. Supporting a war was never in their small and mean minds.

Well, I went home to my quarters to find the resignation of two of my best officers, a perfect Sergeant and a fine Captain. This, of course, would reverberate among the troops, with both resignations and desertions to follow. I asked the two officers to dine with me, and told them of the scene in the Committee. They were delighted, and withdrew their resignation. We drank a toast to the Chairman, and one to ourselves, and said goodnight with hearty goodwill on both sides.

The next day, I was called by the Committee and there I found ten of the leaders of the Congress, to whom I was asked to explain the situation. This, I did in the same way as I had to the Committee. They all were, at first, resentful of my criticism but, as before, I stood my ground and won in the end. I again asked that the Quartermaster General should attend all their meetings and so coordinate, in all ways, the avenue of supplies. My astonishment can be imagined when one member of the Congress shouted in a violent tone,

"Don't ask me to sit down with one of those thieves!"

I picked up my hat and strode to the door. An outcry was raised, and the members of the Congress ran after me. I told them my resignation would be in their hands within the hour. This made the Chairman so furious that he told me I was no patriot. I called him a liar and asked if he had ever risked his life, or made a sacrifice of his peace and health for his Colony. He admitted he had not. Then I left the place, wrote my resignation in a nearby tavern, and sent it by a barman at once to the Committee.

Well, I was packing my belongings when a delegation consisting of two of the Committee and three of the Congress arrived at my quarters, and asked to see me. I sent out word by Terry that I was leaving the city and had no time to spare.

They left, but returned in a few minutes with an apology from the Chairman who had, it seems, been made to resign and was now no longer even a member of the Committee. A note telling me this was sent in, and I then invited them to my room. One man, the spokesman, was most assiduous in his declarations of regret, as were two of the others. I asked what was the purpose of their call, since I was leaving and had little time to spare. This, they saw, was true, for I apologized for the disorder about the room, and made no overtures whatsoever. One, who had been silent, now spoke,

"General Washington, we have apologized and we feel we should be taken seriously. We also have come to see the justice and wisdom of your remarks this morning. Can't you accept our regrets, and continue your work for us?"

I told him it was perfectly clear that the civilian mentality was closed to the whole situation. I could promise no success and on no account risk the lives of my soldiers in a service that was doomed to defeat by the ignorance and prejudice of those upon whom we must depend.

He then began to plead their side of the case, which was so hollow that I begged he would desist, and permit me to continue my packing. They left in silence at that, feeling like a lot of whipped schoolboys. One did turn at the door and say,

"I wish you a safe journey."

I thanked him, and called Jack to see them safely to the main door downstairs. When I was alone, I sat down in an arm chair and went over the whole of the known events, and wondered if I had been wrong in any particular. At that, I seemed to doze. Again, came the vision of the troops led by me, and that strange flag carried beside me. To say I was dumbfounded does not express my complete amazement. I had resigned, and that night would be on my way to Virginia, glad to be free once more to live out the rest of my life in peace.

All these thoughts were surging through my head when I was made aware that Terry was standing before me with a frightened stare. He had, he said, been waiting for fully ten minutes to get my attention. I had not seen him, though he was standing directly before me. He said my eyes had been open all the while. No man ever was so confused, and at a loss to know what the real explanation was of this strange occurrence.

Terry was sent to me by the Quartermaster General, who wished to see me. Of course, I then realized that he had been before the Committee and was coming to report. I had him in, and he was in a rage at the way he had been spoken to by one of the Committee, my old tormentor. I sympathized with him, and we had a drink. Then, he asked if I would be offended if he made a suggestion. Of course, I told him to let go.

"General Washington, I am going to be made the target. I can see that, and all this mess will be dumped at my door."

I then gave him a complete account of what had happened to my demand that he be present at the Committee meetings. He was then moved to say,

"I will see those old devils in hell before I go there again. They are just thinking of making money out of the Army."

I was shocked, for that idea had never occurred to me. Profiteers!

Well, that was a new idea to me. Anyway, I was glad to be rid of all of them, and after telling my officers and men goodbye, I rode off and was as far as Malden, when a rider came chasing after me, begging me to return. This, I refused to do in a polite reply. I continued on my journey and slept that night in a tavern, not far from Malden. In the morning, I was looking after Chancey and my pack horse when another Post rider appeared with an important looking letter for me. Opening it, I found it was a summons to place the whole matter before the Congress, and let there all decisions be made. This seemed to me to be the proper procedure, and I was glad to reconsider and return.

In two days, I had made my mind up as to what I should say, and take no back water. I did this, and the members gave me their respectful attention. During my recital, I saw the men of importance, who were real patriots, exchange glances, and the way they smiled convinced me they shared our Quartermaster

General's opinion.

A member then rose, after I had finished and sat down, a fine type, and I learned later that he had a great deal of influence all through New England, a man I was happy to see there. His name was John Adams. That name is the sign manual to all Americans of an unimpeachable and forthright man in the highest sense. No man ever had deeper love for truth, justice, and honor. I learned in the years ahead to love and to revere this great statesman and noble American.

Well, on we went, with the ball tossed from one to another, and it was candle-light before I got away, though we had met at ten in the morning. We all adjourned to a tavern, and there ate, drank, and talked in groups far into the night. I was happy once more to take command, though I saw a long and difficult road before me. John Adams was my hope, and he never failed in his personal efforts or his contributions of time and money to support our arms.

❀

No Army

DICTATED NOVEMBER 11, 1944

WHEN WE GOT TO the point where we had sufficient food for three months, and ammunition for the same period, with enough wagons, horses, and other transport equipment, I was ready to move against the enemy. The British had been quiet, and taken no steps to attack any town or even to make a sortie against Boston, which was the focal point. I therefore laid my plans to get behind them, drive them toward the Bay and, perhaps, get some sort of hold on their supplies, which were coming by ship into Massachusetts Bay, near the little port of Malden, which is on an inlet. All I wanted was to give them a surprise, take some prisoners, and then hie away to the Northwest, where I'd find a good escarpment in the many quarries that were all about Essex

County.

No man could expect to give the enemy a crushing defeat with the small Army I had, and even smaller supplies and equipment.

Our uniforms consisted merely of the white-cross belt, the hat, and leggings of blue and a pair of boots. For the bad weather, we had simply a piece of black oilcloth with a hole in the center. For warmth, our inner coat of warm deer or other skin, and our linsey woolsey coat that buttoned back at the corners for freedom in marching. We had two suits of flannel underwear for cold weather and cotton ones for summer, with three pairs of woolen socks. All this was not very easy to secure, since the British had bought up the wool in anticipation of the campaign, and we were forced to buy at very high prices owing to the scarcity. Citizens were asked to use cotton, and the women who were at home and indoors were asked to forego their woolen dress for the cold weather. All in all, we were not very well equipped for the bitter New England winter.

My own concern was for my poor horses. Blankets were scarce and, as wool was high, the blankets for the horses were of cotton with little warmth, and my poor horses were dying like flies with pneumonia. This I could not bear, and so made a demand for wool that caused a terrible outcry from the producing agencies. Yet, it was no economy to save money on wool, and lose the price of the horse. When finally I felt I had made my plans complete and was in shape to take the field, I was held up by a new and unexpected obstacle, nothing less than my own illness with an attack of pleurisy due to exposure. I had gone on a tour of inspection up where the accommodations were so poor, and the tavern so badly heated, that a cold had settled in my right lung, and breathing was painful and deficient. I cursed my ill fortune and went to bed. In a week I was able to be up, but still too ill to think of again exposing myself to the cold, wintry blast, for it was now December, and the countryside covered with ice and snow. This weather I knew was a great thing in our favor, since the British hated to be in this bitter climate, and had gone into winter quarters near Cambridge. They had constructed barracks, and made themselves comfortable for a stay until spring. My men were hardened, and I felt they could bear the cold, if they had good food and plenty of it with pup tents and warm blankets.

We were two weeks making our way around north of Cambridge. I counted on making this in ten days. However, we were not very much disappointed, since we knew we were going to be held there for possibly a month or more. We gave orders that no man should be allowed away from the camps, or to mingle with the townspeople. I hoped to give the enemy a surprise. One little event, however, gave the British a warning that we were not far off. This was but a trifle; yet, it gave our location. A small, but earnest candidate for recruiting wished to join us, and I had difficulty in persuading him that we did not need any more men at the time. The poor fellow was so disappointed, that he went to the tavern – and there wept with grief that he could not serve his Colony. The tavern had two British soldiers in it at the time, and these naturally interrogated the landlord, who was an old Tory, and he gave a surmise as to where we might be.

My rage was great, and so was that of my officers. We then made haste to attack, and did so that morning. Already, the British were ready and waiting for us. I took my position above the rise on the left of their camp and was ready to attack, when they fired on us in a volley of grapeshot that shook my men and left them bewildered. I kept my mind on my own plan, and ordered them forward. This was a test they had not been through. To leave wounded and dead, and go forward, they were not up to. And so when they started, only half the troop obeyed the command. One company only was in line when the British gave them a second burst. My mind was made up to get them, and I shouted to my orderlies to go at once and give the officers orders to make no concession to the enemy. We were five hours shoving forward a few feet at a time, and when we finally succeeded in breaking through their center, we were in a very shattered state.

No more disappointed Commander ever made a retreat.

I lost seventy men, either dead, or as prisoners, and had two hundred wounded to care for. I realized that my troops were too inexperienced to be of much use when it came to a real conflict.

I now was faced with the problem of how to meet the enemy in open battle. I saw that I had really not a fighting Army. They lost their heads at the first volley, and went into a sort of hit-or-miss wild scramble, with no idea of what they were aiming at. They discharged their muskets in a single flash, instead of every third man, as I had ordered. This left them no chance to reload, and they simply stood as targets for the enemy's fire. I managed to get a few of the Redcoats as prisoners, and we left twenty dead on the field. Their wounded, I daresay, were far fewer in number than ours. Also, I was bitterly disappointed to find no more ability or sense of responsibility among our officers. They, too, forgot instructions and were shouting and confusing the men, instead of leading them quietly and giving the proper orders in a low, but clear voice.

In other words, I had no Army. I was sick at heart as I realized this, and had it not been for my sense of duty, I would have left the whole business and resigned. This I was not so weak as to do, for I knew my own reputation as well as the Cause was at stake.

No more time could be lost, but a hard and dreary future of drilling and training lay ahead before I could again take the field. I pitied the men, but I was furious at the officers. They were worse than useless.

What to do?

No men were at hand to supercede the lot of incompetents, and these were as worthless as they well could be. My chagrin when we returned to Boston was so great that I was nearly out of my mind. I wondered what I could do to change the prospect, for something radical must be done, and at once. I sent for John Adams to dine with me the very day of my return, and I laid the whole matter before him. He said, in that rich and full-throated voice,

"Washington, you can only do what is humanly possible.

We know your difficulties, but we also know your personal integrity and we have faith in your ability. We shall stand by you. Make your report to the Congress and leave the rest to us."

That was good advice, and I took it. Here, I should like to say that this great man has never received the honor due him. His fine mind and noble character were obscured by the hullabaloo raised by the events in which he moved. Modesty, he ever made a part of all his public work. No man was more worthy of his Country's gratitude than Adams, and no man received less. What this Nation would have been, had he not taken the helm during those critical four years, I cannot imagine. His wisdom and his foresightedness were a rock upon which the infant Republic found its safety.

Well, the Congress was alarmed, as well it might be, for I told them the plain facts. I had, as yet, no officers who could be in battle, and no men steady enough under fire to risk facing the enemy. I was forced to paint a not very glowing picture of our chance of victory over an enemy with all possible resources and experience.

One member rose, and asked if I was making this a prelude to my resignation. I replied that I was not, but that I was at the service of the Congress, and would abide by its decision as to whether or not a better man could take over my Post. He then said, in a rather subdued tone,

"My God, man, what will you do?"

I hesitated, for I did not know what to do. Suddenly I said, scarcely knowing why,

"I can only hope to harass the enemy, and perhaps wear the British down."

That met with a burst of applause. As I spoke, I saw that vision again, as I led the Army with that striped flag unfurled beside me. I knew then that I had spoken under inspiration. A great wave of warmth poured into me, and I felt my whole body tingle. What it was, I do not know, but it seemed to give me hope and confidence. My own voice, I then heard saying,

"Gentlemen, I am always ready to listen if you have any

suggestions to make."

Only one man took me up on this. He rose, and in a slow and deliberate manner said,

"General Washington, how do you expect to win a war merely by small skirmishes?"

I was quite aware that he had a right to say this, but I somehow resented his tone. In an instant, I came out with,

"I shall not win the war. I shall simply make the enemy lose it."

That brought another small burst of applause. When I said that, he bowed and sat down.

When we left the meeting, my friend Adams, who had not spoken at all, said with a slow smile,

"My dear friend, you will be successful. You are acting under the guidance of those who may be depended on."

This amazed me, and I asked why he said that. His reply was,

"I saw three angels, or persons, standing beside you. They are your helpers."

For the first time, I had met a clairvoyant. He then described those "angels" as he called them. They were the Souls, apparently, of the most high and enlightened who were interested in the future of the Colonies. I was not only amazed, but I was also now sure that what I had seen in visions of myself leading an Army was all a part of some plan that was to be supported by the unseen forces that are always at hand, and ready to aid if needed.

We talked until nightfall, with but a light meal in the afternoon that Terry and Jack served us in my sitting room. I had gone into the fullest detail with Adams of all I had done, and what was still to be done. He was in complete accord with my decision to avoid pitched battle and simply act as guerrillas, annoying the enemy when and where possible and, perhaps, in the end, wear him down. We parted with mutual expressions of friendly good will, and the promise to meet again soon.

My next day was spent in writing a full report that was for the Congress. This, I believe to be extant and in the Collection of my Revolutionary Reports. After that I held a meeting of all the officers, and my words to them were plain and to the point. This led to ten resignations. All of them were of men who had never been fitted to their work, and I was happy to part with them. Another cause for their leaving was their terror of again facing action. No further words need be wasted on them.

The day following this was given to making my plans for a small force to be under my own personal supervision, about three hundred men. When I came to pick them up, I found few who were in any way the sort I needed. Most of the men were of two kinds: the loutish farm hands, and the slight, rather delicate-framed boys from the city shops and warehouses. These had not the physique, nor the steady nerves required and all the former were too slow witted to be what I was after. I began to despair, when a bit of news reached me that seemed providential. The Richmond paper, which I subscribed for, had an article about the disbanding of the Virginia Militia. Here was the sort of soldier I needed: strong, young men accustomed to the open and the use of firearms, trained to fight Indians. At once, I wrote to the Richmond Commander asking for the names and addresses of the officers down to the Corporals. This he sent me, and in three months I had with me three Sergeants and one hundred and twenty Corporals, all of them with military experience in two campaigns: one against the Indians, and the other the French and Indian campaign in Quebec under Montgomery.

In a short time, my troops were in training and my officers were the sort I could depend on.

I began to plan.

If I could get supplies of food, ammunition, and transport, as well as new blankets and tents, I could take the field with some hope of at least annoying the British. I put all this before Congress and, to do them justice, they did all that was possible to give me what I asked for. It fell far short, as usual.

In the spring of 1779, I had a review and was really proud of the showing made by the troops. The people who witnessed our maneuvers cheered, and all was gay and bright to their astonished eyes. My troops were happy to be so much admired, and the officers were in high feather, also.

We still had nothing to fight on, or with, so it was all up to the taxpayers. I made an appeal in the newspapers and that brought a few pounds to the War Fund, but beyond that nothing happened. We, myself and the commissioned officers, were quartered in the old Market Hall now, and the barracks were nearby, so I was in constant touch with all my forces. No week went by without a meeting of the officers to consult on policy and report on the state of our current standing.

Adams was usually present as Head of the Military Affairs Committee for the Congress. He was my only hope, for that man spared no effort to waken the people to the real cause of all the delay and disappointment.

One day, as I was nearing the end of my hope and, also, my patience, he came to my quarters in a state of agitation that was most unusual for him. It was caused by the fact that he had just received a letter from a friend in New York who said,

"If Massachusetts will but let us take command, we will defeat the British."

I was, of course, delighted and only too happy to resign if they desired it. Adams then suggested that I come to the day's meeting and say so to the Congress, after he had read the letter. This he did, with the result that both the letter and my resignation were accepted with warm expressions of gratitude.

I was a bit dashed by the complete absence of any expressions of regret or any words of appreciation for my years of unhappy and frustrated effort that were the result of their own failure to provide means with which I could fight. Adams rose and made what amends he could, but the silence that greeted his remarks told the story. Well, I rose with a feeling of defeat such as I shall remember so long as I retain my consciousness.

I bowed and left the room, but was no further than the street when Adams ran after me to say they were all in a tumult, and it had so taken them by surprise that they sat like dummies instead of grasping what was happening. He told me that as soon as I left the room, a man rose and said in thunderous tones,

"There goes the one man who has borne the brunt, and taken all the blame. Yet we let him go without even a word of thanks or appreciation."

That broke the spell, and they all cried out,

"Get him back! Get him back! He must not resign. He is all we can count on."

Anyway, I was in no mood to return. I told Adams I could be reached at my quarters. He returned with that, and the meeting framed a very high falutin' memorandum and sent it in an hour to my quarters, with a request that I return the next day and advise them in the matter of the letter.

Adams dined with me, and we talked the letter over. I had served in New York Town and knew the topography of its surroundings and even the whole of the State. So, I was familiar with its fine waterways and its splendid forests and game. This gave me a real and much needed lift. Also, I felt that our troops would be in a new environment and, perhaps, be ready to show their mettle to the New York Colony.

Now came my heartbreak...

A message from home telling me my brother Charles was dying. This was a blow I could not withstand. I asked for a furlough for three weeks, but it was denied, so that I never saw my beloved brother alive, and even had no way of letting him know the intensity of my feelings, though I dispatched a rider with a long letter at once.

Charles, alone, with only his slaves about him at Mount Vernon!

Martha had not been aware of the illness he had borne for ten years – tuberculosis. She merely thought it a chest cold that would, in time, disappear. That saint left this mortal world with no one of his kin at his bedside. The funeral was conducted by our old foreman; and a beautiful one it was, for all was simple and sincere. The old man read the Ninety-First Psalm, and then all the slaves knelt. As the prayer went from him, the old man wept and sobbed, and all watered the Earth with their tears as they threw it on the coffin. Our choicest flowers were transplanted above him by the slave women, and a wreath of mountain laurel was laid at the head.

All this was written me by one of our people. Martha was not at the funeral, but her slaves came with flowers and Frederick, also, was represented by his valet.

❀

BACK TO NEW YORK

DICTATED NOVEMBER 12, 1944

MY OWN FEELINGS had to be put aside in the face of all that was now taking place in the Army. The letter was announced by Adams, with the Congress acceding to the proposal for New York to take over the Army under my command.

At once a message was received to march the men to New York Town, where their Committee on Military Affairs would take over the responsibility for them. I was glad to say goodbye to all but Adams. That man had been the rock that was my salvation, and I clung to it. He, however, promised to write and to keep me posted in all ways possible, and I was to do the same in writing him.

All this I set down to show the American people, and those especially of the State of Massachusetts, that in John Adams, they had a patriot and a man of such high quality that nothing I can say in his praise is adequate to his merit. God only knows how I could have borne the years in that Colony without his sustaining friendship, and his constant endeavor to uphold and help me. May his name shine ever brighter as the years pass, for there stood the foremost of all the Americans of his Colony.

When we arrived in New York, we were at a loss as to where to go. We were on the Battery, and there stood my old quarters and the converted warehouse that the British had used as barracks. We bivouacked there that night. I rode to the Court House, only to find the Mayor out of town, and with no orders left as to our reception. Fortunately, I had the address of the Chairman of the Military Affairs Committee. His name was Hamilton, a fine type of man of affairs, a merchant, and a rich man. At once, Mr. Hamilton came to the rescue with a hundred pounds for provisions, and called on his fellow citizens to do likewise. All this by means of a meeting that night, where he led off with a great address. Many subscribed, still we had no quarters. I was at the old Inn that I knew so well on the left of the Battery, and the officers were billeted on several families who had volunteered to board and lodge them for a modest charge. It was a week before arrangements were made to clear the barracks, now used as a warehouse, and get them fitted up for the men. Also, we had trouble as to the way we could cook our food. We finally made an arrangement with a professional cook to come to the barracks, organize a kitchen and get the meals, with the men's help in preparing, serving, and clearing up. We managed to turn one big room into a dining hall and, with boards on treaties for tables we were soon having pleasant surroundings for the men, who enjoyed this new way of getting their food. No cooking, only taking turns at the incidental tasks in the kitchen and dining hall. I told them that they could now see how clean and wholesome they could make their meals, but no slacking. At the first sign of it, I would put them in a camp to prepare their own meals.

The cook was a very much honored and spoiled individual by the end of week, and ruled the men with an iron manner that was so new to them that they found the Sergeant almost a relaxation. I had my meals in my quarters but occasionally, and always unexpectedly, I would join them and thus get an idea of how things were. I soon found that the cook was stealing, and so got in a woman who was by far the better as a cook, and honest as well.

This old-fashioned woman became the ruler of the barracks. Her name was Katy, and her age was somewhere in the fifties. She had a face that was like that of a clock, so round and so full of wrinkles. Her hair, still black, was brushed into her cap so that not one hair ever escaped into her creations. The men loved her and obeyed her, and she came to feel a motherly interest in them. This dear old soul was such a fine influence, that I had far less trouble reported to me after she came to us.

॰

As for me, I found great relief when I received a letter from my dear old friend Franklin. He was coming to New York and wished to see me. He arrived looking a bit weary, but with his customary jovial spirit. We enjoyed a week of companionship that has always stood out in my memory. He had lodgings at the inn where mine were, so that no moments of my leisure were spent apart from him.

John Adams.
Painting by Gilbert Stuart
Courtesy National Archives

When Franklin left, I was only two days with a feeling of having parted from a perfect friend and companion when John Adams appeared, and that meant another delightful series of evenings with much serious talk over the future prospects. He brought some very useful information. I was deeply grateful for his notes on all that pertained to the war feeling in Massachusetts and the situation as to the British. It seems they had received reinforcements and orders to clean up and be done with it.

Here was a real war facing us, and not simply a force of pleasure loving troops enjoying the hospitality of the enemy's territory. My work was now cut out for me. I must be ready for attack and, if possible, be ready to take the offensive myself.

Adams was a Godsend, and he and I were poring over the maps and discussing transport and supplies far into the morning hours. Now that I had something to face, I was energized and stimulated. I longed to bring the situation to an issue. This I could only do when the needed ammunition, food, and transport could be had. At present, I was neither equipped to fight or to march.

I went at once to the Committee with Adams's report. This took them by surprise, and they were not in the mood to rise to the point of meeting the situation. I poured myself out to them as best I could, but they were not able to come to any definite, or even the least sort of attempt at a decision.

Again I felt the utter hopelessness of trying to conduct war in such an insecure and even dangerous state of things. As I was telling Adams goodbye, he said with great feeling,

"My friend, if this ever comes to real war, I know you will win. It is this killing delay, and inability of the citizens and the Congress that is taking all your power."

That was faith, but there was no denying that my power was at a low ebb. Even my voice became much weaker, my nerves were jumpy, and my optimistic nature was souring as a result of these years of ridiculous pretending. There was no war and never had been. Half a dozen small skirmishes and some marching, a little shooting, and that was all. Yet several had died, and more were maimed. A few were prisoners and, from what we learned, they were dying from mistreatment and bad food. But these things were not war.

I stayed in my quarters and studied, and brooded, and cursed the civilians for their laziness and stupidity.

Why ask for war if you don't want to support it?

As for myself, the record was far from impressive. My only attempt at strategy that made an impression was the taking of Cambridge, and after that the Malden affair that was a defeat. My other attempts were mere skirmishes, and even these the men were unequal to. So taking all in all, I was not too proud of myself.

Still, my only desire now was to get my supplies and take

the field. This I concentrated on, and went to every length to move the Committee to secure them for me. Finally, after two months had passed and they showed no signs of giving me what I must have if I were to act, I told the Committee I was either going to be given supplies or I would resign, that I was weary of inaction and talk.

This seemed to galvanize them, and in another week I had enough at least to make a start. Now, to show the enemy that we were more than enough for them. Alas, I reckoned without my customary attending disaster that always followed any piece of good fortune. While making a jump over a puddle of water, I slipped and fell, breaking my upper right leg bone near the knee. This simply made my life a blank – I decided to go home and send in my resignation.

I was about to do so when we received word that the enemy was marching on us by way of Connecticut. I was not able to move from my bed when the news came. Of course, I could do nothing but plan. However, that much I did do, and I had my Generals with me every waking hour, while the Colonels were busy drilling the men and making a redoubt on the Battery, which I felt commanded any approach from the north or east. Then, I ordered Katy to come to my room and make a list of what supplies she had on hand. She was a tower of strength and gave me such help as I never before had from a Quartermaster.

Katy also gave me her time off to dress my leg, and keep my bed neat. Even now, my heart swells at the thought of her good face and warm voice. She, too, is here and we often speak of those days before I was up and about. My Quartermaster General also found her of the greatest aid in his work of allocating supplies.

We were planning on meeting the enemy above the town, and stopping him there. Or, if coming from the sea, to give him no chance to land. In either case, we needed to encamp in both directions. All seemed in order, when again word came from the spies that the enemy was well into Connecticut, and would reach us in a day or so.

My despair at being laid on the shelf, when at last we were

ready for action, was too deep to express. I wept, even when I was alone, at the thought of all this.

❀

THE DAY CAME, ALMOST a week later, and I seemed to be given such new strength that I managed, with Terry and Jack's help, to get into my clothes and my left boot. With the right foot in my slipper, I had them bind on with bandages. I decided to get on my horse and see for myself how things went.

We marched northward as far as Spuyten Duyvil, and there met a sentry coming back to report that he had seen the enemy's sentry just above the North River. Untying the boat he had moored to the north bank, he at once rowed across to warn us. I kept my outpost sentries out of uniform and looking like farmers, so if the British sentry had spied him, he would take him for a citizen.

We marched up to the west bank of the river, and waited for the enemy. It was not long before he appeared, with a force three times as large as mine. I had no artillery beyond one cannon, but that was a ten pounder. I also had ten cannon balls and a supply of grape shot. My gunners were good—two old experienced Naval men. The width of the river was too great for the Infantry's musket range, but I got in two or three cannon.

This sent the enemy retreating as they, too, found the river an impasse making the musketry useless. When they had disappeared, we had no idea where they went, as there was heavily wooded land just above the north bank, and it was into this they had gone. I withdrew my troops a few yards from the south bank, but in an hour we saw them advancing from the east. At once, all was confusion in my ranks. I rallied the men, and we turned to meet the Redcoats, who must have had boats ready and waiting to cross the river. They advanced on the double quick to within twenty yards of our lines, which I had managed to get into formation. I shouted to the men to hold fire until the enemy was within safe hitting distance. They were too confused and terrified to remember and obey. The result was they fired too soon and wasted their load, and then all but two men threw themselves flat on the ground to escape the enemy's returning fire at closer range. We lost six men dead with twelve wounded.

No prisoners were taken, for the enemy again retreated after that one volley. My two small regiments were in a panic. My cannoneers had no more cannon balls, but they gave the enemy a belly full of grape shot. We saw five Redcoats drop. We did not know whether they were killed or wounded.

When I saw the British were pulling back, I tried to rally my men to go forward, but they were too frightened to obey their shouting officers' orders. They were simply so many targets for the enemy. My disgust was profound, and they saw it as I rode past them. This so enraged them, that they cried out,

"You don't have to take it. We do."

They were too panicky to know what I was saying, or to obey their officers shouting orders. The men stood like wooden images when the orders were to close with the enemy. I then gave the order to retreat.

I was too sick at heart to try to make anything of these men, who would never in the world make soldiers. Like those in Massachusetts, they were not of such stuff as fighting men are made of. The only thing now was to get them back to the city and there try, if possible, to fend off the enemy if he attacked. To my astonishment, the British did not follow up my defeat, and my spies reported them as taking to their boats and crossing to Long Island. This enabled me to rejoin the third regiment, left to guard the Battery.

I had no doubt as to what I now faced with my report of what was in effect a rout of our troops. We buried our dead and sent the wounded to the hospital. Their injuries were slight.

HAARLEM HEIGHTS

DICTATED NOVEMBER 14, 1944

NEXT TO THE ONES AT Valley Forge, these were among the blackest hours of my whole life, which contained its full meed of bitterness. Drinking at the fount of bitter waters was a test that I had been put to from the time of my disfigurement. Now I was in such physical agony with my leg that I became almost crazed, along with the frightful spectacle I had witnessed of my own troops in a panic and running pell mell from their positions facing the British. I gave up all hope of ever making an Army of soldiers out of these farm lads, town clerks, and the riff-raff who enlisted as a means of support.

All was chaos. The officers who had shown ability and reliability in the engagement were in my own frame of mind. This was only a third of them and the rest promptly resigned and all disappeared. All the volunteer officers followed suit, except four Sergeants and sixteen Corporals.

I didn't give a picayune what any of them did, I was so disgusted and in such pain. My leg became swollen to twice its size, and the surgeon gave it as his opinion that it should be amputated. To this I refused to consent. I dispatched Terry, with a letter to Martha begging her to leave everything to the cook and overseer and come immediately to me. Jack engaged a room for her opposite mine in the Inn, and so I at least had that happiness to anticipate. In a week, she arrived in a state of exhaustion, for she had ridden all the way and both she and her horses were scarcely able to stand. However, both were soon rested and fit.

In the meantime, I had been kept under the influence of opium at night to allow of some rest, for my days were one long agony with my leg. By the time the swelling came to a point where it was bursting the skin, Martha then took charge of the treatment and began to apply hot poultices of bread and milk. The surgeon furiously refused, and abandoned the case. Martha continued this treatment with the addition of a hot blanket always on the leg, and a little old time opiate of clover blossom tea to keep my nerves quiet. In three days, she had reduced my leg to its normal size. I had slept well, and with no bad effects from the clover tea. The opium had made me nauseated all my waking hours. The surgeon never forgave me for recovering with my leg intact. With the aid of two canes, I was hobbling about a month after Martha arrived. She decided that she would never leave me again, no matter what the penalty of leaving the estate to be run by hirelings. I never said a word to my surgeon about the leg, and in a month he was affable once more.

The state of things in the barracks was a disgrace. Katy reported to me the utter demoralization of the men, who were carousing and making of the barracks a perfect pigsty. No discipline and no sign of self-control could she discern. In short, Katy left. Well, I was able to get on my good foot and hold a meeting with what Generals I still had. They but corroborated all Katy had said. One General reported ten officers as being arrested on the street for drunkenness, and three for desertion. My Sergeants reported all Corporals as a lot of sots who were unfit for the service. My Captains' report showed that not only laziness and insubordination were common among the men, but also that they were beginning to bring prostitutes into the barracks in the daytime, as well as at night. My Lieutenants were not present, nor my three Colonels. These I called in at a later meeting. The Colonels reported that the Sergeants were as guilty as the men, and so were the Corporals. The Lieutenants I had left in charge said they had no control over the men, who defied them and refused to obey orders.

These reports I copied and posted to the Congress, with my own personal report of our terrible conduct and defeat at Spuyten Duyvil, along with my opinion that New York did not seem made up of men capable of making good soldiers. I asked them to consider engaging only men who had seen Indian warfare, and to recall those from Virginia, New Jersey, and the western part of Massachusetts and New York. I begged them to rid themselves at once of every man now in the barracks, except such officers as I would name. I frankly anticipated my own dismissal and would have welcomed it.

❦

ALL WAS NEARLY AS BAD as could be from my standpoint, so far as an Army was concerned. We were recruiting as I suggested, only men well trained and experienced in Indian warfare. That assured us of their marksmanship and obedience to their officers. Also, it meant a certain amount of both moral and physical courage. The recruiting was slow, however, and the pay was too low to be any temptation. I suggested better pay for the men, but the Congress did not find the idea acceptable. We were in all ways a failure, with no sign at all of ever being anything else. My own humiliation was so abject that I became a recluse, except when I was obliged to accept and return invitations to social affairs. We came at last to see that Americans were not ready to either support the Army or to fight a war. This conclusion prompted me to say as much to the Committee. Immediately, they were at my throat, and even Hamilton, a good friend whose home I rented for Martha and me, was up in arms to resent this reflection on his Countrymen. I apologized, but added that I spoke entirely from an experience of four years, which had only made me feel excedingly foolish for calling myself a Commander-in-Chief of an Army that never could meet the enemy without turning tail. This rather dashed them, and they were not very happy when I asked what their own views and plans were.

The result was a compromise, as usual, and I was told to order my supplies for the spring campaign.

What a prospect!

No amount of advertising had resulted in a full regiment of recruits. Where was I to find the soldiers? At last, I said to the Committee to raise the pay a third more and see if men would enlist. They did this, and we at once were flooded with the riff raff of the Colony and of New Jersey and Massachusetts. I weeded them out and found only a regiment of old Indian fighters. Then I began an intensive training that was a terror to most of them, for I drew upon my own experience and made each man capable of holding his own in close fighting. We wrestled and also practiced with our hunting knives. I knew the British soldier would never stand up to that. All in all, they seemed a fairly toughened lot, and I ordered supplies.

❀

When the April rains were over, I made up my mind to stir up the enemy, which was in winter quarters about six miles up the Hudson at the place we had met them, near the North River. They even had the boldness to come into the city to visit the taverns and bawdy houses. Their officers were quartered in the City of New York, and we often saw them at the theatres or in the shops.

Rumor had it that their Commander, General Howe, lived in seclusion about two squares from my own house. We never met, so I am not certain that this was true. We could see the lights from their campfires at a distance, and often I had longed for a troop of cavalry to make a nice raid on them. That, of course, was out of the question. All I could do now was to get ready to go up and fire away at them in a surprise attack, if surprise is possible when you have a lot of rowdy and ill-behaved soldiers, who never had the least consideration for their officers or their orders. Anyway, I had to do the best I could, with what I had to work with.

❀

EARLY SUCCESSES AND CONSTANT FRUSTRATION

IT WAS A DULL, FOGGY morning on the 20th of May when we went by the East River in small boats up as far as the first island. Then, we made a feint of going on past the enemy by the river road and the main body deployed around west of their camp. We opened fire at 7:00 a.m. and were happily surprised to see they had not looked for this. They were at their morning tasks and not at all prepared for battle. No one seemed in command, and they were seen running helter skelter all over the camp after their muskets. We had them in a pocket and gave them plenty of gunfire, one third of the men at each volley. All my cannon could do was to plaster them with grape shot. When we ceased firing at 9 o'clock that morning, they were our prisoners to the number of six hundred, while our men were not taken, except a few of the ones who had made the feint on the river road.

We were not very many miles from our Post and marched back that afternoon. This skirmish had been called a battle, but it hardly deserves so dignified a name. The men were elated and said they could lick the British and that, of course, was a boast that needed to be proven since we caught them unawares and with no chance to defend themselves. Many of the officers also made childish boasts of their superiority of skill. The Generals, I am happy to say, were not so idiotic and knew the day's work for what it was, a successful surprise raid and no battle at all. Many of the historians give this as a fine example of my strategy and my troops' valor. This is a lie I wish to nail. I made no such claims for either myself or my troops for this little incidental bit of good fortune. All I ask is that my record be kept straight – nothing added to the plain facts and nothing taken from them.

IN THE ATTEMPT THAT I next made, I had a slightly better result than I expected.

The British were up the Hudson, near the present Haarlem or Harlem, as you spell it. They were to be seen in town often, singly or in groups, both officers and men. Any encounter with our men on the street or in taverns was a signal for a brawl. The officers, especially, were always wearing court-plaster on their faces and, occasionally, a broken head had to be sewed up. I used to hope the British surgeon would be called for like attention to the British combatants.

My life was spent in begging and cajoling, writing pleading letters for supplies and making appeals to the Committee in as heart-rending speeches as I could contrive. Not that they did not want action, or themselves fail to give their proper share of money to the cause; it was the tight-fisted average well-to-do citizen that presented the most difficulties and lack of support.

I had to go to Virginia and make a speech in the House of Burgesses in April to find funds to make a small action possible. There I found the Aristocrats were losing their old power and the Farmers Party, which I had worked with in its formative years, was now the dominant political force in the Colony and its Legislature.

Many men of means contributed at once. Petitions were sent to distant Counties and small contributions were rolled up into sizable figures. All in all, I collected 10,000 pounds from Virginia. I bought what supplies that Colony had to sell, and at a fair price. Also, I gave out many small, but excellent Posts in my short-handed military organizations to those Virginians who had helped to raise this money in the various Counties. This, in your histories, was called my unjust and unfair favoritism to my own Colony. It took the Colonies of Massachusetts and New York four years to furnish 20,000 pounds, and I raised 10,000 in Virginia in one month. Yet, the latter was poorer than either of the other two States.

❀

With the supply money from Virginia, all was ready for the spring campaign by May 30ᵗʰ. Although we were well aware of the enemy's intention to start an early move on us, I wished to make the first attack. By this time I had made it a rule to take the men out on a march twice a month, and make them shoot at a 40-yard target. So far, they had been fairly good, and I hoped for some sort of steady improvement. Our ammunition did not admit a great deal of this sort of training, and I had to rely on their ability in action.

We always went out to Long Island for practice, and there I was able to also find many good inlets for the landing of our small boats. Many times I wished that the true account of my Long Island trips would be told. They are always described as futile attempts to get at the enemy, who actually was not there then. So goes the historian on his wrong way.

We had a fairly good share of our usual misfortune, such as illness among the troops, several thefts of supplies, and the customary bad weather; but on the whole, I was not inclined to grumble. I wanted to make the enemy aware that we were not lying down and, if possible, to instill a little fear of us in his troops.

We went along the Hudson for a few miles, and then turned east toward the Heights of Haarlem. There, we saw they were in camp and not expecting us. We lay in a wooded tract along the river for an hour and our patrols spied out the enemy's position, so that we knew pretty well here to make the first attack.

We gave them a good pasting with our grape shot, then followed with infantry in a rush that caught them unaware, and we managed to separate a large body of them from their main camp.

All went well, except for my own desperate feeling of another panic that might at any moment seize upon the troops. None had ever been in this sort of battle before. Indians, they knew how to deal with; but a lot of British Redcoats rather captured their admiration, and they hated to attack them in close fighting. My officers were fairly good and made themselves helpful, but still the élan was not there and I saw it, so I drew off this body and sent in a fresh lot who wished to show that they were real soldiers. They gave the enemy twenty minutes of hot and fast work, and we took 1,000 prisoners and saw many dead and wounded. I then took my third lot and came up on top of them from the north. This gave me a real sense of success and I was in the mood to go on to the limit of our strength, but I feared to trust too much to these inexperienced troops. So with what I call a small feint at the enemy, I took our prisoners, our 22 wounded and 4 killed and marched back.

This was my only success that summer.

A depiction of the hanging of Nathan Hale as a spy by Howard Pyle.
From Harper's Weekly, October 1880.

❈

A MENTION OF NATHAN HALE

In speaking of my failures up the Hudson, I forgot to say that one of the hardest blows that came upon me was the loss of that young patriot – Nathan Hale.

He came to me at Headquarters in Boston and offered his services in whatever way I could use them. He had a beautiful face, as pure as a child's in expression and a voice so sweet, that I felt at first some hesitation in asking him to enlist as a private and take up his life in the barracks, where the customary ribaldry and habits of the men would be a constant jar on his nerves. Also, it seemed to me, his fineness of appearance might be a source of awkwardness to him, for the common soldier resents a comrade who seems a cut above him. Hale would have borne it good naturedly, but I wanted to make him something more useful to me, and less boring to himself.

I asked him if he would act as a spy. At first, he hesitated and then said,

"Would I have to betray anyone?"

I told him he would have to bring me information as to the enemy's whereabouts, his strength, and also his intentions toward us. This he was willing to do, but not to betray a single man personally. His end you know. He knew the penalty, and paid it with his last words making him immortal, that his only regret was that he had but one life to give for his country.

May I add that here he still remains and is one of our group who meet often, and in our talks he is always the same charming and simple scholar and patriot that I found so hard to lose when he failed to return from a scouting errand I had sent him on.

All was, with him, a perfect realization of his dream of service.

✽

Victory and Defeat

Dictated November 17, 1944

After our successful action at Haarlem, we wished to follow it up with a more extended engagement. This, however, was not yet possible, as we had used up all our ammunition. No amount of supplications, demands, or even threats of defeat could move the Congress to put into operation another arms or powder factory. This was the narrow and stupid attitude that prolonged the war. My own position gave me no power to do more than advise. We were always at the mercy of the damned politicians, who never see further than their own local or personal interests and have been ever the curse of all countries.

Our Army, small as it was, just four regiments and some half a dozen troops of cavalry, with but four pieces of artillery could only rot out in idleness, always the ruin of a soldier's élan.

My wife came to me one day in late August with the complaint,

"Darling, we can't remain here in New York any longer. My friends tell me that you are beginning to be the subject of personal attacks in social gatherings, even where we are guests. Let us retire to Virginia and leave the war to the Congress."

Of course I knew this, and had known it for years. It is always the way. The Commander is made the scapegoat for the failure of the politicians. I was not surprised or even moved by Martha's words, and told her I had long known what she had but now found out. She wept and raged at the Congress, the people, and even at me for not declaring myself. I told her in a few words what I felt, that I must see the thing through now, and not leave it to be a failure charged up against me. I was too well-seasoned to pay the least attention to gossip of civilians, and too well-aware of the truth contained in their criticism to resent their abuse personally. I begged my wife to be patient, and share with me the discomfort of the situation.

❀

DAILY LIFE

So WENT THE WINTER months. All I could do was gather supplies, and see that the men were kept in good trim as to their health and training and try to keep Martha as content as possible.

We went out on a foraging bout now and then, up north and on Long Island. We salted down the game we shot, and the pork we bought from the farmers. We caught fish and salted that down also. My own food supply was none too good that winter. Martha was often at her wits' end to get hold of enough fresh meat or vegetables to keep us in health. I became very lame with rheumatism in my bad leg, and even Martha began to have swollen knuckles for lack of fresh fruit and vegetables. However, she was never one to give up and we often rode into the county, stopping at every farmhouse where she endeavored to coax some cabbage and turnip out of the farmer's wife by paying triple prices. Now and then, we got a windfall of a box of apples and some presents from Mount Vernon, but there the fruit trees had been neglected and they bore very little. Still, we survived, and were lucky to be no worse.

We came to March with a supply of ammunition for a full and extended campaign of at least a month. I had worked out a plan that I hoped would give us success, and have the men in accordance with it. We saw at once that the British were also making their own plans and wished to surprise us.

All were on the alert and ready to receive them, but I wished to be the first to take the field. By March 15, I was on my way to Haarlem Heights again, this time taking my men directly there by the Boston Post road, and that took us straight toward them with no detour. We attacked by artillery and then the infantry in force and scattered them to the east and north, but left their west wing ready to close with us if they wished.

My cavalry, with no more than 300 men, gave a brilliant account of themselves when they charged that western wing of the British. Our count told of 67 dead Redcoats and, no doubt, we wounded three times as many. Our losses were 14 men killed with 3 horses, 17 prisoners, and 46 wounded. This, I thought a good two hours' work. When they retreated in great disorder to re-form on the plains above us, we knew better than to give them such an advantage and withdrew with our wounded and our prisoners. However, we had created a camp north of them by means of boats on the Hudson and we therefore made a feint of retreat for a mile, then turned east and came up to their camp in less than five hours. We gave them a good plastering with our cannon and grape shot, while the infantry and cavalry passed them. Our cavalry protected the artillery's retreat and so we got our position above them, half a mile or more to the north. Our supplies had gone up there by boat the night before with a small detachment, and we made camp after sending the sentries, spies, and patrols out.

Only one fact worried me. We were not ready for any very great engagement, since I had to split my forces in half. We had them beneath us, but they were well off for ammunition. As usual, I was limited.

We gave no thought to the west, and there I was at fault. My patrols saw them coming in force from that direction just before sundown. We were ready for them with grapeshot and cavalry. Now came my worst hours of the Revolution, save those at Valley Forge. My band began to retreat in the face of the enemy's terrific fire, and we were with such limited supply of infantry that I was fearful we would be driven into the river. Nothing we did could stop them. They came on in serried lines, and closed the ranks as the wounded or dead fell.

My men, less experienced, would yell and run as each man fell. Our officers could not rally them. I rode out in front of them to lead them and made a fine target; but nothing hit me, though my poor horse was killed. I tried to rally them, but they were like rabbits hunting their holes. In the end, we lost 76 men dead, 157 wounded, and 465 prisoners. On our side, no prisoners, and we never knew what we made them pay in dead and wounded. I got my men drawn off to the northeast, and then got down to the river where I had several boats waiting. We were all night getting back to town by water, and our camp equipment was in the hands of the enemy.

Later by exchange of prisoners, I got most of it back, but again victory was snatched from us, and the end was a defeat. This event is known as the Battle of Haarlem Heights. The first two engagements there are called "the attempt to take the Heights."

Von Steuben and Lafayette

Dictated November 18, 1944

The last man I ever expected to meet in New York came to see me shortly after our return from the field. His name was General Von Steuben. He had only been in the Colonies a few months, and was greatly interested in the way I had managed to keep the skeleton of an Army together with nothing of importance to go on.

Von Steuben was a General and a retired Army officer. He had become disgusted with

Baron Frederick Wilhelm von Steuben
Copy of painting by Ralph Earl
Courtesy National Archives

Europe and its never-ending wars, and decided to emigrate and take up land which he had done in the vicinity of Schenectady, a village north of New York Town, three days' journey by horse.

To receive a visitor of such experience was very interesting and, to me, important. The man was a gentleman and a fine soldier, as well all know. His charming manners made an exceptional impression on me, so that we were in a few moments discussing the war with easy frankness on both sides. To my astonishment, he asked if I would consider giving him a command. This was manna from heaven, for I had no Generals who knew anything about war that was not based on their experience with the Indians. We were now fighting an enemy that was trained to fight under European strategic methods. I jumped at his offer, and it was hours before we parted, having gone into all the pros and cons of the situation.

We met again the next day, and the next, and I was so absorbed in this new acquisition to my staff that I began to see now a better prospect ahead for success. Von Steuben was too well-trained to have any false ideas as to the task I faced, and I appreciated his very frank and well-expressed views on the whole situation. In the end, he saw the supplies were the key to all my past defeats and lack of success, and asked if I had thought of making an appeal directly to the people. Of course, I had not. It would have brought down the Congress on me, and I could not then accomplish anything as they held all the power.

Well, we were in a quandary as to what could next be done. I had seen another long wait and idle men growing soft or even deserting and resigning. Von Steuben was quite sure that up in his county the farmers would raise extra crops for the Army if they knew the Committee would buy them. We estimated the needs of the command and he left with a definite idea of canvassing that section to see if the citizens would cooperate. We could do nothing about the ammunition, that was all in the hands of the Congress.

Many years later, Von Steuben gave me a word picture of his missionary work in his county and the difficulties, as well as the success, he had when he asked for help for the Revolution. The Tories were bitter against the Revolution, but the Nationals were keen to aid it in such ways as they could. In the end, he recruited sixty-five good men, and made contracts for all the crops to be sold in his own county and six adjoining ones. This was indeed a Godsend.

All through the rest of the war, Von Steuben was a strong support and constant aid in every possible way. He was never fully appreciated or rewarded for his work, which was of inestimable value, and I wish here to say that without Von Steuben, I feel we could not have gone on.

Another fine and valuable friend appeared at this juncture, the great French patriot, LaFayette. He came from France with sixteen fellow countrymen who were fired up by our efforts toward freedom and wished to find in the Revolution not only adventure, but experience in a war that seemed to these young men noble and inspiring.

LaFayette was a youth of but nineteen years. His companions, also, were young and filled with ardor for our Cause. They had no experience in this sort of warfare or, for that matter, in any sort of military service beyond the smattering they had picked up in Paris when serving as officers in the French Guard of Honor that was a feature of the Royal entourage.

We were delighted to greet them, but somewhat embarrassed when we found they had no idea whatsoever of the conditions under which we labored, nor the poverty of our resources.

My first impression of LaFayette was one of a schoolboy who was ready to go any lengths for adventure. I soon found my judgment changing to one of deep regard and profound respect for the principles which lay at the bottom of this extraordinary youth's mind. Also, he had in his manner a sweetness that won my heart almost at once. No one could be in his presence long without loving him, and I came to love him as a son.

Only great and good things can be said of LaFayette. His traducers will write in vain. He stands

The Marquis de Lafayette
Painting by Alonzo Chappel
Courtesy National Archives

today, in the Spirit Realm, a symbol of great and lofty manhood. A patriot, a man of unimpeachable honor and, in all human relations, an exemplar. My own love for him has not overlaid my appreciation of this great Soul.

What to do with this delightful youth was a problem. And, what to do with his sixteen friends?

My first thought was to suggest that he come to my home, for I now had taken another furnished house, to live with Martha and me. I decided against this because of the gossip it might create, and perhaps the idea of a foreigner in my family would be criticized. So I arranged for this French contingent to live with my officers in their quarters. They were all a lot of happy-go-lucky boys ready to take life as they found it. I was hard put to know how to rank them.

Rochambeau was a Captain, and could be trusted with that office as soon as he learned the ropes. This Frenchman was at least thirty, and the senior of the rest. He was charming, as they all were, and in every way a gentleman. Still, the men did not like an officer whose speech was so difficult to understand. In the end, I made him an aide-de-camp and we got on very well indeed, except for the fact that he never understood orders. The complications arising from this were often most serious, and took much time and trouble on my part to get Captain Rochambeau to comprehend what was to be done.

LaFayette, on the other hand, seemed to divine everything, and we always worked in complete understanding and harmony with excellent results. Here again, some historians have been all wrong in their estimate of LaFayette. The moderns especially have tried to smirch his record both here and in his own country. I found his contribution to our efforts was ever helpful and always constructive. Let posterity understand that.

ALL WAS STATIC THROUGH the autumn and winter, which left time for more social matters. My new European officers made the town very gay, since they were at once lionized and made much of socially. Several of them, like LaFayette, were titled men and that made a great flutter in the social dovecotes. Ambitious mothers were set to capture these boys for their daughters. LaFayette and three others of the sixteen were already married, but that still left a fine prospect and the chase was on. All escaped the matrimonial noose but three, and they were soon captured.

There was Count Rochambeau, who married one of the Carringtons of Richmond. Another was the Chevalier de Croissant. This lad was a beautiful and talented boy, who was even then writing his immortal poems. His fate, he found in one of the daughters of my old friend, Hamilton. The third came to his freedom's end in the arms of a lovely maid, whose name escapes me. Her father was one of the Congress and the marriage, I understand, was a very happy one.

Among the other Frenchmen was a small chap with merry twinkling eyes, who was a great raconteur. He was the Chaplain of the outfit and his name, Audrienne. Father, or Pere, Audrienne was the favorite companion of LaFayette, and so close was their friendship that the little priest forsook his clerical career to accompany his boyhood friend on this adventure to an unknown land. Audrienne never was a soldier, and was not a very ecclesiastical personality.

We were happy with these lively French boys, and often gave them a party at our home with our American boys and girls. Martha was ever in her element with a lot of youngsters making merry about her. She became their confidante and counselor in their small dilemmas, which sometimes arose through their ignorance of our provincial ways.

All in all, my life was brightened and broadened by the coming of these foreign volunteers, and I value every one of them as a dear contribution to my otherwise unhappy life at that time.

❧

BACK TO THE BUSINESS OF WAR

THE SPRING WAS IMMINENT when Von Steuben appeared, and with only good news and helpful counsel. We pored over our maps and worked out various plans and devices for action. He was all for an early attack, and felt that we might crush the enemy if we had enough ammunition to last through a week's hard fighting.

We had given the men special training in close fighting and, also, in marksmanship. I, myself took charge of that. No amount of training, however, can be a substitute for experience under fire, and that had been the trouble from the first.

All we might expect was a quick and sudden effort, then a withdrawal and an attack from another quarter. When we finally came to a complete outline of a campaign, I went to the Committee and was astonished to learn they had made no calculation on a spring offensive, and had no more ammunition than the usual output for practice purposes.

Then, I told them my frank opinion of them, and added,

"You had better surrender, and not ask me to sacrifice the lives of any more poor fellows. You have failed us at every turn, and now you seem content to kill your citizens in order to keep the British Army here to fill your pockets, with what they must expend in this Country."

All this time, I had to stand off my French and American officers, as well as Von Steuben. The latter blamed me openly and in the press for my delay in taking the field. I could not answer without betraying my weakness to the enemy.

LaFayette was my only confidante, and I gave him the facts. He was horrified at my situation, and left for France on the next ship sailing to see if he could raise funds for our cause. All know how he tried and failed, but returned with a contribution of his own to equip his little band with weapons. All was such a horror and misery to me, I wished even for death to end it.

❧

MY OWN SWEET MARTHA now saw that there would be no peace for me unless I could make an effort to oust the enemy. She talked to all and sundry of my position, and was of the greatest aid in awakening a sense of the situation among the people she met. This bore fruit eventually, but at the time it seemed futile.

❧

AARON BURR

IN THE MEANTIME, I had a call from a young officer, a veteran of the war with the French. He was a small, slight chap with the most beautiful cast of features and a distinguished carriage and manner. His name was Aaron Burr.

He asked for a staff position, and I was happy to have such an intelligent and finely educated man with me. I also counted myself fortunate in acquiring an officer who might help me in the task of getting my orders obeyed, by merely taking them himself. However, he was of too independent a disposition to do that, and always changed them to read a little differently, but mean the same thing. This, naturally, I resented. Burr could not bear to let anything be told him, unless he first argued about it. My training did not admit of a superior officer having to argue for the benefit of his junior officers.

Aaron Burr
Painting by Gilbert Stuart

The end came when I gave him an order to be delivered at once, and he waited three hours before getting it into the hands of the officer for whom it was intended, too late to be of any use. This brought on a rebuke from me, and Burr then asked to be transferred. This, I was most happy to accede to, and got General Von Steuben to take him on his staff. Later, Von Steuben told me that he had the same trouble, and asked to have Burr transferred to another command. I did not wish to interfere, and asked Von Steuben to try and argue with Burr about his strange conduct. The upshot of the matter was that Burr resigned and raised a troop of cavalry, which he financed himself and asked me to accept.

Now came the rub. If he could not obey orders on the staff, would he do so when in command of a troop of his own? I put the question to him. He was fair and open and said,

"General Washington, that is my failing. I conceive a thing, and cannot see it any other way. I fear I shall be of no use to you, unless I can act on my own initiative."

This, at any rate, was frank and I respected his candor. However, I told him I could beg that he would leave the strategy to me, as I was the one who had to bear all the responsibility. At that, he smiled and said,

"Well, I may have the privilege of siding in some way that will not interfere with your strategy. Cavalry can be of great use in certain ways that may not come under your plans, and yet may further them."

I agreed, and said in as good natured a manner as I could muster, since the implication was clear that he had no respect for my plans,

"Captain Burr, you have small knowledge of the difficulties I am at all times confronted with. The Army is small, with little experience, and in no sense trained to meet on equal terms with the British. I have so little support from the Country, and with one thing or another to make my task difficult, I dare not issue carte blanche to anyone. In the end, I have to account for all that happens."

This he saw was only good sense and was man enough to say so. I asked him what his objection was to leaving the strategy to me. His reply was,

"I am no use as someone who can take orders."

"Then why seek a military career?"

He was frank in his reply,

"I love the adventure and, also, I long to be of service to my Country."

We sat down and talked over the situation. In the end, he came to see how foolish his idea had been, for when we parted, he was quite of my own opinion as to the unreasonableness of his attitude. We agreed to consult often, and to try to cooperate. Later, I came to call upon him for action and he was most difficult, and in no way inclined to accept my opinion. This ended in my losing my temper, and asking him to refrain from any further interference with my ideas. I suggested that he offer himself and his troop to the enemy, since his love of adventure would then be satisfied and he could do, perhaps, less harm to the Country than when mixing up the strategy I had in view. This made what I expected would be a rift that would never be closed. Later, when he was again with Von Steuben as a guerrilla, he did some good work and I am grateful for this opportunity to acknowledge it.

❀

BURR AND HAMILTON

MANY APPOINTMENTS MADE it necessary for me to have on my staff a young officer with tact and a good appearance, who could make the callers feel that he was an authority on anything concerning my affairs. Alexander Hamilton had all the qualities to fill that post. I used to marvel at the way he made all my affairs his own, and the manner in which he would take credit for all I did, and often seemed to think that he was in reality General Washington. It was amusing at times, but this attitude became so inherent that he would tell me to my face that he had changed my orders, and decided on better ones. Here was another genius with no military experience whatsoever. Burr had been a gallant, and even heroic soldier. Hamilton was not even an American, and was quite at sea about the many Colonial matters always involved in my decisions and plans.

Alexander Hamilton from Leslie's Magazine, 1887.

Still, I found Hamilton had a special aptitude for figures and was useful in keeping my accounts. When I had him on the carpet for telling a very important citizen who called that "General

Washington left all important matters to him for decision" the gentleman raised hell, as he should, and sent a letter to the Congress asking where this young English upstart came in.

Hamilton could be made to see the point, but he did not swerve from his egotistical belief that he was the bright and shining star of all humanity. Later, I had to dismiss him. He seemed to feel this was merely jealousy of him, and said so publicly.

The tragedy that ended in Hamilton's death and Burr's disastrous adventure made me see how these two highly gifted men stood ever in their own way. But jealousy always exists between genius minds, and Hamilton was by far a soul who incarnated for the task of founding America. I missed Hamilton more than words can say. What foolishness is such hubris.

❀

TRENTON AND AARON BURR

DICTATED NOVEMBER 19, 1944

TO MEET A WELL-CONDITIONED enemy with such poor equipment as mine was, perhaps, foolhardy. Still, I was supposed to be the head of an Army, and the least I could do was to make some kind of an effort to show that we were still alive. That was the most I could do and so when the winter of 1779 was over, I was in the mood to see if I could do a bit of damage to the British.

Howe was now entrenched in New Jersey near Trenton, a small town near Philadelphia on the Delaware River. This came about through the effort Burr had made to scare the British away from New York. His guerrillas were well-trained, and of magnificent morale. In spite of his arrogance, Burr himself I have always considered a genius, filled with such a spirit of devotion to any cause he espoused that he could do more than was seemingly possible when he met with insurmountable difficulties. This drive of his was an example. He had not more than sixty men, cavalry, and he did work that would ordinarily require ten times that number.

I saw at once what he was up to, and wished to follow it up with my own efforts. True, I had no such troops as he. My men, only one regiment now, were sick of the war. They were hungry most of the time, and with no real victory to make them feel their power to win against the enemy whom they knew to be well fed and ten times their number.

What to do?

I decided to make an effort when spring came to get over on the Jersey side, not far from New York Town, and go up to the Haarlem Heights, cross above them to Weehauken and then go straight south. We would then harass the British in such ways as we could.

Remembering my experience in New Jersey as a young man, and bringing our starving men back from Montreal, I hoped and believed the good Jerseyites would help us and give us food. I forgot that New York citizens had been generous at that time also, but now were only concerned with profiting by the British occupation. My disillusionment was complete.

We went up to Spuyten Duyvil in May, crossed by ferries to Weehauken and made camp above the town. We got enough money from the Committee to purchase a week's supplies from the Jersey farmers. Game was scarce, and we suffered from want of meat. Still, we could exist on grain and vegetables if we could find a bit of bacon now and then.

I was disappointed in the attitude of the people, for they seemed but lukewarm for the Revolution and, in but few instances, were not even decently polite to our officers when they asked to purchase their produce. The exceptions but proved the rule. However, I knew I must work fast or perish. So we marched south, bivouacking in the suburbs of Trenton one night, eating our supper of cold food in the dark. I had made preparations for an attack by my Cavalry at dawn and then to send out the Artillery, followed by my regiment of Infantry.

Captain Van Rensselaer had said the morning before our

Washington at the Battle of Trenton. December 1776.
Copy of engraving by Illman Brothers after E.L. Henry.
National Archives

arrival,

"General Washington, I am fearful of this. I feel a dreadful premonition of disaster."

Of course I was moved by this, but I could not then do otherwise than go forward as planned. The premonition was to be fulfilled by his own death, as he fell when leading the Cavalry charge. He was killed instantly by a saber stroke from one of his own men, who miscalculated. This was a grief to me that I still feel, though my young friend is still here, and we are as close as ever in our relationship. No man was so valuable to me and to the Cause we both served.

We had to ignore all but the objective, and so I was not able to stop for an instant, though I saw the horrible deed and his body fall from his horse, decapitated.

The Artillery worked well and we had really surprised the enemy, so that it was half an hour before we had to meet them in formation. All the morning and until five in the afternoon, we pressed forward and made them retreat. They made a stand then, behind an old mill. We knew better than to try to take that, for we were weary and our ammunition low.

We withdrew to the town of Trenton, where we found the citizens in a panic, but I made an address in the public square and reassured them. I told the troops to protect every home and every citizen, to behave as gentlemen, and win the respect of the Trentonites. This, with a few exceptions, was sufficient to put the men on their mettle, and in the end they won the respect of all the townspeople.

We were there three weeks and, what was more, we were admired and fed as the defenders of the town. In New York, there was not a sign of life when we gave out the news of taking Trenton from the enemy. We were still short of ammunition and I begged for supplies. This, as usual, was in vain.

Burr came to me with his usual offer of help, and did splendid service as a scouting outfit. I knew every hour what the enemy was doing. The lack of ammunition was my worry, and he saw this. What did he do? He simply went to Trenton, entered one of the banks, asked for the loan of two thousand pounds credit and went on the note personally.

When Burr came to me with that draft for two thousand pounds, I was faint with surprise and emotion. I looked into the handsome young face, and he was weeping. I could only grasp his hand in both of mine, and when I could find my voice, say,

"Half of this is my debt, and I shall see that I keep my obligation."

He was at first inclined to refuse, but I asked him to permit me to share it, and he then threw his arms about me and wept like a woman on my breast.

What a scene for those who try to present Burr to posterity as a cold and calculating villain! If ever there was a great and gifted man, with a heart and soul above his fellows, yet ever sensitive to their need and appreciative of their merits, it was Aaron Burr.

Allow me to step out of sequence and comment about the famous duel between Burr and Hamilton. Dueling, as my own life shows, was common among men in that period. Burr avoided the challenge until Hamilton's insults became so frequent and so public, as to even be offered in the press, that as a man of spirit and self-respect, no other choice was left to Burr than to call him out. That his bullet was fatal was not what he had expected. Burr was never a good marksman with a revolver. Most of his military work was as a cavalryman, and his training largely as a scout.

This I wish to say, since I know from all parties who witnessed this affair that Burr was not angry and hoped a few shots would be sufficient to clear the air. It is said in print that Hamilton fired in the air and Burr aimed point blank at his heart. That is not true. Hamilton fired point blank. His bullet whizzed over Burr's shoulder and was found in the tree behind him by Hamilton's seconds. In after years they admitted that, but as they were Burr's political enemies, they kept it a secret. Burr's seconds were too busy getting him away from the scene to observe what the others were doing. Burr ran to Hamilton, throwing away his pistol, but the doctor caught him and actually pushed him down to the waiting boat and gave the boatman a pound to hurry away across the Hudson where their horses were waiting.

Had the doctor not done this, perhaps Burr's fate might have been very different. Burr weighed but a hundred and fifteen pounds at this time, and was never strong physically. The doctor was a two hundred pounder, and almost carried Burr to the boat, though he was protesting his desire to attend to his fallen foe.

Now to return to our business that was imminent in Trenton. We were only twenty-four hours in the town when we had created an arsenal and manned it. Burr was the leading spirit and, since he was a man of that Colony and his father a distinguished citizen, he could get things done in double quick time with no moments spent in the investigation of his record. His word was good with every man in Trenton.

We were now ready to go at our enemy and so, in forty-eight hours after their retreat, I was ready to give them a jar. I sent my Cavalry around to the east and my Artillery up the river to a little village. With the Infantry, I made a detour of four miles and got behind them to the south. Our supplies I had sent the day before, and so was able to get into action with a free mind.

After we started to march out, it took twenty-four hours to be in position. We waited to hear from the Cavalry and Infantry; these were in command of Burr and my Artillery Commander.

The Cavalry did well, and threw the enemy's camp into confusion as they dashed through it, shooting as they rode. They had no sooner gotten away than the Artillery opened with grape shot and was effective. We had no cannon balls. My men now began closing in from the south, and we were able to keep their lines from forming until twelve noon. The battle raged until nightfall, and when darkness came we had taken three hundred prisoners and saw by count sixty dead. We imagined three times that number wounded.

My officers were all elated, and the men as well. Now followed the usual disaster that always dogged me. My leg was injured when my horse fell on me. I was about as crushed as a man could be. Burr was at my side at once, and wept over it. He had the softest heart for other's suffering of any man I ever knew. He helped carry me to my tent, and the doctor soon had the leg in splints. I made up my mind to take it as a fortune of war and not let it interfere, if possible, with our plans. Burr stayed with me all night, and when the pain would be too great to admit of sleep, he diverted me with his fund of amusing stories and anecdotes.

That day, LaFayette was in his glory. The boy had command of a company and was in the thick of it. He gave no quarter, and received a bullet wound which grazed his left hand. Fortunately, no muscle was injured, but he was proud of his bandaged hand. LaFayette was also at my side and made tea and toast for me.

Burr and I began to plan the next move that night. Our scouts brought news of the enemy withdrawing across the Delaware into Pennsylvania. I was amused at that, for I could not imagine the Quakers giving them a very warm welcome. This gave us time to make more ammunition and to leave the enemy alone a week or so. Apparently, Howe was not keen to turn on us and did not know how weak we really were. This was an amazing fact to me, that his large force was never really used against us in an attack at this stage. All that I can surmise is that he enjoyed his comfort, and did not wish to make the effort. It would have been easy for him to annihilate us at any time. One of my officers used to say,

"General Howe has an engagement and can't be bothered with us."

Burr was all for going after them, but I knew that was what he expected. I preferred to wait until I had a better position than that western bank of the Delaware. I waited for two months and when I saw they were not coming after us, I made a feint down the river where I thought they might be drawn. This, however, they ignored.

In the meantime, my leg mended, and I was able to mount a horse with help. I rode all down the river, looking for a good crossing that was not too far south. I came back the other way as far as the mill, south of Trenton, what seemed to be a good crossing point. The result was that we decided to cross to the other side in the night and then encircle them, but with a small force left on the east of the river to get at them when they were crossing.

My own feeling was that Howe was wearing out his welcome in Pennsylvania and might wish to get back to Jersey, but this was not a wise conclusion. It seems the Quakers were lionizing him in Philadelphia, and the money he spent for supplies there at the time made him the most popular man in the city. Still, he was not happy in this dull and solemn environment. Even Trenton had far more social attraction and he was counting, so I learned, on returning to that town as soon as I evacuated, as he was a man accustomed to the comforts of civilian environments rather than the field.

By July 10th, we were again on the march. My own part was to get my Infantry to the west of his force and let our Cavalry and Artillery take the same course of attack as at Trenton. I saw later this was a mistake for it was just what he expected.

The Cavalry charged into them and were met by grape shot. The Artillery could not operate for fear of hitting the Cavalry. My Infantry, also, was met by a volley and promptly mowed down. I withdrew and so did Burr, but we got a blasting that had killed sixty of our men and wounded seventy-two, with four-hundred gone as prisoners. In the exchange of prisoners, I got two hundred back, but we wasted our ammunition and the battle of Trenton was canceled out by this defeat.

I was heartbroken, and so was Burr. We never again came together in battle, for he withdrew his guerrillas and hammered the enemy from the outskirts of Philadelphia, while I went into winter quarters at Valley Forge.

❀

VALLEY FORGE

DICTATED NOVEMBER 20, 1944

HISTORY HAS MADE THE winter of Valley Forge a synonym for starvation and cold, death and the horror of an army deserted by the people it fought for. I do not intend to harrow the reader's feelings by detailing the unutterable suffering we endured there from November until March. It is a tale of the human being, against every odd, willing to keep the faint flickering flame of his life still unquenchable.

My most terrible moments were when, in the old ramshackle barns we had to use as barracks, the poor fellows lay among the hay strewn on the floor and in the lofts. I said a prayer for the dying, knowing it was only lack of food that had taken their life and no one was to blame but myself.

I tried to persuade myself again and again to surrender just for bread, just for warmth, just for the chance to live on, but something mightier than my own mind would seem to take

The Prayer at Valley Forge.
Engraving by John C. McRae after Henry Bruekner, published 1866.
Courtesy National Archives

possession of me, and with such power that I was unable to resist. This was a conviction that Charles' vision and my own astral self were under the guidance of the very Spirit of Life, and that by holding out I would accomplish what I had been destined for.

All that winter, I came to feel more and more this Finger of Fate. It saved me from going insane. It prevented me from ending my own life. It gave me the power to live from one day to the next, with no hope of relief. It even stilled the pangs of my own constant hunger for food. It gave me the strength to stand the groans and cries of my starving men, and even their curses. It left no room for anything, but its own dictum, "Survive and win!"

Martha had come to look like the wraith of her own self. She was always at my side, and was constant in her care of me and of the men who were unable to walk. She came to be their only comfort. She talked and read to them from the Scriptures when they asked her for this distraction. We had to be so careful not to let the enemy know our condition and that prevented some help that might have been given us.

The men ate the horses. Then, they ate the bark off the trees and the roots. We even beat up the shrubbery for the insect nests, for what nourishment might be in spiders and ants. We caught the rats and ate them. We made traps for rabbits, but only three were ever caught. We had no ammunition and could not hunt. We starved, down to the last ounce of flesh on our bones.

We also were now all but naked, for our clothing had to be slept in, as well as worn in the day time. Our blankets were now thin and verminous rags. Men let their beards grow for warmth, and we tied the hay around our feet and legs to keep them from freezing. All the men were like wild creatures, and gave up all attempts at either cleanliness or even decency.

Of the six hundred who went into camp, four hundred had gone when March came, some to their homes and two hundred and fifty to their graves.

How did we keep going? Now and then would come a bag of wheat from Burr, a sack of beans from Von Steuben, or a bit of money from Franklin or Adams with which to buy flour and make bread.

One man never forgot us for a single week Aaron Burr. He would send something, even if it was but a pound of money or a pair of rabbits. What can one say of such a friend, I think only that kept my men and me alive. When I would mention his name, there would be a low murmur of "God bless Aaron Burr." When we were trying to dig the graves with our weak hands and bury our dead, a little moan of sorrow was all we could muster when one or two would fall with exhaustion. My own great natural strength failed me, though I was the last man to fall to my knees when I attempted to bury a shovel in the frozen earth. When that happened, I knew the end was near for me and them.

This happened on a cold and bitter winter day in February and I lay where I fell for a time, and said again "All is well."

No words but these ever came when the last ditch was reached. When I managed to stand and to pick up my shovel, a young farmer, who had seen me fall, climbed over his fence and came to my aid. When I told him what I was doing, he was very much touched. We, he and I, buried my poor starved soldier and put a bit of evergreen over the grave. The farmer then asked what he died of, and I told him "Of starvation." At that, he seemed incredulous and evidently did not believe me, and walked away. Again, I said to myself "All is well" and went to the Forge to rest, exhausted by my efforts.

Martha, too, was lying down. There was no other way of keeping from freezing. We had scoured every inch of the roadside and woods for fallen branches and odd pieces of sticks. Now there was nothing with which to make a fire.

It was about six o'clock in the afternoon and still daylight. I was roused from my thoughts by the pounding on the door, and the young farmer asking if I was in the mood to speak with him. Of course, I got up and welcomed him. He had been thinking over my poor soldier's death by starvation, and could not believe it.

Valley Forge—Washington & Lafayette. Winter 1777–78.
Engraving by H.B. Hall after Alonzo Chappel

I asked if he would care to see the others. I took him to the barn where the poor fellows burrowed in the hay in their clothes and blankets. They came to attention when I gave the command and their sorry appearance in their rags and bearded faces, hands like claws and feet wrapped in rags with hay, all made the farmer stare in shocked astonishment.

"How did this happen?"

"It is because the Colony of New York that offered to keep us if we would fight for their freedom has now deserted us. We have had no food, ammunition or money from that Colony for five months."

This was the signal for an outburst of anathema from the men. I went on to say that many had deserted and gone home. Of the four hundred left, half were now dead of starvation.

My voice, now weak with hunger, began to grow even fainter and I fell in a faint on the barn floor. My men came and pulled me over to a pallet, doing what they could do to restore me by rubbing my hands and getting water down my throat. Nothing seemed to work, so the farmer ran across to his place and in a few moments returned with a jug of whiskey. This was the life-saver, and I was soon sitting up. The men stood about silently, with wistful eyes at the life-giving jug of whiskey. The farmer, however, did not weaken and present it to them, though it could have been purchased for two shillings. Instead, he pounded down the cork and left.

The men grinned at each other faintly and shook their heads. I got up and went to the forge determined to sell something, if I still had anything salable, and get that jug of whiskey for the men. In a few moments, the farmer reappeared with two jugs of the premium stuff and presented them to me. I almost fell on his neck. That night, the men were drunk and happy in oblivion. One jug sent all off to the land of Nod. I kept the other for an emergency. My plan miscarried, as the men stole that jug the next day and drank it all up. I was never to see the farmer again, for he ran away from me as if I had been a pestilence when I said;

"I am George Washington, and I wish to thank you."

Such was my reputation with my fellow citizens.

A Message from Above

I was all but unconscious one day from cold and hunger. Martha was with me, and almost in as bad a case. I was in the stupor that hunger brings on when I suddenly saw Fanny Ball, my grandmother, even more clearly than on that first occasion when she stood before me. In a compassionate voice she said,

"My dear George, you will never be left to die here. Help is on the way."

That was all. I spoke of it to Martha and she, as always, took the cheerful view and seemed to be strengthened by it. In two hours, a man arrived with a letter from Aaron Burr that also contained two pound notes and the words:

"All I have at present. More as soon as I can lay hands on a debtor of mine. Never give up the fight. Yours to the end. Aaron."

I was all but prostrated by the emotion this dear message caused. Martha knelt, prayed for him and blessed him. This, once more, showed the divine soul of Aaron Burr. That soul that has been burdened with such sorrow, cruelty and calumny as have been the lot of few men in human history.

※

In a week the winter broke, and I began to realize that this was my time to get my wits together and see what could be done. My own forces were practically nothing. LaFayette had a thousand men down at the south of us, and was being lionized by the Pennsylvanians. His men were all well and in excellent fettle. His popularity, and above all his title, made him the center of attraction and he had no difficulty in raising funds to purchase food for the winter. Also, he was so charming that the ladies could never get enough of his society. Balls and parties were given in his honor from one end of the County to the other. His Headquarters were at York and he was all over the countryside, meeting many of the wealthy men of the Colony who were also in love with his personality and delightful manner.

We met only twice that winter. Once, when he rode over to see the men and brought a gift of two hundred pounds. This, I at once expended for food, and it kept us going for a period of six weeks. He came to see later what I had been through, and asked why I had not revealed my plight to him.

Then I gave him the truth. Hatred of me had grown to be so great that the very mention of my name was enough to hurt him in the public's eyes and that, I hoped, might not happen. I gave him the account of our sufferings and he wept. Once more, he came with money and saved us. He brought one hundred pounds. This was in February, when we were spent and dying. It was the thing that put me on my feet. I knew I must survive, and so I got myself a side of bacon, a sack of flour, a pound of tea, with a jug of molasses and a sack of corn meal. The rest went for the men.

We are happy to have this chance to tell the plain facts of what we owe to LaFayette. This has not, to my knowledge, been told before.

One other savior I must not fail to mention, John Adams.

In December, I had written him the whole story. He set about collecting money, food and clothing for us at once. In January, he came on horseback with a wagonload of grain and salted meat, and in his wallet was a draft for two hundred pounds. In the wagon there was also a bale of blankets and a pile of warm clothing including socks, moccasins and boots, mended, but serviceable. Abigail Adams, his glorious wife, had spent all her spare time knitting, mending and begging for us.

This came in time to sustain us for three weeks and aided us in keeping warm. Adams, too, wept when he saw me, and realized what the desertion of the Congress had meant. We were now simply a band of derelicts with no standing in the Colonies, and no name but mine was ever mentioned in connection with our recurring defeats.

Adams was, as always, true to his principles and no weathercock. He knew we must be free to become a nation. He alone in Massachusetts was bold and brave enough to stand by me all through the war; Von Steuben in New York, Burr in New Jersey, Franklin in Pennsylvania, and my own Colony, Virginia gave me the only other help. There was one more, and he gave until it endangered his credit—William Claiborne, who died a martyr to his sense of duty. Claiborne was the one man to seek me out at Valley Forge, and when he saw the emaciated men and my own thin and strained face, he gripped my hand as he said;

"God Almighty, Washington, you are all dying men. Give me a week, and I'll have the money to put you in trim again."

He was better than his word, for he had an account in New York and exhausted it to give me three hundred pounds, which was what made our survival possible in March.

I love to speak the name Claiborne. It was borne only by good and brave men in those days.

❧

MARTHA HAD EXHAUSTED her funds at the bank at home, and my own had long been drained out. When we wrote to our overseer for money, he replied with the information that the taxes and the poor crops had consumed all our resources that year, and even made it impossible for him to pay his own wages.

Corinth, my body servant, wrote me from time to time but I knew there was nothing to be had from Mount Vernon. I had been obliged to borrow a hundred pounds on some of the land when I was last home. The attempt to borrow more had failed, unless I would mortgage my father's home. That I could not do, even to save my life.

To those who wonder why I was so visionary and impractical, I can only say I was still not dismissed and neither was the Army. We were the employees of the Continental Congress even though the men had not had any pay for many months when we went into winter quarters. I wrote each week and even oftener, and sent my reports to the Military Affairs Committee. They knew the exact situation. It did not seem to me possible that they would ignore my reports – but they did, all but John Adams. We hoped against hope that each month would bring relief. None ever came from the political arbiters.

Let this be known.

It seemed incredible that a body of elected men could ignore those reports, and neither discharge or succor us. Neither would I surrender unless they ordered me to do so. I wrote them for orders. None ever came.

Now let this be known to the American people.

Despite all the whitewashing, back-scratching, and falsifying of history that has gone to cover up the sins of that Congress, the fact remains it was they who were the poltroons and the deserters.

We survived thanks to five patriots – Burr, Adams, Franklin, Claiborne and a foreigner – LaFayette. They were our saviors and incidentally, the saviors of the Revolution.

✿

YORKTOWN

Dictated November 22, 1944

We did not like to speak of our bitter hunger to strangers and so, perhaps, the people never really knew why I could not stand when any visitor came to my poor shack that I called my quarters at Valley Forge.

It was the old forge, abandoned by the farmers of the village near us. I was glad to be free of rent, so I did what I could to make it habitable and with Martha, made it our home for five months, from October, 1779 to March, 1780. We took pains to keep it clean, though naturally the flooring was of dirt and we had no skins to lay over it. I used to put my feet on a stool to keep them from freezing. Martha, also.

We had no furniture, but for my chair and table that were always carried in the transport wagon, and a couple of camp stools.

We had the forge for a stove, and thank God, that was all that made it possible to survive. A small window, with no panes, was all the means of getting light when the doors were closed. We put my old shirt over it and a bit of light, enough to see to move about, would seep through the edges.

No candles and no wood, except what we could pick up in the forest or find by the roadside. We used to go on a hunt for the dried twigs and fallen branches, and were happy if an hour's search would yield an armful. Soon, they were ashes, but they took the damp chill from the air. My God, when I think of Martha and her cheerful way of saying,

"George, I really feel quite comfortable in this old forge."

This, when she was dangling her feet from the top of the forge, or lying on it with a blanket wrapped about her, and a bit of straw in a pallet to break the pain of the hard stone under her. When spring finally came, she looked eighty years old, and she was not yet fifty. Later, with food and care, she regained something of her old freshness and color; but her hair was now snow white and the lines so deep about her eyes, that she always was aged in appearance after that winter. I, too, not much to look upon in my youth, was a terrible spectacle before the spring came.

Our lives were spent in silence, mostly, or in prayer. I prayed to the God I felt was unconscious of my plight and with, perhaps, small faith in a divine personality who would hear and send help. I knew in my Masonic work that immutable law is all there is, everywhere and at all times. This is the thing that makes one pause before committing an irrevocable action. All that was happening could easily be traced to my own decision to persist in my endeavor to free this Country from Britain. The law was indifferent and impersonal. I had made the choice. My Countrymen, with the few exceptions I have mentioned, were either uninterested, or ignorant of the situation.

The Tories and Aristocrats wanted to keep the settlers in perpetual servitude to Britain. The ordinary citizen was either too poor to give aid, or unaware of the suffering our fight for his natural rights had occasioned.

We came to the 30th of March with but enough strength to sit up, but not to stand for more than a few moments. My men lay under the hay in utter weakness, past even the pangs of hunger. One was dead, and the others unaware of it for two days, as the still frosty weather had arrested decomposition. One of them came to me on his knees, for his legs would not support him. The distance from the barns to the forge was about two hundred feet. He brought me a little bit of cheer, for he said,

"General, I'm being taken home by my folks. They are out here and would like to speak to you."

I tried to rise, but could not. He saw that, and began to weep. Martha was able to sit up and stand, and it was she who went out and spoke to the poor fellow's family. They gave her a side of bacon, a jug of molasses, and two sacks of flour. The father and a young brother of our man brought this in to the forge. I begged them to give me but a little of each, and take the rest to the men. This they did, and it saved us to live on a few days more.

The parting with this man I never forgot. He was only twenty when he came with the regiment, but now looked forty-five. His father wept, as did his brother. In fact, all were in tears. We said goodbye, and my soldier went down on his knees and kissed my hand. I tried to embrace him, but my arms were too weak, and I could only speak the words my heart felt so keenly. We never met again, but he wrote me after a year and said he was well, now married and happy. That letter was a great comfort to me, and I replied fully and in detail.

Martha, ever my comforter and inspiration, was certain we were now to be blessed in some unexpected way, and seemed to really believe what she said. I, less hopeful, but never dampening any cheerful idea of hers, did not feel so confident of any such miracle. It did happen, much to my astonishment.

The Jersey Congress gave me the credit for Trenton and now they had heard of my poor men and myself at Valley Forge and, it seemed, considered it a poor reflection on their Colony to have men starve in their midst. Too late to save the seventy-five who had died of privation and cold at Valley Forge, but it was more than we could expect after what we had experienced when we appealed vainly to New York, Massachusetts, Virginia, and Pennsylvania.

At once, they sent a message to me from Trenton with a draft for two thousand pounds. I had to receive the messenger in my chair, and when he told me what the envelope he laid before me contained, I was too weak to control the tears that came. He, too, was affected. I learned that he had broken down before the Congress at Trenton as he described all he had seen at Valley Forge.

To their credit, I now wish to say that they lost no time but individually came with supplies, each man bearing his private contribution. In two days I was able to stand, and when one man offered to go with me to get the orders placed for supplies and ammunition, I was able to get into a carriage and attend to the business. All now was up to me again. Martha said at once,

"George, we shall now move to Trenton and you shall be tended to properly until I can get you strong. I will arrange the matter of our quarters while you see to your men." This she did so quickly, that within twenty-four hours, I was housed in a tavern and before a warm fire, receiving those who came to contract for our ammunition and food. I got the men well-placed in an old warehouse and sanitary arrangements made, so that in forty-eight hours, they were brought in wagons to the new barracks. We burned the old barn for sanitary reasons.

Clothing, boots and new blankets I got and all old garments and blankets were burned, even old knapsacks, and new ones supplied. Once more we slept, bathed, ate and drank in comfort. The men, most of them, soon were able to walk, and to even go about the town, but five of them had died on the way to Trenton. I was with them, and went back and forth with the wagonloads.

The people of Trenton lined the streets and saw the poor soldiers lying, like ghosts, on the clean straw in the wagons. The men cheered, but the women, most of them, sobbed when a skeleton hand would be raised to wave in acknowledgement. The crowd about the warehouse was dense and when the men were carried by lusty young Trentonites to their clean pallets with fresh husks, they, too, moaned in sorrow at such scarecrows.

One hundred and thirty-two survived. They were fed and nursed back to health, but never fought again. That was not possible and even I, with my more than average constitutional strength, was not again able to mount a horse by a leap from the ground, or to lift a log at a house-raising, as I once did. That story often has been told in print.

However, all now was hopeful activity. LaFayette came to see me, and we were now able to think and to plan. He was all for action, and I was happy to pore over my maps and notes once more. We had no scouts, so I could not make any calculations as to the enemy's exact position, much less his strength.

Franklin wrote me that the news was seeping out that the British were about ready to strike the forces of LaFayette, which were only about two regiments. I wanted Burr to join him, but did not wish to ask that, knowing his preference for individual action. I got a messenger to him and said as much, but no reply came.

When I led my men myself out of Trenton to march to York and join LaFayette, we were but two hundred strong. We had no artillery and no cavalry, only foot soldiers. My plan was to support LaFayette, who had two regiments and a force of twenty cavalry and four cannon. I had the ammunition and supplies for a month, with my small force of men who had the muskets and knives of my old regiment. I took along three doctors, medical supplies, litters, and hospital tents.

My horse was a fine strong chestnut, and I soon had him trained to the sound of firearms. He was a great animal to cavort and make a show. This I wanted to cure him of, but had no time to spend in that sort of work, so he made me very conspicuous when we were out.

Martha never was so happy or so busy. She became the heroine of the hour, and was entertained in most of the homes of the members of society in Trenton. She always wore very simple garments, but her lovely voice and fine sense of dignity as well as her very lively conversation seemed to delight her new friends, and all that made me feel a sense of gratitude to these good people of Jersey. All in all, the people of that Colony seemed the most natural and kindly of those I had met in any of the Colonies.

When we started off, I had only two Sergeants, no Corporals, no Captains, and no Lieutenants. I had to teach the two Sergeants, fine young farmers, how to care for, and how to drill

Washington Receiving a Salute.
Print by William Holl after John Faed.
Published 1860s. Courtesy National Archives

the men. I gave them a few instructions in the art of marching and how to make the most of musket reversed. Also, I gave them a bit of advice about the way in which they must use their knife, and that they were not able to do. One said,

"I can't kill a man the way I would a pig. Give me a pistol."

I did so, and then gave him target practice, and found he couldn't hit anything. However, he was all right to help the Sergeant in many ways, and I let well enough alone. Later, I found he was near-sighted and could not see twenty feet ahead of him, so he had to be used as an orderly. Terry and Jack had long been gone and both were lost to me now, so I used this nice fellow, Ben, for a messenger and to assist me in my quarters.

At last, we were ready to start for York. The whole town turned out and cheered us. My men were fine, healthy, and willing young chaps, and I was proud to see how well they had responded to the drill and training. The wagon train was in good hands, and

I had once more a fine horse under me. I tried not to think of the past, but said farewell in my thoughts to the sad months and their tragedies.

We made camp at nightfall only seven miles from York. All was in order, and I hoped we might be with LaFayette in twenty-four hours. This, however, was frustrated by a small, but unfortunate accident. My Sergeant, who was of most use, was impelled to go scouting around and he ran upon a bad piece of news, nothing less than that we now were simply lying three miles behind the enemy.

This made me change all my plans, and I withdrew the next morning two miles, and then asked the Sergeant to get some information as to the roads outlying. He did this, and I found I was in a pocket.

I marched all night to detour, and in the morning was safely out of danger but with the loss of three days, and the men not pleased to find I had not known the enemy lay before me. I addressed them and tried to raise their opinion of me, but I found that I was in for immediate criticism if anything chanced to go wrong. I now had to reach LaFayette by a much longer route, one requiring a march of sixteen miles to the south and four miles north again.

However, we did this in three days, and were in good condition when we arrived back of LaFayette's lines. He had his sentries posted a mile behind him, and they were on the watch for us. I gave my Sergeants orders to follow and rode into York.

We were received with a spirit of cordiality that was as new to me as it was heartening. LaFayette gave me his quarters and went to a tavern. I found myself in the home of a very charming widow, who did not seem entirely to relish the change. However, I tried to win her over by a few well placed remarks, and she soon was most charming and friendly.

We now gave every moment to planning the attack. I was sure that if we did not delay, they might be taken off guard. We went over every detail and I spoke my mind frankly as to my own contingent being far from a fighting force. LaFayette was most understanding, and we laid the action out in detail as to the position and manner of attack. All was to be coordinated by the time we got into their front. I wished to avoid any semblance of my Trenton strategy and so decided on frontal attack to open with, and a flank movement to turn them back on their center. We then would come up in the rear and make a diversion.

All this was the plan. Whether we could make it work was the question. I wished to open with a shower of grape shot, immediately followed by an advance of infantry. Then when they were spent, to have a renewal of cannon and grape shot while our Infantry reloaded and so on, but all would depend, of course, on the enemy's maneuvers.

We were well into the midst of this plan, when I saw a flaw in it that made me jump and exclaim,

"God Almighty! We are making it easy for them to turn over our left flank!"

So, we began all over and tried a dozen plans, none of which were practicable. I was weary, and so was LaFayette. I suggested that we both lie down for an hour and rest, and then come at it fresh. This we did. We were wakened by a noise in my boots. This turned out to be a large cat that had somehow got in and chased a mouse into my boot, which was at the head of the bed. We had a merry chase after the mouse and cat, and finally drove both of them out in the hallway. By this time, we were wide awake. I saw my own course clearly, and by the very manner in which the cat had pocketed the mouse.

I called LaFayette's attention to the way the cat had made a feint one side, drawn back, and then circled round and cut off the exit of the mouse into the hall. Whether this was all an accident or a divine interposition I shall never know, but the whole thing had a very great significance to my mind, for how the cat got into my room with a locked door and closed windows, I do not know. There was a low fire in the fireplace, and the cat could not have come down the chimney.

All the rest of the night, we worked on this and had all

in order for execution by dawn. LaFayette went home to bed, and I threw myself in mine and was unconscious until noon. We marched out of York three days after our arrival, and reached the enemy in two days. Howe's forces were in a little valley which made them difficult to get at. This was a complete cancellation of all we had worked on. I saw at once that he was in a pocket and could be held there if I could get in behind, in front, and shove him. So I was not ready to attack for another twenty-four hours.

In the meantime, I had given orders for all to be quiet, build no fires, and to be cautious about firearms and let none go off and alarm the enemy or my plans would be upset. For once, no one disobeyed and I believe our surprise was complete when we attacked them at both ends of the valley simultaneously and with force.

First grape shot, then muskets, alternately. We had a hundred men on the hill blasting away to their left, and the same on their right. In half an hour, it was all over. They ran up a flag of truce, and I sent LaFayette into the front with instructions to ask for an armistice and to say it must be a complete surrender with all the British now as our prisoners.

Howe was there, and LaFayette said he was white with fear and trembling like an aspen. In half an hour more, LaFayette rode back to me with the sword of Cornwallis, the General in command of the Hessians, and the armistice agreement in his hand, signed by Howe.

So far, all was well. I was so happy that I hugged LaFayette and he was crying like a schoolboy, his face all dirty from the stains of his soiled hands that had been inked when his quill spattered as he wrote out the terms of the armistice in French, for he could not read or write English, though he now spoke it well, but with a strong accent. I washed his face, and we both had a good laugh.

He then told me the details, and I was glad to learn that Howe was in mortal dread of me. He said to LaFayette,

"That man Washington is like a cat. He has many lives. I have beaten him several times and he always comes back. I cannot win against such an animal. He is either more or less than human.

Here I surrender."

No such words ever got into print. What was given to the public were the two simple words: "I surrender."

Anyway, LaFayette repeated this to me, and I was glad Howe had the fairness to say I was still unbeaten.

We celebrated by giving the enemy, as well as our own men, a cask of whiskey and what we could muster of food. All fraternized in the evening and no unpleasant incident occurred. I sent off the news by messenger to Trenton, another to New York, with a third to Philadelphia. This done, I called in all the officers and congratulated them.

Then, I ordered all the troops out and in review I addressed them and gave them my compliments and my thanks. I also told them of their dead comrades whom I prayed might, in spirit, share this victory.

Martha was in Trenton, and I had given the messenger a special letter to her, so that she should be first to know the good news. On his return, he brought a little note from her that only said,

"George, darling, I knew you would win this time."

So all was well.

Surrender of Cornwallis at Yorktown, Virginia, October 19, 1781.
Lithograph by James Baillie, circa 1845.

Surrender

Dictated November 23, 1944

My own emotions were of such power that I nearly fainted when LaFayette gave me the news. I wanted to be alone, to fall on my knees and thank God in words that I knew would sound too extreme to other ears. I wished to invoke the spirit of Charles and tell him the glad tidings, and to call to my father and mother and ask them to share my joy. Above all, I longed to speak to my dead soldiers, and give them the credit for the victory that had come too late for them to share in it.

All I could do at the moment was to share with this dear friend the happiness he had brought. We finally got ourselves calmed down so that we could plan what was now to be done. I had no food for six thousand men, and I could not pretend that I had. The only thing was to sign the Peace Pact at once, and free the British. This I decided to do that very day.

I got my old writing case out, and began to compose the Treaty even before I told the men of their victory. They must be fed and the food I had would be gone by morning, unless I got the Peace Pact signed.

My words were few but explicit, and are to be found in the archives. I demanded complete surrender, evacuation of the British Army, a recognition of the independence of the American Colonies of British rule, a full recognition of our position in the family of nations as an independent State, and the customary rules of conduct between the signers now and in the future. All this, with specific demands for indemnity for destruction of property, the amount to be placed at a *million pounds sterling* my troops were to receive the British colors that day, along with the British weapons and ammunition.

So much had to be left to the future that I dreaded leaving a loophole, and so had a chap look over my terms who had been a lawyer in Trenton, and was now a Sergeant. He said this covered the essentials, and to make it clear that the details would follow, but the major conditions were to be at once in force and the ceremony of surrender to take place that afternoon.

All this I embodied in my Peace Pact and copied in duplicate, so that it was four o'clock when LaFayette faced Howe with it. He read the terms and exclaimed,

"By God, that man Washington is a demon and there is no use shilly-shallying with him. Give me my quill."

He signed both copies, and gave LaFayette one to return to me.

In the meantime, I had my few troops drawn up in review formation. They looked so few, so poor, so shabby but I was all the prouder for that. When I gave them the news, they simply looked stunned until I took the flag from the standard and made the Sergeant kneel and take the oath of allegiance. This was very simple, and is still in use with you. He repeated the brief words after me.

By that time, every man raised his hand in salute and kept it there until the Sergeant rose. Then I asked the other Sergeant to do likewise. Following him, the officers of LaFayette's two regiments. These forty officers marched in line and saluted the Flag, knelt in front of me, and repeated the words of the oath in unison. They returned and marched their men, a company at a time, to the front. They would kneel and take the oath, then rise and march to the rear. My own little regiment came last. As they took the oath and rose, a mighty cheer went up while they marched to the rear.

Then came my own oath. I knelt on one knee and with the standard held by my left hand, I raised the folds of the Flag to my lips and kissed it. By six-thirty the Peace Pact was signed, and I asked to have the British troops in their ranks by eight, which at that season was not quite twilight.

This, Howe did. With my friend LaFayette, I rose to his quarters and he took me to the field where more men than I had ever faced stood at attention as I, in my shabby uniform, passed before them with my hand at salute, though I could barely sustain the position, I was so weak. I said in the few words, which I believe have been recorded, that I was happy to have the honor of receiving a signed Peace Pact from their Commander and I wished to express my appreciation of their valor personally, and hoped that all good fortune would attend them in the future at home. I also said our troops, through me, desired to express the same sentiments.

When I finished, they were silent and I walked away. My horse was near, but I dared not try to mount him, as I was feeling faint. LaFayette gave me his shoulder, and I made an effort to say goodbye to General Howe; but all grew dark and I fell forward and lay unconscious for two hours. This seems never to have been repeated or, at any rate, recorded. General Howe was said to have remarked,

"The poor chap has never won a victory before. It is too much for him."

LaFayette told him of Valley Forge and that starvation had been the cause of my weakness, upon which the choleric old General blurted out,

"Then by God, he ought to be put out of his misery. I hope he dies."

Well, I didn't die, but I came damned near it; and when I was on my cot, I lay there four days in a sort of stupor. The men were dispersed, but I was in the care of a doctor and the orderly, Ben, with LaFayette and a man I knew who had been with me in New York. I was in a tent and near a fine spring, so we lived practically in the open. My entourage slept in blankets on the ground. My horse was tethered to a nearby tree, as was LaFayette's.

No one knew where I was. Franklin got the news and came to Trenton. There he learned of my prostration, but did not know how to get to me. On the fifth day, I was able to sit in the saddle and managed to stay in it for the six miles required to make Philadelphia. Martha joined me there, and I was made comfortable at an inn that she found, where Franklin could be nearby and run in of an evening.

We talked over plans and ways and means to get my own ideas into the minds of the people. Franklin made a great splurge on the front page of his paper, calling me the Savior of the Colonies. Men of importance called on me and asked to be made the head of the new government. Naturally, I had no power to promise or even to suggest anything at the time.

What I wanted was an invitation to lay my ideas before a Congress of the thirteen Colonies. This, Franklin suggested and in the end, after four weeks, that was done.

I was quietly and, in a way, prayerfully regaining my strength. I kept to myself and LaFayette came to see me daily. I longed to see Burr and Adams, but all I got was a brief note from each, congratulating me and wishing me well. I felt a terrible sense of isolation. I wanted Burr especially to be with me; but he was ill, and lay in the house of his wife-to-be. Adams was too far distant and could not leave his farm in Massachusetts. I wished so much to have his wise counsel. Also, I hoped Hamilton might come to see me, and tell me how New York State was taking the victory. Of course, I learned later that in both Boston and New York the people were parading and joyously ringing bells. Meetings of prayer and thanksgiving were being held, the merchants were decorating their shops with bunting, women were making flags, little boys were wearing their hats turned up on three sides, men wore a white cockade on their hat, and ladies held high their heads that were ornamented with a white cockade. All in all, the people were happy.

The Tories, however, were in a panic and many were closing their businesses out and planning to emigrate to Canada or the West Indies. Many did go from New England, but the New Yorkers did not take fright and stayed on to take their luck with the new regime.

I was busily formulating some sort of Constitution, or Magna Carta, that could be presented to the people. I had been close enough to Colonial politics to understand where we must be strong in our new regime. We must have a form of government that the people could participate in, and also understand. It must

be one that represented all classes and also gave each a fair share
of responsibility. I knew the local administration was but the
miniature of what the whole State must be. Each Colony had its
peculiar problems and they must each deal with them, but with
an eye to the general welfare. I hoped to make some outline that
would serve as a nucleus for a Magna Carta.

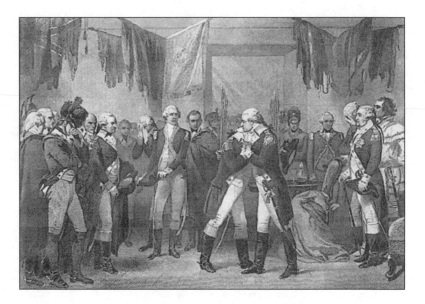

Washington's Farewell to His Officers, 1783.
Engraving by Phillibrown after Alonzo Chappel.

The inauguration at Federal Hall, overlooking Wall and Broad Streets, New York on April 29, 1789 when Washington became President.

Howard Pyle, Harper's Weekly, 1883.

CHAPTER SIX

CONGRESS,
THE CONSTITUTION,
AND
PRESIDENCY

❦

DICTATED NOVEMBER 24, 1944

MY PLANTATION WAS ALL but ruined by the shameless neglect and mismanagement of the overseer who, it seems, came to feel the place was his own to do with, or to neglect, as he chose. The house presented a perfect picture of the whole estate: the quarters of a lazy, dirty, stupid man who would not even in his own interest exert himself if he had sufficient to exist on.

My plans were made to take over my father's estate, which was now mine, and in good condition because of the excellent work of our overseer, Carey. He was getting old, but he had been diligent and wished to make as good a showing as possible. We had so little stock that Mark was able to care for it all without help. There were now at Mount Vernon three house servants, my old cook, a maid, and Corinth. For the field work, there were Carey, his wife, and two other couples. Only a small crop was possible, but it was enough to support everyone and give food to the stock. In the stables were my prize mare Belinda and two work horses, with a horse that I had raised called Canby, a fine animal for the saddle. We also had two old cows and some sheep and pigs, with a number of dogs who were getting old, and the poultry. Belinda and Canby were simply ornamental, and of no use in my absence, as I never permitted anyone to mount my own saddle horses but myself.

Mount Vernon
Courtesy National Archives

The house Carey had closed, and it only needed a few repairs to be in perfect order. We went to live at Mount Vernon. All were making the homecoming a cause for rejoicing, and I saw once more how the seeds my parents had sown in the hearts of these dependents had come to bear rich fruitage in their love and loyalty.

After returning from the war, Martha and I felt as if we had to start all over again. I wished to replenish the stock, and that would do it. Also, I needed new machinery and tools, and repairs were needed on barns and the slaves' quarters. Carey and I worked over the plans until we saw how we might make Mount Vernon once more the prosperous estate it had been under my father and Charles. Martha also bustled about, and with the house servants soon had the old home bright and shining, and in every way comfortable as in the days past. When we had the kitchen moved and whitewashed, all the cooking utensils scoured and shining, a little passageway was built to connect it with the dining room door. I was in such a state of joy that I began to feel like a young man once more, though I was now a broken-down wreck of what I had been.

The change in my feelings began to show in my face and body, and the old muscular strength returned, so that in six weeks I lifted the main timbers we used to replace the old ones under the roof by my own hands alone. This I did, while the servants stood by and cheered. I wanted to test myself, and when I met the test successfully, I felt a glow of happiness that I had not known for many years.

I set this down to show the great and beautiful response of nature when one can assist Her with a spirit of joyfulness.

All was humming with life in a few weeks, and I began to think my life was overflowing with blessings when the call came from Adams to come to a meeting in New York to give my views on the founding of a new and liberal form of government. I was dashed at this, for I could not see my way to go when I had so much to do. Still, I knew how much would depend upon the grasping of the moment if the Congress was to be, in fact, a going concern by their own efforts. All I could think of was Mount Vernon, I could not bear to leave again. Martha was in despair, and said,

"Surely now that you have freed the Country, other men can do what has to be done?"

IN THE END, I HAD to make my personal desire a secondary matter, and was off on a good horse, Canby, to Baltimore.

Arriving in Baltimore, I found a wait of three days and so called on the Commander at the Post. I was glad I made this trip, for in the end it freed me of all illusions, and I had a clear picture of where the strength in our Country lay and where its weakness. I found this young man quite impossible in his manner and his attitude toward the Revolution, and so cut my call short. I also called upon the Carringtons. The wife was still living, and the home was in the care of her daughter and husband. Mrs. Carrington, also, was quite British in her sympathies. Then and there, I ceased to feel as a Virginian and became an American.

No fealty to that old Colony, as against the others, remained. I thought of Governor Patrick Henry, of William Claiborne, of George Rogers Clark and all his heroic deeds, and I thought of the money Claiborne had robbed himself and his family of in order to save our Cause, and of Henry's taking his own money to equip Clark's little band, and of the magnificent results to the Cause.

My decisions made in that Inn in Baltimore, where I lodged those three days, were the ones that underlay all that followed in my work in this mortal life.

The packet made a fair voyage to New York, and the old Battery was a familiar sight when I came on shore. Adams was stopping at my favorite tavern and had my old quarters there. He was representing Massachusetts in the present session of the Congress, which had thirteen representatives, one from each Colony.

The meeting with Adams was a deep joy to both of us, and we remained together most of the night, conferring on the task ahead. My own contempt for the members of the Colonial Legislature I had been the victim of made me none too hopeful of the results of any body of politicians. Hamilton and Adams naturally tried to soften my aspersions, and said,

"You will get nowhere, Washington, unless you keep the Congress in a sympathetic mood and refrain from any reproaches. They are well aware of how they mistreated you, but they do not relish being reminded of it. You won in spite of them, and they know that, also. Try and curb your feelings so that you save their face, and you can then accomplish something."

I knew this to be good advice, but a bitter pill for me to swallow when I remembered all they had done, and left undone to harm my poor comrades. Hamilton, also, tried to make me less bitter. I promised I would do my best to ignore the past, and think and speak only of the future.

❧

The Constitutional Convention

On the day that I met the Congress in May, 1787, I wore my old uniform and cloak, for it was cold. I was rather pleased at the way they received me. All stood, including the President of the Congress, and a seat was given me beside him. When the members were seated, Hamilton made a brief speech about my services and that I had never deserted my men or my Post. He told of my sacrifices, and my wife's, to procure food and ammunition.

Many had not known this, and the information came as a shock. They also heard of the help Adams had given when we were starving, and still I would not leave my men. He spoke of Martha, and her sharing of my cruel hardship, until we were all but dead when help came. He gave the figures that told of the soldiers who died of starvation, and lie at Valley Forge in unknown graves. In short, he paved the way, and said all I wished to say of my poor men and their sufferings. When he finished, I felt well satisfied that these men knew what they had done by their neglect.

All was stillness when Hamilton finished. No sound was heard, and the sense of quiet silenced every man. I then rose, and paid tribute to Martha, and pictured Adams and his dear Abigail as they strove and gathered supplies, and how Adams arrived at Valley Forge just as I had become too weak to even rise to my feet.

At that, they rose to their feet, and one man fairly screamed,

"By God, we should all be on our knees."

At that, they all knelt and the man who had spoken went

on, something in this fashion,

"Almighty God, take this moment of contrition as a sign of our shame and humiliation. Give us the light and the sense to, from this time forth, behave as our fellow members, Hamilton and Adams, have acted. Grant us the divine wisdom to so act in future that our labors may, in some measure, stone from our terrible sin of neglect in the past. Give us to make what reparation is possible and bless our efforts with success."

The "Amen" that followed was strong and determined. I had sat with bowed head, and so had Hamilton. As the members rose, the voice of the man who had prayed was heard saying,

"And now to work."

All this I set down, fearing it has never been reported to you.

You know from the record how I spoke of my plan, how I had outlined it and how it was discussed and, at last after several days, drawn upon to frame the Declaration of Independence. This was a great step forward, and I was well content with it.

We had to now try to form a Central Government to operate with the separate State Governments and that, too, was a heavy task. My own notes were worked out in a series of suggestions that covered many sheets. Adams and Hamilton at all times were with me on each and all ideas and paragraphs, so that they are really co-authors with me of the second paper placed before the Congress.

When we had presented it, the members then took each paragraph and opened a discussion on it. I became bored with the picking at every word, and finally rose one day, and said,

"Gentlemen, I fear I have not long enough to live to hear the end of your discussions of this clear and simple plan of action and so, if you will excuse me, I will return to my home and my personal affairs, which are in sad need of my attention."

This was received in silence and, with a bow, I departed. Adams told me that when I had gone, the member who had prayed, said bluntly,

"Good riddance!"

Adams then rose, and asked if he was speaking of me. He replied that he was, and now saw what had been the trouble in the past – I was too self-important. Adams appealed to the Chair, and Hamilton said in rebuke,

"The Member is indulging in a similar manner to that he is charging to General Washington."

The Member rose, left the room, and the next day resigned from the Congress. He was from Connecticut.

In the end, I had to go back the next day to receive an apology from the whole Congress. After that, we made progress. This instrument we simply held in abeyance, and each took a copy to study over the pending vacation, which lasted over the Christmas, New Year's and Boxing Day festivities.

By now, Virginia saw that we were taking action, and sent Thomas Jefferson to me in New York, where I remained, as I wished to see the thing through before time for my spring planting. Jefferson had with him Madison, of the House of Burgesses.

James Madison
Painting by James Durand
Courtesy National Archives

James Madison was a very astute and talented lawyer, and a neighbor of Jefferson. I had long admired Jefferson as an exception to most of the Aristocrats in his views and his distinguished career in the Colonial Parliament, the House of Burgesses. The same could be said of Madison, who, though belonging to the part of the Aristocrats, was not a rich man, but one who had by his skill in the legal profession acquired a competent income and was looked upon with deep respect by the Aristocrats.

I welcomed these two gentlemen warmly. I knew at last Virginia was convinced that we would become a Nation. We at once found ourselves en rapport, and I was happy when they approved in the main all that we had done, and were planning to do, in the way of forming a new kind of government. I wish here to give Madison his due at last. The Constitution was practically his wording. Jefferson wrote the preamble, but the meat and body of that instrument were worded by Madison. My ideas were all couched in the best possible terms by Madison, and I am happy to say so here. This does not detract in the least from the beautiful and perfect philosophy of the preamble by Jefferson. That gentleman is as eager now, as I, to let our people know the service Madison performed.

꧁꧂

THE CONSTITUTION was adopted after months of much debate, criticism and argument. Discussions continued for days on determining the difference between a federation and a national government. Would there be a "supreme power" or would each state be left to govern itself? By July I was so frustrated at the opposition to a strong central government, I could only see America fail if every state were to be allowed to be a nation unto itself. The future of more than America was in our hands. Adams and Franklin both confided in me their deeply held belief that the work we did in giving birth to this nation of free men was a sacred act on behalf of all of humanity – and so it has come to pass. Would that all Americans truly understood their obligations to maintain liberty for all people – can you not recognize that your precious liberty is now at risk?

Many changes were made, but not such as to weaken the great charter of the people's government. We had no words to express all we felt when the work was done, and I returned home, having had the time during a brief ten-day break when they were drafting the Constitution to visit Valley Forge once again. It had been many years since that painful, horrible winter. Now the land had grown back to lush green – how far we had come.

꧁꧂

Back at Mount Vernon

Jefferson had been to Mount Vernon to see me twice since the Constitution was adopted, and we had spoken of the second instrument to insure beyond doubt each man's rights.

Martha and Jefferson had a pleasant time playing their instruments together, she the harpsichord and he the violin, which it was his habit to take with him wherever he went. I recall so vividly a picture of Martha, seated at her harpsichord in a lemon colored dress of a very thin gauze material, and Jefferson, in his long-tailed blue coat and beautiful waistcoat of yellow silk, playing together in our parlor; while the house servants gathered in the halls to listen, and I sat by a window, happily looking on and listening. Many such evenings we had with Jefferson and always his presence was a source of enjoyment, not only because of his talent for music, but his delightful flow of ideas. We were wont to remain up until the small hours before we could bear to end the talk and exchange of views and experiences. Always, we wound up at two a.m. with a steaming punch and a story or two. No better company could be found than that of Jefferson. We loved to dwell upon those delightful times when he was with us.

Thomas Jefferson
Painting by Gilbert Stuart
Courtesy Boudoin College
Museum of Art

All in all, it was a time of delight. The crops were good, my new stock was healthy and multiplying. My new horse, Canby, was a fine one that seemed to be happy in our companionship and my mare, Belinda, seemed to be glad of our return. This had to come to an end, like most peaceful periods, and in September I was again called by Hamilton to New York. I made no calls in Baltimore this time, and spent the waiting hours in my room at the tavern, or riding over the familiar roads on my horse.

Hamilton met me at the landing and we went at once to the Congress, where we poured over the minutes of the meetings held since my last visit. All was, as usual, contention and quarreling over non-essentials. I was disgusted. Hamilton said, at one point,

"My dear General Washington, you don't know what it is to preside over a lot of egotists. All politicians are that."

I cited himself and Adams as exceptions that proved the truth of his remarks. When I had finished reading the minutes, Hamilton then told me I had been sent for to form a ministry or government. This staggered me. I assured him I was no politician and could not bear talking things to death. He was quite firm in his belief that this was all the more favorable to success.

No plan had been made as yet for the make-up of a governing body, and we had to make a Constitutional Amendment to affect this.

The day on which I appeared before the Congress was a dark and gloomy day, with rain and a high wind. Few of the members came out, and only seven were present when I finally brought out the fact that we must vote for an Amendment. This did not conduce to make for amiability, as it meant delay in closing the day's work. Again, I was attacked by a member who said,

"General Washington, can't you make a concession and leave this matter to us? We are quite capable of running the Congress."

Again I bowed, took my hat, and started for the door.

However, cries of "Stop! Wait!" in a chorus made me pause at the door. The offending member came running up to me and apologized, and I said bluntly,

"I came up from my home at your request. I assure you, it gives me neither pleasure nor profit to be here."

At that, one man rose and with a sneer, and said,

"My opinion is, General Washington, that you feel a cut above us and you are not willing to cooperate."

I answered to the effect that I had been sent for, and at great inconvenience had come in the hope of being of service, but I could plainly see the members as a whole resented my presence, and so I would be happy to withdraw.

No one rose, and so I went out and was packing when a delegation waited on me, begging me to remain, and promising a better atmosphere when the full membership was present.

✿

TWO DAYS LATER, I went to the Congress, and there we passed the first Amendment.

Then came the matter of selecting a President. I suggested either Hamilton or Adams. No one seemed inclined to second either one, and I then kept silent. Finally, John Adams rose, and made a speech I shall ever remember for its eloquence and its poignancy. He had, it seemed, been at great pains to sound out the more influential members, and asked them to name their preference. None had any. Each feared to take the responsibility, or to place it on a fellow member. In the end, he said the only man fearless enough to undertake such a gigantic role was the man who had won the Revolution. This was received with some applause, but not enough to indicate a popular vote. I rose, and said I had never even dreamed of such a thing, and begged them to think of me as quite outside their consideration.

Whether to spite me, or because they had confidence in me, I shall never know; but when the vote was taken, it was unanimous and I was made the first President of the United States of America.

✿

President

Dictated November 25, 1944

My first feeling was one of horror at this new and terrible responsibility, just as I had begun to feel free once more to live my own life. This, of course, was soon replaced by a sense of destiny and a feeling of profound humility that in my weary hands would be confided the welfare of the Republic.

As soon as I could find my voice, I thanked the members briefly, for there was neither goodwill, nor even the pretense of it in their faces. Hamilton, Adams, Livingston, and a half a dozen others were sincere and warm in their attitude, but all the rest of the forty-two members were grinning as if to say,

"Now you are among us for four years. Let's see what *you* can do."

I left the meeting and went at once to my room in the Inn. There beside my table, I fell on my knees and prayed for guidance and strength to so use my office that the people would find in my administration justice, and all the freedom I had fought for. I remained there in a sort of exhausted daze when standing before me, on the other side of the table, appeared again my astral double, this time attired in black velvet and wearing a white court wig, tied with a black ribbon, a fine lace fall and ruffles and with silken stockings and silver buckled shoes. The figure looked as I had never looked in my life. My hair had grown thin from lack of nourishment, but I was not bald. I still wore it in a loop, tied with a narrow black ribbon. Like most people, I did wear a court wig on gala occasions.

The figure was smiling, and seemed happy. I was too astonished to think clearly, and simply stared in awe. Soon it spoke,

"I am now content. You have done your best and you have won your Cause. Now you will rule over the Republic for eight years. Do not stay in office after the second four years. Men who stay in office longer lose all perspective of their own rights and become tyrants. Give all the citizens your love and devotion. Your great and splendid record of service will be a light to lead other patriots in other lands."

Then, it seemed to pass through the table and into me in some way, and I fell over on the floor and lay there in a sort of dreamy, half-conscious state that must have lasted two hours, for I was aroused by the sound of a long and loud knocking at the door. Rising, I admitted Adams, Hamilton, and Livingston, who had come to offer their personal congratulations. I pulled my old self together and ordered some refreshment, and we sat down as congenial a quartet as ever met after a political battle. I was greatly touched by their expressions of loyalty and friendship, and told them I should lean very heavily on their wisdom and counsel.

We parted at nine in the evening, and I promised to be on hand in the morning to organize a Ministry.

❦

I LAY CONNING THE situation for an hour after I retired, but was too weary for any very clear thinking. Awake by seven, I came to my shaving with a strong feeling of confidence. My double had perhaps given me hope that I could meet the situation with some sort of ability, and so I got myself dressed and off, with no qualms of fear that I was unequal to the task given me.

When I arrived at the meeting, the chair on the platform was vacant. All were present, and there was an air of expectancy that made the place electric to my senses. I strode to the platform and sat down in the Chairman's seat. I picked up the gavel, though the silence was complete, but giving one whack, I laid it down and said,

"This meeting is now in order."

The silence was now broken by a titter from my erstwhile attacker. I paid no attention to him, and neither did his fellows. One member, after a brief pause, rose and asked permission to say what he thought should now be done. I gave him the floor, and he proceeded with a long, dry, and boring dissertation on government. The members coughed, shuffled and even tittered, but he was adamant and persisted for two hours, and at the end seemed pleased with his effort to explain what government meant.

At the finish, I decided to take the bull by the horns and cut off any more such wearisome and useless exhibitions. I then addressed the Members briefly, and the essence of my remarks was that most of us present were well aware of the meaning of the word *government*, at which someone laughed, and that was contagious. I fancied I caught Adams there. I explained that our duty was to take the form of government, detailed and ready for use, in the Constitution as we had adopted and begin to apply it in practice. This got a round of applause which heartened me. I fancied Hamilton's fine hands led off.

Then I dwelt briefly on a division of labor of consolidating the interests of the Colonies in certain officials, to be appointed to serve in their separate ways to offer the people the help needed to go forward in their private business. This, too, met with applause.

Then I said I had made a list of these departments and should like to submit it to them for their approval. By this time, the whole membership, with one or two exceptions, were seriously listening and I felt hopeful of their cooperation. I spoke of the Cabinet, for I could think of no better name. I had never heard the word used, but I wished to attach to our new form of government entirely new designations and Cabinet did indicate a close and intimate condition that expressed my idea of an official family.

I named the following Departments: State, Army, Treasury, and what I designated as the Department of the Republic.   All were silent as I mentioned each office, and the duties pertaining to it.   At last, one man said,

"What is the Department of the Republic?"

I explained that I hoped to make it the Department for the aid of settlers, by collecting information regarding the land, waterways, the quality of the soil, and any knowledge that would assist a prospective settler in choosing his location or in transporting his crops. This met with loud and long applause.

Now I was beginning to gain confidence, and I gave a more detailed account of the situation in the Western lands, which I had seen, and the need of much help before that section would support settlements. They seemed astonished that I knew all this from personal observation, and again applauded.

At this point, I asked if it was their pleasure to recess for an hour for refreshment. The motion was made by my old enemy and heckler in a thunderous tone, which said clearly,

"I've had more than enough."

It was seconded and carried, and the meeting adjourned. Adams, Livingston and I went to a nearby tavern and got a bite of lunch and some ale. We laughed over our friend, whom ever after I dubbed 'The Nuisance', and all seemed to feel we were getting on very well so far.

Of course, the inevitable reaction came, when in the after session a member asked what was to be my salary. I begged to be excused from having any voice in the matter. This was not received very well, and an argument arose when Adams suggested two thousand pounds. We then realized that our money should be our first consideration; and I asked that a Financial Committee of four men be selected to consider the matter of our form of money and, also, to have charge of all matters concerning expenditures, this to be headed by whoever was appointed as the Head of the Treasury Department. This was applauded. I then asked, who was their choice for the office of Treasurer. With one voice, they shouted "Hamilton." He accepted, much to my joy, and so far all was well. The rub came when his Committee was chosen. I took no part in all this, merely trying to keep them in order and to carry out the wishes of the majority. No progress was made, and at six o'clock we adjourned.

My poor friend Hamilton was ready to resign. I did what I could to persuade him to stick, and so did Adams and Livingston. We got our heads together that night and made out the list of members. It was clear that money was the tender point. We found four men who were of sufficient means that we felt sure they were above all suspicion, and Adams said he would be on hand early to try and make some friends for their appointment. He was as good as his word and when I arrived, he gave me that ineffable wink of his right eye, with a nod, and I knew he had done the trick. The air was changed that morning, for all had been thinking over yesterday's proceedings, and the picture was beginning to clear. When I called them to order, they were all very serious and I fancied somewhat more respectful in their attitude to the Chair.

I called upon Hamilton and asked if he had considered the personnel of his Financial Committee. He said he had, and would like to submit the names. The first was received with silence. The second caused someone to shout "No." The third, silence, and also the fourth. I asked if there was any discussion and the man who said "No," rose and said that Member was too busy to accept and it happened to be himself. Laughter greeted this. We had a fifth chosen, and a sixth in case of such a situation. The Chair tried to make the matter one of straight business, and then offered Hamilton the fifth man. This was well received. I then asked for discussion. None was offered. Adams, seconded by Livingston, moved the Committee adoption and it was carried unanimously. One hurdle, and I felt it was the most difficult, was taken.

By this time, I was ready to again assert myself and I spoke of the need of a man in the Department of State who had known and studied Europe and our relation to its different Countries. This, I felt was necessary for our trade and also our harmonious relations with the various Countries, all over the world. My remarks were applauded and I could feel I was gaining their confidence and, perhaps, in some cases, even their loyalty. My own choice would have been Livingston. He was, by far, the best informed and equipped man for the office. Adams, however, seemed to be the man they wanted. He was proposed by Livingston and seconded by the Member from Virginia, Thomas Jefferson. The vote was divided, but a large majority in the affirmative. The minority, I found, favored Livingston. By this time, all were feeling in good spirits and decided to finish the Cabinet appointments, and then adjourn for the day.

The Army was a ticklish appointment. We had no outstanding military figure and no popular man in service. I finally suggested a name, because I was keen to have him with me. I spoke of Burr's service all through the war and his generous contribution that made Trenton possible. This was not met with favor as few knew him, and only my friends spoke for him. The Members resented my interfering, and so I am to blame for not having him with me from the first. I should have asked Adams to bring up his name, but we had never discussed any but State and Republic Heads. I was disheartened when I saw the small and mean attitude of the majority, and never again in the eight years of my service as President did I ever suggest an appointment.

I may digress to say here, that the way in which the present Executives reserve all the offices in order to gain power is something to make the angels weep.

The third day we found no Army Head, and so went on to that of the Department of the Republic. Livingston was chosen, but declined. Then, a man was put up who failed to get a majority. No one was chosen, and I began to see that all were selfishly obstructing the appointment of any man but their own selection. I asked them to consider the urgency of our situation and try to come together on names offered. They resented this, and one man declared he was not going to attend another meeting when the Chair dictated their proceedings. Adams was on his feet instantly, and asked the Member who had discovered any dictation from the Chair. The man said,

"I am opposed to a Chairman having any voice in appointments."

Adams replied the suggestion of Burr had been made because the Members had failed in their duty of presenting a name. This silenced the Member, but the atmosphere was tense. All I could do was to ask the will of the meeting. This was the signal for adjournment and, since the next day was Sunday, we had a rest from each other.

My Sabbath was spent in writing to Martha, and to Franklin. He was the one I wanted near me and, with some qualms, I asked if he would take office if requested. I slept twelve hours and got up a bit groggy. My feelings were more than depressed. I did not care for the body of men before me, except for those superior ones whose names I have mentioned and who have ornamented the pages of our history. The rest were very ordinary men of egotistical manners, ill nature, and of such a suspicious turn of mind that I was unhappy in their presence. One man especially, not 'The Nuisance', but a Member from New Hampshire, was such a glowering old demon that I disliked even looking upon him. However, I knew I had to face them, so I stood it with what spirit I could summon.

The meeting had a dour and gloomy atmosphere. Several were absent, and there were only seven above a quorum present. However, I decided to make what progress I could – and there was Adams, also Hamilton and Jefferson, and a man I was coming to like, though as yet I had not been introduced to him. This was a Member who had never spoken, but whose presence was so impressive and his conduct so correct that I instinctively marked him as a friend. This was a member from Pennsylvania named Schuyler, a man of great height and weight with a fine, intelligent face and courteous manner. He was a very accomplished scholar, and had emigrated thirty years previous from Germany. I came to love this man in the time that followed and to treasure his opinions. We were never close friends, but if he has descendants, I wish here to say that Schuyler was in all ways a great aid and inspiration to me. His opinions were free of narrow prejudice, and at all times he gave most diligent and selfless service to the Republic in whatever capacity he was filling.

Well, when the day ended, we had chosen a man for the Republic Department who would, perhaps, be able to survive their all but destructive criticism of every man suggested. His name was Elbridge Gerry, of New York.

It was not very long after we had been in session that day, that I realized the members were by no means all loyal to the Republic. One man was vehement in his remarks about the dangers of giving the people so much power.

We were now in some quandary as to what to do next. I wished to be free as soon as possible, but made no suggestion to that effect. We did get this done – we made an appropriation of funds to enable the Committee of Finance to remain and carry on their work. They were to report at the next session, which would be September 1st, when we would adopt our own official currency.

❧

FELLOW STATESMAN

DICTATED NOVEMBER 26, 1944

WE CAME HOME IN A moody state of mind, for we could foresee no happiness in the future if I had to deal with these men who seemed to feel antagonistic toward all of my own convictions. My heart was heavy, and I saw only a repetition of all I had just been through. Still, my three or four staunch friends would be with me, and I tried to let that thought comfort me.

Martha had been busy with her new home, and it was in such a state of shining order that to enter it drove all gloomy thoughts away. We were so happy to see the place in perfect condition that my mind could only rest on what was before me.

My own den was a precious relic of my father's life, and I had in it all his pictures, maps, books, and writing outfit, along with my own. My wife was very much of the same mind, and my mother's sitting room upstairs was a little museum of their belongings.

The lawns were not yet in condition, but within a week I had made them smooth and freshly green with watering pot and scythe. My fields were not in their old wonted state, but that could only come with time and labor. The barns and sheep folds, pens and out houses were all freshly white-washed, and so I was content as I looked upon my loved and cherished home.

My wife had been so engaged with all her affairs that she had really worn herself down, so that I made her now take a rest, and let the house servants do all that needed doing. We had a happy week, and then the devil began to show his tail. A letter arrived from New York asking me to return in another month and open the session of Congress, and address them with suggestions and plans for the future of the Republic. Also, to hear the Report of the Committee on Finance and arrange for the issuance of the Republic's currency. Of course, I was aware that all this was important, but I did not relish the responsibility of having to be always the leader, yet with no followers. So far, the slightest suggestion on my part, except for that of arranging for a Cabinet, had been met with adverse criticism and even antagonism.

A letter, also, from Adams was received and that was balm in Gilead, for he said in it that the sober second thought of the majority of the Members had resulted in a wave of enthusiasm for the great clarity and sense of all I had done. They were even in the mood to think I was the best possible choice they could have made for a leader. This, naturally, soothed my feelings somewhat. Still, I dreaded the work ahead, and wished with all my heart that Adams had been the choice. Nevertheless, it was a good sign for the Republic that the sober second thought had worked for harmony, rather than dissension.

❁

RETURN TO NEW YORK AND THE CONGRESS

AT THE TIME OF MY arrival in New York, I was suffering severely from a low fever that was one of the aftermaths of all I had been through, mentally and physically. That being the case, Martha decided to come with me until I was in health once more. That, too, comforted me, for now we found our greatest happiness in our companionship, and she was ever the one to make of each circumstance either cause for joy or gladness.

She would find an amusing side to it, and so turn away its sharpness. Such a comrade as Martha made even my pending ordeal less difficult. She had made many friends in New York and so was in no danger of loneliness when my duties were absorbing.

We had a safe and not too uncomfortable voyage on the packet, and on our arrival at the Tavern in New York, I found a suite of rooms, freshly papered and furnished with charming new curtains and chair covers, and the vases filled with fresh flowers. These attentions made me feel that this was to be a different experience than those I had known in New York.

Martha was at once overwhelmed by the attentions of the people of the city, and she was obliged to immediately call in a seamstress to turn our chamber into a bower of bright hued satins and silks, pretty bonnets, and all sorts of falderals that gave me a thrill of joy whenever I looked in there in the daytime, and saw the business that was so charming, and resulted in Martha looking so pretty.

I began to feel rather shabby in my old uniforms despite new falls and ruffles, and yielded at last to Martha's demand that I look like a President and ordered two new suits. One of blue cloth, the other of black velvet such as I had seen on my double. My shoe maker was appalled at having to fit me to three pairs of shoes and two of boots. My shirtmaker, also, was overwhelmed and my hairdresser came twice a week. All in all, I felt a bit foolish, but I wanted the Congress to feel I was glad to expend the money paid me to do credit to my office.

My horse and Martha's, I had brought with us, and we had to have new riding clothes. Martha, on her chestnut in a black habit with a light blue gauze veil on her little stiff hat, and her gauntlets of soft gray, looked charming as she rode well. She and I were quite a success with the people when we rode in the late afternoon on the bridle path that ran along the Hudson. Also, she gave them, in each case, a charming smile and nod. I was always proud of her, and she seemed to be always in the picture as the great lady she was.

All this I set down because it was the brighter and happier side of life at the time.

The Business of the Congress

I gave myself up to the business before me, except for our daily ride along the river. My ideas were beginning to crystallize, and I was sure I was not making them too grandiose for practical purposes. I wished above all to have our work made clear and plain to the people, and to make them see the reasons for all we did. I loved that part of the work, and was really happy in conceiving ways and means to help all the people, in such ways as to make their lot simpler and easier.

This, of course, was not a very high ideal from the standpoint of the well-to-do classes. What they wanted was more business. However, I knew that was sure to follow if the people in humble circumstances were prosperous and contented.

All in all, I had it in my mind to be thankful for the opportunity to in some measure aid in bringing the Republic into practical use. The first meeting of the Congress was a very brief and informal affair. We met, called the role, and when that was done I addressed them in a somewhat formal manner as a prelude to our tasks that were to follow. I then asked their pleasure, and Livingston proposed that we adjourn until the next day in order to have a little private session of the Finance Committee and make ready their report. All were agreeable, and we adjourned.

I invited the Committee to dine with us, and they did. In the evening, we went into an informal session and got well into the matter of the new currency. We decided on a simpler scale than that of Britain, using a decimal system. I suggested this as being the easiest for simple people to calculate. My suggestion was at first a shock, but on discussing it, the whole Committee realized its merit and adopted it. Our silver coinage was to be confined to a five and ten cent piece. A paper currency of fifty cents and a hundred cents, with a further extension to come of 500 and 5,000 cent notes.

We had never been accustomed to a currency and coin, except the penny of copper alloy and the silver shilling. We decided to keep the silver shilling and the half penny or cent; but not the penny, the two-cent piece. The designs were not worked out for these coins or the paper notes. We left that to be undertaken by another committee. Also, we made a budget and the cost of maintenance of the government as it was so far organized. We had to look to the matter of taxes and decided to also put that over to another committee.

All in all, we were in good shape to start things going when we said goodnight at 10 o'clock.

The report of the Finance Committee was read by its Chairman and was debated with little opposition to any of its recommendations. Questions were merely intended to clarify points, and the morning session was ended by voting the adoption of all the points.

In the afternoon, a member asked what we were to do about the Head of the Army. I decided not to make any further suggestions. This was a marked jab at them, and they took it. I said I had made but one suggestion since taking my office, and that had been received with such contempt and even insult that I should never again try to name a person for office. All were silent, and then Livingston rose, and asked if he might ask a personal favor, and that was to reconsider his own choice for Head of the Army. I put the question and the result was a unanimous affirmation. Then, Livingston asked if the Congress had considered the remarkable fitness of the President to conduct the military affairs of the Nation. This, too, was acclaimed, though I was none too pleased at the thought of this added burden. However, it seemed for the time to be a practical idea.

Then came what has proven to be a disastrous appointment: the President to be automatically the Commander-in-Chief of the Army. What it has cost in lives and treasure, we shall never know. It is my hope that this stupid and useless imposition may now be abolished, and a regular Head of the Army to be always in the Cabinet; as well as a Head of the Navy and Air Forces, along with the Secretaries of War and the Navy, who should be responsible for equipment and supplies.

To resume. We made that session a great advance in the

spirit of cooperation and speedy discussion. We appointed three committees, and they were at work that very night. These were the Committee on Design for our money, the Committee on Taxation, and the Committee on Foreign Affairs. The Chairman of the first was my old friend Adams, and of the second, a member from Massachusetts, whose name I cannot at this moment recall. Livingston was the third.

I went to my rooms, well content with the events of the day, and the spirit of the Members for each other and myself.

❦

WE WORKED FOR THREE months, and the records show what we did.

Martha left for home during the second month, and wrote that she found all in order on her return. Her housekeeper and my head stock man, Mark, had done well by fields, home, and stables.

We had a real jollification on the night before we dissolved the session. My own part was to entertain them at a farewell supper. This was a big expense, but I had decided to use my salary to keep up my office, and never for my private life. So, I personally provided the spread and had a banquet served in our fine room at the town hall with thirty men serving good food and plenty of wine. That put the capstone on my status, and never again did I have a sign of disrespect from any Member of that Congress.

❦

IN SUMMARY OF MY TERM OF OFFICE

ALL I CAN SAY OF MY term of office was that it was a period of great satisfaction, as we went forward step by step. Each day, as I came to know the men with me in this great adventure in government, I realized that some Divine guidance had placed together so many great and unselfish men, whose talents and

sound minds were of such an unusual character. I think upon
them with such respect and fond admiration, as to persuade me
that it was my happy lot to know intimately and work with the
greatest galaxy of minds ever assembled in a cause. Oh, to see
them in their moments of inspiration and listen to their words as
they stood among us and in their voices, the ring of truth, as their
wise words of counsel would pour forth in a stream of eloquence
that ornamented and enriched the annals of English speech! I
often sat in silent wonder at these great men and women when
they gave out their hearts and minds in such words as are now
immortalized in the records of their great service.

My part was to preside, and to see that all was fair and
clear and in the interests of the people. I felt often how privileged
to be with those men, whose stature seemed to me often to be so
much beyond my own in statecraft. Aa a soldier, I had not realized
the work, the responsibility, and the strain put upon the minds
and emotions of those who are the lawmakers; and the men who
envisioned the codes and modes that shall keep order, advance
progress and make plain to the simple men their edicts intended
for the good of all. Now I had come to understand the core and the
vital part of government. I wanted a Nation of patriots, of those
who loved their Country, and were ready to serve it in such ways
as I myself had tried to do. I came to see that only the wisdom of
statesmen could direct that love of Country into channels, where
force and bloodshed need not be the driving power. An army
should be the protection, the strong arm that in danger from alien
enemies or even from enemies within, would safeguard and defend
the sacred rights the statesman had created for citizens.

I was happy to have this enlargement of my consciousness
of the work I now presided over. I went out of my way to show my
colleagues what I was learning from them. John Marshall said to
me one day,

"President Washington, I have never met a man so self-
effacing in a high position as yourself."

That remark seemed to me to be correct, for I knew my
own capacities and did not underrate them. Also, I knew what

these men were, and I felt honored myself, in honoring them.

All in all, the first year was the best of all. We had only the ground work to plan. Events were not pressing upon me.

Our foreign relations were simply nonexistent. We had our trade with France, and through LaFayette's influence, it was quite brisk. Britain, naturally, had no dealings with us; only the Canadians got their trade. The Principality of Saxe-Coburg sent the first minister to our Capital in the second year, if I remember correctly, and Spain and Austria in the third. Italy was also friendly, and had a minister in Philadelphia before the first year was over. The Scandinavians and Russians did not send a man to represent them until the third year. We were likewise slow in going over to Europe.

I was not very keen, and the Congress was slow to take up the matter. Finally, we got Livingston to go to Britain and see if they wished to make friends. He was a master at diplomacy, and soon trade was going on freely in both directions between us.

Franklin, my dear old friend, was closest in those days and we were almost daily in each other's company. I persuaded him to go to France. I had brought him and LaFayette together in the war, and they loved each other. The young Frenchman had the liveliest appreciation of Franklin's greatness, and so that Post was perfectly filled by my old friend.

Another man who, at this time, came to be of distinguished service was the great Adams. He never quite thought of himself as a statesman, but that he surely was; and his clear mind and lofty feeling made him a power whenever he spoke. I used to watch with silent, but keen observation, the effect he never failed to produce when he spoke either for or against a measure. His powers were instinctive rather than trained, and he was so modest that he was quite unconscious of the effect he produced.

One man, too, whom I wish to speak of here was the man to whom we always turned when clarity was needed. This man was the son of a very great lawyer and he himself was but twenty-two at the time, but his faculty for simplification was even then notable. He had no record behind him, yet often his words were those of the law when it was passed and, in some cases, bore his name. That name, so well known in Delaware, is that of its greatest statesmen, Lorillard Sr. History has not made this name important, but we who knew and worked with both father and son know it belongs with those who now ornament the pages of our Country's history.

All were gentlemen. I am aware that this is now considered a term of reproach. To indicate culture, or even good manners as desirable, is now supposed to be undemocratic. The spectacle of boorishness and rude speech is now taken as a sign of strong character, rather than of ignorance, and appears to be much applauded. I am glad that in those days, we had the grace to respect each other and ourselves, and to use a code of manners that smoothed the sharp edges of debate and made our work the easier for its consideration, each man for the other.

I had seen what boorishness could do in the early days of my office, and I saw to it that no other man should suffer, as I had, for the ill conduct of those who had no sense of propriety in the conduct of public affairs.

Alonzo Chappel's portrait of Washington

CHAPTER SEVEN

OLD AGE

❀

Wisdom and Commentaries

DICTATED NOVEMBER 27, 1944

Now I come to the closing chapter. A man who can say when he comes to his sixtieth year, "I have lived, and now I am ready to go," is in the very prime of his power, if he but realizes it.

My own is a case in point. Fortunately, I had a powerful constitution and in all it had been subjected to, it seemed able to withstand every assault and recover its normal power. My teeth were my greatest affliction. I mention this because of the evil taste of those who have taken it upon themselves to administer my belongings, who have exhibited the set of artificial teeth that I was obliged to wear when I was seventy-three. They seem to fascinate the public to such a degree that I feel sure no item in my history can compete with them in their dramatic appeal. They were an affliction that made me feel like a demon. I cursed them daily and wore them with the sensation of a dragon, about to gnaw out the vitals of a victim when I ate my food. Take those damned teeth out, and destroy them if you are patriots or even decent human beings. Thank you.

✺

DEFEATS

DICTATED NOVEMBER 30, 1944

IT IS TOO LATE TO SAY what should have been said long ago, when I had the opportunity to speak as one who had the authority and office of the President of this Nation. Still, it may inspire some response from the people who may read this story of my life and deepest thoughts and hopes concerning this Country.

So far, I have said little of the way I tried to assist in forming the policies and methods we should pursue in our National life. However, this was not because I had no ideas and no formulated plans. It is because I found the representatives of the citizens, who were the Congress, bent upon making themselves, in all ways, paramount.

It is one thing to be a Congressman, and quite another to be the Executive of that body and administer laws that one feels and rates as contrary to both the desire and the well-being of the citizens. A man who can suggest to the Congress what he notes is needed for the welfare of the Nation is a happy Executive, but in my case the majority and less thoughtful representatives were, from the first, determined to make their will, and theirs only, the government.

It was by the help of a few of the greatest minds in Congress that I was able to carry on. Even the Supreme Court, the balance wheel of the Congress and the Executive, was flouted by the power-drunk set of men who came from a very simple mode of life into responsibility utterly strange to them. It went to their heads, and since they were in the majority, the Constitution made it possible by their numbers to override all others.

❀

Defecit

Dictated December 1, 1944

My third year was the most trying, for the people had not yet come to understand fully the part they were to play in the Government. They still looked for a ruler to tell them what they could, or should, do in the matter of their own affairs.

The most of the trouble came from those who looked for some sort of public office and, as we were so few and so new, we could not offer much in that way. The Post was carried on as a service, but the messengers had to be changed every few miles and so it was not much of a position for thrifty men. That is, we found a man who was willing to spend his waking hours on a horse to take letters from one Colony to another, and for each ten miles he covered, he got twelve cents. He made about twenty cents a day, which a man could just about live on then.

Another office was that of copyist for the Congress. It required seven or more to do this work of making duplicates of the minutes and speeches, as well as the laws passed. The men were paid little for their valuable labor, but there was little to pay with at this time. Not much of a temptation to many but very young and aspiring boys, who wrote a fair hand and were keen to hear and learn the many laws made, and watch the proceedings of the Congress. Several of these boys became important lawyers in their maturity.

We had also to engage several people for the purpose of making uniforms for our new troops and seamen. We purchased a large warehouse in Philadelphia and fitted it up for a factory where our own cloth was woven, and a score of spinning wheels were installed with five weaving looms. One room was given over to the dye vats and another to the tailoring of the uniforms.

Also, we had a shoemaking shop, as well as a smithy and farrier concern for the care of our Cavalry horses. An arsenal we made of an old abandoned barn that was made partly of stone. We tore off the wooden superstructure, and made the whole building of the stone we picked up from the public land, outside the city.

No waste was permitted, but still we found our budget would not cover the expenses. We decided on an impost on our exports, and so with a fractional tax, we managed to meet our expenses. It was clear we must have more citizens if we were to continue, and so we made strenuous efforts to get settlers by advertising in the European newspapers.

Also, we set apart much land for those who could pay but little. While this was good wild land, we could not expect much tax money from it until it had been under cultivation for a year or two. Many times, I came to my bed at night sick at heart and wondering where I was to find a way to help the poor settlers realize the money they must have to pay for their land, and give us a little to carry on the Government. All I could see ahead was the long road of pinching to get funds to pay the Army, Seamen and the few other employees of the Republic. When I look at Washington now, and see the hundreds of idlers gossiping or reading and killing time while the people try to meet their huge taxes, I marvel at all the waste and folly that goes on at the Capitol in the name of Government.

My lot was to pinch every penny, and poor Hamilton's also. He was never happy after he took over his post as Head of the Treasury, for he used to say he felt either like a robber or a bankrupter all the time.

Well, we squeezed through that year, and I made a contribution of two hundred pounds to the Treasury. Hamilton gave a hundred pounds, and so did Livingston. Adams gave twenty pounds and the same amount came from Jefferson. Also, we had a windfall from the *Pennsylvania Gazette*. Franklin started a fund to sustain the new and poor Republic. The people who were patriotic gave their coins until Franklin sent us the sum of five hundred pounds.

I gave my first year's salary, and half of Martha's savings to use to pay bills. Livingston and the men who had private means, such as Hamilton and Jefferson,did the same. Also, many of the

Colonies started Franklin's scheme and raised funds in their principal newspapers.

The Aristocrats, though they benefited by the abolishing of the Crown taxes, never contributed a penny.

All that season, we pondered how to manage and still keep up appearances. Finally, I sold the last of my own land that I had first purchased and let my field hands go. They had been freed years before, but wished to remain in my service. They were good men, and found employment immediately with the man who bought my acreage. This money settled many of my more pressing debts, but the relief was only temporary.

I refused to consider mortgaging Mount Vernon, and I could not bear to think of selling a single acre of my father's original estate. It came to the point, however, when I found myself in debt to the tune of six thousand pounds. I knew I should be forced to part with some of Mount Vernon. I sold twenty acres of the forest and forty of the meadow land; and for this got two thousand pounds, as the timber was now of fine growth and very valuable for its hard maple, walnut, and other excellent woods, in demand for paneling and fine furniture.

This relieved me somewhat, and I paid a good interest on the outstanding four thousand pounds.

All this time, the people were grumbling and making life a burden for me because they seemed to be expecting some sort of miraculous benefits, such as a golden shower from the government. They were better off than they had ever been, but they were not content to live as simply as they had before the Revolution and seemed to feel no sense of responsibility for their own future. They gave little to support the Government, but seemed to think it was an institution for their personal support and gratification of their excesses. My heart was sore at the way they would rail at us for our pains, and many a time I lost all faith in popular government because of their childishness and stupidity. In fact, it was only when we came to the point of losing all confidence in the people's ability to govern themselves that something occurred that restored our faith.

This was the small incident of the attack made on me by a citizen while I was out riding in the country. The man was a farmer and when he saw me, ran into his house, got his musket and then following me on his own horse—I was unaware of his purpose—and coming alongside of my Canby, he fired at me point blank. Somehow the shot went wild, and I was not hurt. I dismounted and gave the man a piece of my mind. He was terrified and wished to get away, but I drove him before me into town and delivered him over to the sheriff.

At his trial for attempting to kill me, he said in his defense that he was a British subject still, and would never pay allegiance to the American Republic or its President. He made such an ass of himself by claiming to be a loyal citizen of the British Crown, that the people of the city began to make this the cause for meetings to discuss who was disloyal to the Republic, and who were the citizens to be counted on to support it.

Franklin, of course, made it a sensation in the *Gazette.* Other newspapers in New York, Boston, Baltimore, and even in Williamsburg told the story and I received numerous letter of sympathy from citizens expressing their indignation.

No time was lost in sentencing this man to a year of hard labor. His family carried on his farm, and made no demonstration against me or the Republic. That was a sign to me that the decent and dependable people of the country loved the Republic and would, if called upon, defend it.

❀

ALL WAS SO CALM IN the summer of 1792 that I felt a new man as I worked in my den at Mount Vernon. The many visitors made our home a sort of public house, but it was still home. I was never so happy as when living in the old place, and enjoying the sweet memories that ever clung about it.

Martha was tired after her strenuous season in Philadelphia, and was wont to say,

"George, I am going to sleep around the clock for a week."

But she never did. She was always up and superintending the maids and the gardens by eight and, from then on until bedtime, she was never idle. She had many friends in Philadelphia, and always one or two came to spend a day or two with us, so that the house was usually full of visitors.

When we wished to be alone, we rode out on our horses and took a long stop in some spot we loved, where we dismounted and let the horses graze. I was still able to lift her into her saddle easily, as well as mount from the ground myself.

All this, I set down to show you how my life was enriched and filled with the beauty of my dear Virginia home and all the associations. My beloved wife, too, so close and ever in tune with me in all I felt and did. A man would be an ingrate who did not acknowledge, with a full heart, such blessings as were mine at this time.

❧

WELL, IT WAS NOT to be!

I mean, I was not to be left in peace at Mount Vernon. The political pot was boiling, and an election of the President was due. I had told my close friends to be sure and make plans for my successor, and leave me to my private affairs. I wanted to propose Franklin as the candidate, for I knew what a great and splendid leader he would be. Poor Franklin, however, was feeling very weary and when I approached him on the subject while he was paying us a visit that summer, begged off, saying he was growing too old to take on such a responsibility.

I then asked Adams and he, too, feared to tackle such a job and was feeling he was unequal to the financial strain the Presidency would put upon his means.

I got nowhere with Livingston, who was now back from

France and filled with horror at the Revolution there. Jefferson, however, had taken his place and enjoyed it. I talked with several other men, any one of whom I felt could do the work as well or better than myself, but none would face that four years of worry and labor.

Often I am amused at the way it is all presented in the histories and my biographies, as well as the many special articles and magazines. They seem to believe it was all honor, glory and state balls; a triumphant and satisfying term of service filled with harmony, progress, and public acclaim. God knows, it was far from anything of the sort. Every move was a battle, and I lost most of them when I was the keenest to win. My own ideas were, in most cases, reversed. Because I yielded with no outcry, it did not make the disappointment less.

The greatest defeat was in my fight to make eight years the utmost length of service for any President. I saw only too clearly the evils that accrue when one set of men retain hold of a government too long. I begged and pleaded with my fellows to consider the danger. My pleas were in vain. All were convinced, but a few staunch believers in my acumen that a man well suited to the Presidency could handle the work and the accumulation of dead wood without risk.

Another defeat that I see now was tragic was due to my fight for the maintenance of a fund to set aside for the relief of our people in time of disaster, or what we used to call "hard times" due to crop failures or other causes of business depression. This was not even considered, and we often saw the terrible and unrelieved suffering that was due to the neglect of this provision.

Now I come to my bitterest disappointment. I was never a factor in the rash, and almost insane system, of making of any and all people beneficiaries of the suffrage. I counseled against giving the vote to a new settler until he had known the experience of our way of life that would fit him for citizenship. This can only be accomplished by many years of work and residence among us, and a gradual merging of his original concepts of life with what he would find here.

The cry was all for immigration and a building up of the population. What sort of people came, and how they thought or behaved seemed of little importance compared with the advantage of numbers. Fortunately, those who did come in those years faced such hardships and stern conditions in taking up the cheap land and laboring in such a new environment that they were of sturdy stuff.

In the end, I am most grateful to those who stood by me in these battles: Adams, Franklin, Madison, Paine, Hamilton, Livingston, Pinckney, Jay, Jefferson, and many more whose names you will not recognize; all of the men who so bravely served under me to whom you owe so much. You owe them your gratitude for your nation and your freedom. We succeeded at the impossible, but under the hand of Providence this great Nation came to be born. This is a Nation with a destiny one that continues to be fulfilled so long as people cry out for freedom.

❀

Home

Dictated December 9, 1944

Now I shall tell of the last days of my Presidency.

We were all in a dither, tearing up the accumulated papers and correspondence, of looking up the ways and means of getting our belongings to Mount Vernon and of saying farewell to our friends.

Martha had a lot of shopping and sewing and presents to prepare for our return to Mount Vernon. All was just a series of small, but necessary, activities and so we were rather weary when it came to the final goodbyes. I had made my farewell speech to the dear friends and fellow workers in the Congress, and I made no attempt to conceal my emotion at the parting. I felt my time was short, and I loved these great men so dearly that to think of life without them seemed now a hardship too difficult to face.

My own passion for the welfare of the Nation was too great for me to be calm when relinquishing the helm. I knew my own example must be the pattern for those to come. The people seemed fearful of a change, and asked me to remain in office. They even went to such extremes as to ask me to accept a royal title, and rule as king.

That so horrified me, that I felt concerned for the future. If they could view all I had done to give them a people's government and then entertain the idea that I would ever consider a monarchy to replace the Republic, then they were indeed far from appreciating my sacrifices and my labors.

Of course I could only refuse in as polite terms as I could command, with my heart aching at the very thought of such a reversal of all my hopes and aspirations for the Republic.

WELL, WE DID GET off and the last I saw of the Executive Mansion was on a rainy morning in May, when Martha and I, with her maid and my man, Corinth, packed ourselves and our belongings into a coach and a wagon and started for Mount Vernon.

We were two days and one night making the journey home, with a stop in Baltimore for the night. I was happy to visit my old post and saw the General in command there. He was highly pleased to take me over the barracks, and they brought back so many old memories that I felt impelled to tell the men of them. We had a beautiful and memorable time, and I left feeling a glow of satisfaction that soldiers of every generation are always able to speak freely to each other, and understand one another in a unique fellowship.

HOME AT LAST!

There were no more than eighteen of our people left at Mount Vernon, but the shout of welcome they gave as we arrived sounded like ten times that number.

We tumbled out into the arms of our old overseer, Carey, and from him we went to the embrace of each one. Martha looked as tousled as if she had been in a fracas by the time we got in the house, and I was not in very good order, myself.

All was in perfect, shining condition and our rooms, open and airy, were a sweet and welcome sight.

Home!

I saw it as I had always seen it, the sweetest place under Heaven.

I could see in my mind's eye my father at his desk, my mother teaching the little cousins, and Charles, always conning some inner happening that to others was unknown.

I saw our other brothers, tall and handsome chaps, more dignified than we were, always courtly and well mannered.

Home!

The land was as smiling as ever as I turned to the window and saw each tree and bush and patch of lawn. How sweet the air was! How blessed the peace that seemed ever to brood over this beloved spot!

My eyes closed for a moment, and I seemed almost to lose consciousness. Then, a sense that I was not alone came over me. I opened my eyes and there, facing me once more, was Myself.

Now I seemed to be looking like an old man. I saw the white wig, the dark lines under my eyes, the two blackened places under them and a faint, sad smile was on my lips. I was an old man, weary and spent.

My own senses were so much affected, that I simply stared in dumb wonder at the man before me.

"Now I am content. You have done all that was set for you to do. You can now rest."

A moment of silence, and he seemed to come close and disappear into me.

I sat for a time, marveling at this and suddenly I saw him again, standing as he was, but now his face was immobile and his color that of the dead...

"I am now to be translated to the Realm of Spirit. You will remain for a time, and I shall still be with you, and I shall be preparing the way you must take when you leave your Earthly body and live only in mine. Be of good heart. You shall still serve the Republic."

At that, he seemed to fade into a dim vision that disappeared entirely.

I sat there in my chair for, perhaps, ten minutes and then fell into a deep sleep. Martha found me there and woke me. It was now time to be unpacking and settling my belongings. I rose, and found my strength was not great enough to undertake such a task. I lay down on a sofa and rested until the hour for dinner.

※

AFTER THAT, LIFE WENT ON happily and busily. We had many callers and visitors, and Martha was ever busy with her tasks of hospitality. I kept much to my den, where my books were, and made my life one of reading, writing, and studying.

We loved the mornings when the frost came, and Canby was persuaded by a lump of sugar to exert himself and take me for a ride. Then home, and a hearty breakfast, and after that a look at the stables and the animals.

All the fields were in the state of getting ready for winter, and my crops were in and marketed. No more deficit had appeared in the Treasury, and so I kept what I had and was grateful that it could be so.

※

THE NEWS OF OUR SUCCESS as a new Nation was now common talk in Europe, and so I laid myself down each night in a peace I had not known for eight years.

❀

MY DEATH

DICTATED DECEMBER 10, 1944

WE SAW VERY LITTLE of our neighbors during the year 1798. We had so much to do to get the plantation and home in order and, then, we found our old fount of energy was not flowing as it once had and we tired quickly. Martha, also, was slowing down and, though we kept four slaves in the house, we were put to it to keep things up to the mark set by Martha's standards.

All seemed to be as usual one fine autumn evening when I felt a certain peculiar twitch in the heart beat. I sat quite still until it became unbearable and I began to gasp for breath.

Martha was sitting with me knitting. I had been speaking of the way our people were making up for lost time in the matter of seeking to take all possible means for the Nation's defense. My ledger carried a fine review of the military plans and, also, the way the Militia was making its mark in New York and Massachusetts, as well as Virginia. This, naturally, gave me a little thrill of satisfaction and I was in my armchair under the candlelight smiling over this pleasant bit of news, when that devilish catch came in my heart.

I did not wish to alarm Martha, and yet I could not breathe. Finally, I began to make the little sound that always precourses a death rattle. Martha looked up in alarm, and when she saw my drawn face, she screamed for Corinth, who was dozing in his chair in the hall. He came running in and loosened my stock. Then, he dashed out for a drink of whiskey from the dining room sideboard.

At his return with the whiskey, I had come around again and was able to speak. I tried to reassure Martha, but she was in a perfect terror and was kneeling at my side in bitter tears. I was able soon to rise and, with Corinth's aid, to go to my bedroom and undress.

Darley's drawing of the death of Washington

I did not get up the next day, and lay thinking what was still to be arranged in my affairs before I laid them down.

My lawyer was sent for the next day, and I made a codicil to my will that left all my slaves free. That would leave Martha with her own slaves, enough to carry on with.

All this took several days, during which I remained in bed. Only when I felt all was in order, did I try to get up. Now I could take chances and, if I was rash, it did not matter. I was ready to go. My thoughts at this time were of my youth, and of my parents, and all the events that went to make up my mental outlook and character.

Martha was ever beside my bed, either reading to me or silently watching me. Her terror at the coming separation was my greatest sorrow. Try as I would to make her understand that I would always be at hand in my Spirit, she could not believe it.

We were very much in love still and, old as we were, liked the touch of each other's flesh. She would lie beside me, even in the daytime, and put her hand on my face in a caress that spoke of her constant love. My own feelings were stirred, and I would kiss that little hand and hold it.

We had no words then. Our thoughts were clear to one another. My love had never waned, neither had hers, and we both were so sure of all this that there was nothing to say.

It was Corinth that gave me the most concern. He was unable to face the parting, and I was obliged to try and teach him all I could put into simple language, of the way we survive. I assured him and explained how only the body could die, and that I, alive in my Spirit, would still be there at home, and one of our slaves, Lemuel, a field hand who had etheric sight, would very likely be able to see me.

Corinth, then, made up his mind to go with me. I am sure that is what brought him after me within two months of my own death. He had no illness and was simply found slumped in his chair in the hall. With never an outcry, his Spirit freed itself and I found him standing beside his body as I, in my own etheric body, looked in on the family, as I did every evening after my death.

❧

When I emerged from my mortal body, I was so amazed at the ease with which it happened that I did not at first realize that I was a Spirit, in a Spirit body.

This emergence seems to be a merging also, for I saw for an instant my Double, smiling at me as I rose above my flesh and moved away from my bed. Then, I seemed to be that Double and that is what I now am, but with all my memories, emotions, and mental characteristics.

❧

I WAS SO HAPPY TO meet my dear parents and Charles at my death. They were at my bedside and smilingly greeted me, as I emerged, for the last time from that body that had ridden and wrestled and hunted and fought.

My father's first words were,

"Well, George, its all over and we're glad to have you with us again."

My mother said,

"Darling, now I am happy once more about you."

Charles smiled, and merely said,

"Hello, George!"

It was all so simple and natural and so like old times, that I scarcely realized what had happened until I looked down on my bed and saw my weary body lying there in the arms of Corinth, who had lifted me up at the last moment and now was weeping with his head on my breast.

When I emerged from my form that lay still and pale on my bed, it was a joyful moment, for I had not looked down on that body that had served me so well for seventy-five years. I merely saw about me those three beloved people. Their tender smiles were so sweet and their words came to me in such loving tones, so that the ecstasy of the moment was all I could feel.

I shall not dwell upon what was said. Those moments are sacred and every Soul knows them. All again was love and understanding. We kept speaking for some time, and then suddenly, I heard Martha's cry of agony. She had come into the room and seen poor Corinth lying across my body and heard his bitter weeping and calling on me not to leave him, but to take him with me. She at once came to me, and throwing herself down beside me, put her lips to mine, trying to breathe life into me, but the heart had stopped and the two seconds allowed for resuscitation was past. Her weeping was terrible to bear.

I went to her and tried to comfort her, but she was now too far gone in hysteria. Corinth, ever ready to serve, rose and coming to her, knelt down and began to pray to Almighty God to comfort her. Finally, his voice reached her consciousness and she became quiet. Corinth said, in his sweet voice,

"Miss Martha, we will be with him when the good Lord takes us, too. Don't say you've lost him. He will hear you. Say only what you want him to hear."

She was quiet in another moment. Her spoken words to me I shall not reveal, except to say they were so much more than any man can ever prize enough.

❦

Soon the sad and terrible rites, that seem to me to only increase the sorrow of parting, were conducted.

The Nation seemed stunned that my poor old carcass had at last given up its resistance to life on Earth. It had served me well, and I hoped to make it serve them. I was appalled at the expense of all that was done, for I was aware of all the sacrifice it meant at that time.

My beloved friends like Burr, Adams, Hamilton, and so many I cannot name them now, were struck with the pain of separation. Thank God, I knew it was not permanent!

I was almost in a collapse from the emotion all the ceremonies caused me. My little houseboy, now a man, was the one who begged to dig my grave. His tears fell on every spade of Earth and his sobs were so hard to bear that I, who was beside him all the time, had to be taken away by my father and Charles. My mother kept close to Martha.

The man who was the most helpful was our old friend, the overseer. He attended to every detail, and he made it all as easy as possible for Martha. He was not a man to say much, but he did speak these words to Martha. I heard him say,

"Miss Martha, I don't see how we can git along without Master George. The Country won't know what to do without him to think out things for them."

Undeserved probably, but I consider that the greatest tribute from a free citizen that I ever received. His friendship for me was never close because of our past. However, he was an intelligent man and, simple as he was, he had the good of the whole Country at heart and he felt that I had, too.

Martha, I was with each night and, as she slept, I called out her astral body, which was as lovely as when she and I first met. I spoke to her such words of comfort as I could command. I begged her to try to impress these thoughts upon her waking mind. She said to me, speaking with her mortal voice later,

"George, darling, I know you are here with me, and now I

am satisfied to fill out my days with work until you take me with you."

❧

I WON'T TRY TO SPEAK of the ceremonies and all that came after. I saw it all, and was a part of it all. My fellow workers in the government were most kind, and I was amazed and greatly moved by the way in which they honored me.

My deepest thanks have not been given before. Now I say to all my Fellow Countrymen, who do me the great honor to observe my birthday, not merely as a chance for a stopping of work, but by giving me and my labors for the Republic a thought, or in possibly conning the articles that are written and which strive to be just and fair in spite of all the misstatements, accepted as true, concerning me. I love you for caring to read, for a few moments, of the man whom you think of as the Father of your Country and one who loved to serve the Cause of Liberty.

I love all who love the Republic. They seem to be fewer each year, but the more dear for all that.

I come to the end of this effort to speak my heart and mind to you. I pause and wish I might say much more that weighs on my heart these days. I see you clearly, and I know your troubled and confused minds. I care and I suffer with you.

All I ask, my dear Countrymen, is that you keep the dearly bought Republic and that you see in the beloved Flag the symbol of all whose blood has been shed for it, and that each White Star shall be to you the symbol of the men and women whose toil and privation created the States that each stands for.

We are a Republic that has a past that is a shining page in the History of Mankind.

Take these words from the man who was, and is, one of you and like unto you in all ways, except that his destiny was known to him, and with what light and strength as was given, he tried to keep faith with it.